Making Money in Real Estate

Third Edition

Making Money in Real Estate

HOW TO START OUT ON THE ROAD TO FINANCIAL INDEPENDENCE WITH RESIDENTIAL AND COMMERCIAL PROPERTY

Carolyn Janik

Dearborn™
Trade Publishing
A **Kaplan Professional** Company

President, Dearborn Publishing: Roy Lipner
Vice President and Publisher: Cynthia A. Zigmund
Senior Acquisitions Editor: Mary B. Good
Cover Design: Design Solutions
Typesetting: the dotted i

Published by Dearborn Trade Publishing
A Kaplan Professional Company

Printed in the United States of America

05 06 07   10 9 8 7 6 5 4 3 2 1

Library of Congress Cataloging-in-Publication Data

Janik, Carolyn.
   Making money in real estate : how to start out on the road to financial independence with residential and commercial property / by Carolyn Janik.—3rd ed.
      p.   cm.
   Includes index.
   ISBN 1-4195-1751-1 (7.25x9 pbk.)
   1. Real estate investment.   I. Title.
HD1382.5.J349 2005
332.63′24—dc22

                                                                        2005014809

Dedication

In memory of my grandfather,
Jan Pustelnik,

Who left Poland,
Worked his way across Europe,
Married a girl from home in New Britain, Connecticut,
And bought a farm to make a better life for his children.

Contents

Nothing exists in a vacuum, especially real estate. When investing in real estate, understanding the relationships is critical.

Everybody knows that location is critical, but not everyone realizes that location is in relationship to something. The something includes the infrastructure such as roads and utilities. It also includes other land uses. It is the relationships that make a difference.

When evaluating potential investments in real estate, it is worthwhile to focus on the relationships especially important to that type of real estate. This book, *Making Money in Real Estate,* is divided into two parts, the second of which focuses on different types of investments. These include the following: single-family fixer-uppers, multifamily houses, condos and co-ops, vacation-area properties, mixed-use buildings, and land.

The chapters dealing with the type of property consider the location, but focus on a variety of other considerations, especially time, work, and money; and of course financing. But, the thrust of the chapters on property type is in relation to you, the investor. That is why the chapters on type of property are put in the second part of the book rather than the first part.

Part I of the book lays out a foundation on which you can build your own decision-making perspective. It starts out with a discussion of why to invest in real estate. The answer is more complex than simply to make money. It considers diversification as a way to mitigate risks, but points out: "Most often, the key to successful investment is choosing the right piece of property—

the one that best fits not only your financial goals and limitations, but also your knowledge, skills, and available time."

The key to getting the thrust of the book is in getting an understanding of the relationship between you and the potential investment so that you can make appropriate decisions not only as what to invest in but also how to go about it.

The first chapter discusses control and liquidity, considerations that relate to personal references. Additionally, the chapter looks at inflation and taxes as considerations that favor investing in real estate. And, of course, there is discussion about getting cash flow and appreciation and using leverage to enhance both. All this is in the contexts of the risks that you are prepared to take.

The second chapter tells more about the book and about investing in real estate as it relates to you. You, as the player, are the focus of the next two chapters, which concentrate on the relationship between you and your investment. If you are not into the details, if you don't have an awareness of what is going on about you, if you don't have a touch of creativeness in dealing with issues, you may not be comfortable with investing in real estate as a direct investment. If you do well with reason, are confident, and can develop good strategies and tactfully deal with the other people, you will find yourself in a very favorable, competitive position.

The preceding items relate to time, work, and money. You need to assess the availability of your time for the investment, which is like operating a business. You can hire some help which you need to manage, and/or you can do some of the jobs yourself. In essence, you need a game plan for the operation of the investment.

Whatever your game plan, you will have to deal with other people, which brings us back to relationships. There are tenants, you hope, and agents aplenty. Your decisions relate to whether you want to manage by yourself or whether you want to hire management. If you chose to hire, you will be particularly interested in the professional organizations that provide accreditation of their members. Additionally, the book discusses a variety of other specializations that you may come in contact with. They are represented by other players. How you deal with them makes a difference in achieving success in your real estate investments. Indeed, the skills in investing in real estate are transferable to other endeavors; and you should be aware that you can transfer skills from other endeavors to real estate.

It is necessary to become acquainted with the terminology of the industry in order to effectively communicate. The first part of the book starts you off in this direction, and continues with boxed comments throughout the book to help further. Also included in the boxed statements are tips on "digging deeper." There are also added features such as "stop and think" boxes.

On top of all of this there is a discussion of appraisal methods and making a good deal. Then there is a chapter on negotiating, followed by a chapter on getting it in writing. Part I ends with a chapter on taxes.

This book is an easy read. The reader will get a good feel for what she or he needs to decide in looking to make money in personal real estate investing. It is about relationships, and the lessons are applicable to other endeavors. Enjoy!

Maury Seldin
St. Petersburg, Florida
February 2005

Dr. Maury Seldin is chair professor emeritus, College of Business Administration, American University, Washington, D.C. He is also chairman of the board and president, Homer Hoyt Advanced Studies Institute in Real Estate and Land Economics. He is a Counselor of Real Estate Emeritus. He has published eight books on real estate subjects. Currently, he is working on a book about understanding terrorism and its motivations.

Why Invest in Real Estate?

"More money has been made in real estate than in all industrial investments combined."
Andrew Carnegie (1835–1919), American industrialist

Andrew Carnegie, founder of U.S. Steel and one of the great industrialists of American history, said those words as the 20th century was just getting started. They held true for almost a hundred years—until Bill Gates redefined *industrial investment,* that is. Up to the age of computers, investing in real estate was the best road to riches for most people in the United States. Then came the 1990s.

Perhaps it was our love affair with the chip and with the then-booming stock market that prompted the following lines in *The Wall Street Journal Lifetime Guide to Money* (published in 1997): "Indeed, if you own your home, you should not be concerned if you do not own any investment real estate. Considering both the need for diversification and liquidity in a portfolio, a home is probably all the real estate most people need."

Have Americans become so committed to no-fuss, no-mess paper investments that direct investment in real estate is now too demanding for them? Are we afraid to get our hands spotted with paint or our shirts stained with perspiration? Or are 21st century Americans just predisposed to paper investments on which they can enjoy the roller-coaster ride of minute-by-minute value fluctuations?

So which quotation is correct, classic Carnegie or contemporary *Wall Street Journal*? Actually both quotations hold some truth, but not the whole truth. Money, lots of money, is still being made in investment real estate. And a good percentage of that money is being made by middle-income Americans at a time when very few of us can start up an industrial investment, whether it might be a steel mill or a computer company. But to give *The Wall Street Journal Lifetime Guide to Money* its due, real estate does make many demands upon its investors. It is not an appropriate investment for everyone.

It might even be fair to say that real estate investing is a little like the Marine Corps—for the few and the brave. If you're reading this book, however, you're a likely candidate. If real estate investing is right for you (and you are right for it), property ownership can significantly contribute to your financial security, perhaps even make you wealthy.

Buying property is very rarely the only right answer to the question: How can I secure the future? And for some people, it is never the right answer. But for those investors who are interested enough to learn its rules and strategies, real estate investment can add diversity, security, and big profits to a lifetime financial plan.

DIGGING DEEPER

If you'd like to see how the value of real estate in your area compares with the rest of the nation, you can ask your Uncle Sam. The Office of Federal Housing Enterprise Oversight (OFHEO) publishes a quarterly report that shows by statistics and graphs the changes in the house price index in the nine Census Bureau divisions and in each state individually. This information is invaluable for an overview before investing, but it is not a substitute for local marketplace research. The current quarterly report is available online or by request from:

Office of Federal Housing Enterprise Oversight
1700 G Street, N.W.
Washington, DC 20552
202-414-3800
http://www.ofheo.gov

Let's start by focusing on the two key words in that quotation from *The Wall Street Journal Lifetime Guide to Money*: *diversification* and *liquidity*. These are the two poles, plus and minus, in the arguments for and against adding real estate investment to your wealth-building plan. Both concepts are acknowledged as advantages of stock market investing. You diversify your holdings so that a sudden downturn in one area of the marketplace does not wreak havoc in your portfolio. In this electronic age, the liquidity of stocks is phenomenal. At virtually a moment's notice your holdings can become cash. But diversification and liquidity take on new meaning when applied to real estate investment.

Three Cheers for Diversification!

Back at the turn of the 17th century, Don Quixote, the ultimate idealist, declared, "'Tis the part of a wise man to keep himself today for tomorrow, and not venture all his eggs in one basket." *Don't put all your eggs in one basket* has become the mantra of the financial marketplace. But to understand what diversifying really means, think out of the box on a larger scale.

You can keep yourself very busy diversifying your stock market nest eggs into dozens of "baskets," and all your money is still in the stock market. To get out of that market, some people diversify into bonds, mortgage-backed securities, annuities, and real estate. All are viable and often-recommended possibilities, depending on your age, financial status, specialized knowledge, and temperament. But real estate is different from all the others.

Why? In the first place, human beings need it for survival. We live upon the land and, with the exception of landfills and volcanoes, there's no more land being made. In other words, the supply of real estate is finite and the demand elastic (seemingly infinite in areas where population growth is high). In the second place, it will not disappear. Changes in the value of real estate do not occur quickly and land is considered indestructible. Investing in appropriate real estate vehicles, therefore, may be the most effective diversification an individual can make.

Appropriate is a key word in that last sentence. Different types of real estate make different demands upon their owners. The key to successful investment is choosing the *right* piece of property, that is, the one that best fits not only your financial goals and limitations but also your knowledge, skills, and available time. Part I of this book will help you assess your real estate strengths and weaknesses and give you an indepth view of the process of investing in real estate. Part II will help you choose real estate investment vehicles that are appropriate for you. At this point, let's look at why real estate can add balance and control to your plan for building wealth.

Balancing Act

It doesn't take a lot of imagination to come up with this scene: *Flash! Terrorist attack. Word spreads across the entire nation instantly. Stockholders cry, "Sell! Sell! Sell!" Trading is halted on every major exchange. News commentators take over radio and television; the Internet buzzes; and sales of aspirin and Rolaids, not to mention Zoloft, spike nationwide. When trading resumes, virtually every stock is down, down, down.*

But time goes by and things get back to normal. Soon, investors are back at the game and it's "Buy! Buy! Buy!" So goes the stock market roller coaster.

By comparison, real estate is like riding the Little Engine That Could up the biggest hill in Kansas. Yes, there are cycles of good times and bad times in the real estate marketplace, but they generally occur slowly over time. No real estate investor vacationing in Australia needs to hunt out an American newspaper to see how the value of his or her land has changed.

In addition to trading at the speed of electricity, the stock market is also quickly responsive to national and worldwide events as they happen. While all real estate is somewhat influenced by the national economy, the major determinants of its value are local. Some experts believe that a slowing real estate market is a leading sign of a slowing economy in any given area. On the other hand, increased real estate values often substantiate the beginning of economic upswing in an area.

Okay, so investment in real estate is a genuine diversification of your portfolio, a place for your money outside the immediate influence of the financial marketplace. It balances and stabilizes a portfolio that might include more volatile investments in the stock, bond, and commodity markets.

In addition to investment diversification and the stability of its value, real estate adds tangibility to a wealth-building plan. You can see it, touch it, and walk on it. When you own a half-million dollars' worth of stocks, you have nothing to hold in your hand, nothing to show to another person. When you own a $500,000 rental property, you own something concrete, something you can point to in a particular place, and, often, something that puts money in your pocket each month.

A Matter of Control

Real estate is a hands-on investment. In fact, many college textbooks list among its drawbacks the term *management intensive*. In normal language, that jargon means that work is required. "Work," however, does not necessarily mean cutting the grass or painting the back stairs; you can hire people to do those jobs if you choose. Work can and usually does mean time spent in planning, supervision, and control.

The work involved in most real estate investment is another factor that sets it apart from investment in the financial marketplace. (After you've made the effort to pick a good mutual fund, it will make—or lose—money for you without any more work on your part.) But there are rewards that come with real estate's demands, some financial and some satisfying to the self.

One of the most important rewards is control. A small shareholder has no control over the workings of

General Motors or Microsoft. On the other hand, the owner of a real estate investment can improve it or let it deteriorate, raise or lower rents, change its appearance and (with the possibility of a zoning change) its primary usage, and decide when and for how much it should be offered for sale.

The possibility of sweat equity is another benefit of this "management intensive" investment that simply does not exist in paper investments. Investing in stocks is like buying a pari-mutuel ticket at the track, whereas investing in real estate is like owning the horse, feeding it, training it, and maybe even riding it in the race. In real estate, what you do *can* make a difference. (See Chapter 4 for more about demands and rewards.)

LEARNING THE LANGUAGE

Sweat equity is additional property value produced by the owner's work in improving the land or buildings on it. Some mortgage lending programs allow a purchaser to do work on the property in place of some or all of the required down payment and other costs of purchase. (Read Chapter 9 for more about financing.)

Just How Much Diversity Can You Take?

For some people, buying and selling a home is all the real estate stress they ever want to experience. But people with an entrepreneurial spirit and an interest in property almost always ask an important financial-planning question: What portion of my investment capital should I put into the real estate marketplace?

Choosing a balance among investment opportunities is a very personal matter. Different individuals will (and should) allocate different portions of real estate, stocks, annuities, and other investments within their portfolios. For example, there are intelligent people at one end of the spectrum who wouldn't ever consider being a landlord, and equally intelligent people at the other end who have by far the greater part of their available investment funds in the real estate marketplace.

One of the goals of this book is to help you make the decision of how much real estate is right for you at each of the many stages and decision points of your life. Whatever allocation of investment money you choose, keep in mind that you should always have on hand some investment vehicles that keep your holdings virtually as accessible as cash. Putting all your assets into one basket is, in fact, very risky, even if the basket seems as big, safe, and stable as American real estate.

Working with Liquidity

Real estate is known as a nonliquid asset. In other words, if you invest in real estate, it's not always easy to cash out when you want to. Long-term commitment to investment property gives the investor the freedom to wait for optimum market conditions before putting the property up for sale. But what happens if you suddenly need the money that you used for the down payment on your property?

That's it in a nutshell! Liquidity is often pointed out as the major risk factor in real estate investment. But it is not an unsolvable problem, although many investors will tell you that they don't always like the solution.

That solution is borrowing for sudden cash needs. Because it is a tangible asset, real property can be borrowed against. In today's financial marketplace, mortgages are available that enable an owner

> **LEARNING THE LANGUAGE**
>
> In the world of money, **liquidity** means the speed at which an investment can be converted into cash.

to draw some, if not all, of his or her capital investment out of a property. (See Chapter 9 for more about short- and long-term borrowing.)

The advantage of borrowing rather than selling to get the use of your cash is that you continue to own your real estate, collecting rents, anticipating appreciation, and deducting mortgage interest, expenses, and depreciation on your tax returns. The disadvantage is that you are paying interest for the use of the borrowed money. This additional interest payment could turn your cash flow negative and make holding the property financially painful. (See Chapter 6 for more on what makes a good deal.)

". . . liquidity is really a judgmental factor. Anything is salable at a price."

David T. Goldstick, real estate attorney and coauthor of *The Complete Guide to Co-ops and Condominiums*

But what if you must have your money out and additional mortgaging is not an option? Well, you can sell. Except in rare instances, a nonliquid asset is not necessarily an unsalable asset. To increase salability, you just have to make the price more attractive. For example, if the fair market value of a building is $300,000, it will usually sell relatively quickly if you ask $310,000 and are willing to negotiate down to the $300,000 fair market value. It will usually sell more quickly if you *ask* $294,000 at the outset and negotiate down somewhat— even more quickly if you're willing to sell at $255,000 or less.

"$255,000! That's at least a 15 percent loss!" you cry.

Yes, but don't you know investors who have experienced 15 percent losses in the stock market too? And remember, the 15 percent "loss" we're talking about is the "apparent loss"—that is, the difference between the fair market value and the actual selling price. It is a measure of the amount of financial pain you're feeling because you're forced to liquidate, but it is not an accurate measure of your loss. Your actual loss can, in fact, be less or more painful than the apparent loss.

The real question in a sale to liquidate assets is: How much of your capital investment are you actually losing? Let's consider a few examples at the painful liquidation $255,000 selling price. These examples are oversimplified to make a clear differentiation between market value and investment value.

If you originally bought the property at $225,000 in cash and own it free and clear (without a mortgage), you are still recouping your original capital investment of $225,000 plus about $30,000 profit, minus property transfer costs. Of course, that "profit" does not factor in any decrease in the value of money caused by inflation, nor does it consider your capital expenditures for improvements over time. Depending on how long you owned

---

LEARNING THE LANGUAGE

In the real estate and financial marketplaces, **capital** is wealth (usually money) that is used to create income. Your capital investment in a real estate purchase would include your down payment and your expenditures for improvements.

the property, $30,000 may be a very poor return on your investment or perhaps even a loss.

If you bought the property at its current selling price ($255,000) and have a $225,000 mortgage balance on it, you'll be coming out with your initial capital investment *minus* the costs of property transfer, debt service, and maintenance. This will probably be a cash loss but the amount of the loss is very much affected by how long you have owned the property (the longer the period of ownership, the greater the loss).

If you bought the property recently at market value ($300,000) with a $240,000 mortgage on it, you will experience a serious loss. You invested $60,000 as a down payment. At a sale price of $255,000, you show only $15,000 of your invested money left. Not only are you unlikely to get that amount back, but also you'll most likely have to bring cash to the closing to pay for property transfer costs. So you will have lost your entire investment plus some.

Certainly, that last example is financially painful enough to push the property into the nonliquid category. This kind of nonliquidity is the reason so many homebuyers who bought a condominium apartment in the mid-1980s became landlords. Prices had been in an upward spiral. When the market slowed in the late 1980s, those owners couldn't get their down payments back at the going market prices. If they wanted or needed to move, they often chose to rent their condominiums rather than sell at a loss.

Many of these properties were sold very profitably in the boom markets of the 1990s and early 2000s. Others, however, are still being held because they have proved to be such good investments. This kind of nonliquidity is a very good example of why financial advisors recommend that you allocate to investment real estate only money that you will not need for at least three to five years.

Liquidity is also a problem for those investors who are likely to move (or be moved by their employers) frequently. Long-distance ownership is discussed in Chapters 4 and 6. It can be profitable and produce comforting positive cash flow, but, as you would expect, it has its challenges. When being transferred by their employers, real estate investors who wish to liquidate their real estate investments before moving usually take a cut in potential profit, sometimes even a loss.

Five Reasons to Invest in Real Estate

Diversity and liquidity are the big plus and the big minus that most people perceive when looking into the real estate marketplace from outside its gates. But what about all those people who are now active in the marketplace? Why do they buy and sell investment real estate? Let's look at five of the most common reasons: inflation, appreciation, positive cash flow, tax benefits, and leverage.

Fighting Inflation

There are conflicting theories as to what causes inflation, but virtually everyone agrees that it's here to stay. This ongoing rise in the cost of goods and services seems very much in harmony with the universe— both are ever expanding. So there's not much sense in railing at something so completely beyond your control. Better to find a way to beat it.

The primary measure of inflation in the United States is the consumer price index (CPI), sometimes called the cost-of-living index. This index is determined by a monthly survey by the U.S. Bureau of Labor Statistics (BLS) of the average change over time in the prices paid by consumers in 87 urban areas across the nation. The BLS classifies "goods and services" expenditures into more than 200 categories arranged into eight major groups: *Food and Beverages; Housing; Apparel; Transportation; Medical Care; Recrea-*

tion; Education and Communication; and *Other Goods and Services* (tobacco, haircuts, and funeral expenses are examples of "other"). When the CPI goes up, the purchasing power of each dollar goes down. That's inflation.

So how can you beat it? Real estate (both your home and your investment property) is just about the best weapon available. You see, the CPI is a composite of price changes in all the goods and services that are tracked. But all goods and services do not increase or decrease at the same rate. The rate of increase in the value of real property consistently outpaces the CPI. So just owning a piece of property usually puts you ahead of inflation.

"Making money with no effort, no risk! Hooray! Hooray!" you shout. "This is the start on the road to riches."

Whoa! Be careful that you don't confuse that old truism, "Real estate is your best hedge against inflation," with the potential appreciation of a property that you are considering. Being ahead of inflation keeps you from losing the real buying power of your money; it doesn't make you rich. Appreciation helps you to make money (and it may or may not require some work on your part).

The results of inflation and appreciation combine to produce a higher price tag at selling time. Many novice investors call that sum their profit and, in fact, the IRS taxes you on it. (An exception for most of us allows $500,000 of profit from the sale of a primary residence to be tax-free for those filing jointly, and $250,000 tax-free for those filing single returns.) But don't run to the bank dumb and happy. Your evaluation of your investment success will be more accurate and you'll judge all future purchases more profitably if you can distinguish between the effects of inflation and the effects of appreciation in value of your property.

Appreciating Appreciation

Let's look at how appreciation is often confused with inflation. If the rate of inflation in real estate is 4 percent a year and if a property increases in value from

> ## "Inflation is always and everywhere a monetary phenomenon."
>
> Milton Friedman, Nobel Prize–winning American economist

$100,000 to $104,000, there has been no real appreciation. The property owner may feel that his investment is making money but, in fact, it has just stayed even in terms of real worth. Appreciation happens when the worth in real dollars (not inflated dollars) increases.

Appreciation is the goal of every investor who buys and sells real estate. To choose property that will appreciate significantly (and therefore be profitable), you must know the economic, geographic, and demographic aspects of an area and you must have a sense for those aspects of real property that increase desirability and sales appeal. For example, the knowledge that a large corporation will soon be locating its national headquarters in a certain town will affect the area's economics and demographics and would indicate a probable appreciation in the value of land. A knowledge that younger families with children are moving into an area would prompt an investor who is doing rehabilitation of run-down single-family houses to add an additional bathroom to increase the value of the building (or the potential rent). (There's more about appreciation in Chapter 6.)

LEARNING THE LANGUAGE

In real estate, **appreciation** is an increase in the relative value of a property brought about by:

- Economic factors, such as an increased demand for housing in the area
- Geographic factors, such as a positive improvement in the condition and appeal of the neighborhood or nearby neighborhoods
- The elimination of negative factors, such as the rerouting of heavy street traffic to a highway
- Improvements made by the owner, such as the addition of another bathroom

---

Positive Cash Flow

When you invest in rental property, you not only get to use other people's money to help buy the property (your mortgage loan), you also get to use other people's money to pay for the property and its expenses (the rents you collect). Real estate is the only investment vehicle with this kind of special subsidy. Income from the ideal rental property will pay all the expenses of the property and provide a little extra cash for the investor to spend. At the same time, it will chug right along acting as a hedge against inflation and appreciating, too. Not a bad deal if you can get it—and you can.

There's more about cash flow and how it figures in picking a good deal in Chapter 4. At this point, it's important to remember that cash flow affects financing, maintenance, taxes, and resale value. It must be analyzed carefully with the full awareness that some sellers attempt to manipulate the cash-flow numbers. (Yes, it's that important.) When cash flow is positive, your real estate investment can happily add spendable dollars to your monthly income. Sometimes even negative cash flow can add positive numbers to your federal income-tax refund. (See Chapters 6 and 9.)

Taxes! Taxes!

Not only are there whole books written about investment property taxation, there also are whole shelves of such books in law libraries and whole groups of lawyers who specialize in using them. Real estate, it seems, is the golden child of the Internal Revenue Code. No other investment vehicle is so favored, and no other investment vehicle uses taxes so favorably. Few investors, however, can take time to learn all the nuances of the tax laws. For the individual investor, the best approach is to understand the basic concepts and then to rely on a tax specialist, lawyer, or accountant for advice on details, procedures, and compliance.

Chapter 10 will help you get a handle on those concepts. Among the tax advantages to look forward to are:

- **Depreciation**
- **Deductibility** of debt interest, property taxes, and operating costs
- **Tax credits** for historic and low-income housing
- **Tax-deferred exchanges**

In addition to the real estate tax breaks available for all Americans, Uncle Sam also gives a special nod to older folks. As you probably know, anyone who con-

> **"A taxpaying public that doesn't understand the law is a taxpaying public that can't comply with the law."**
>
> Lawrence Gibbs, IRS commissioner

LEARNING THE LANGUAGE

In the world of investment real estate, **cash flow** is the amount of cash left after gross income from the property is used to pay the property taxes, all operating expenses, and the debt service (mortgage loan payments). It can be **positive cash flow,** which means the investor receives income, or **negative cash flow,** which means the investor must put in money to meet carrying costs.

tinues to work after claiming Social Security benefits risks the reduction of those benefits. (Reduction is on a sliding scale by age and income, but it can be as much as $1 for every $2 you earn if you are under the full retirement age of 65.) Now here's the good news: Rental income is not counted when calculating the amount you can earn before benefits are reduced! This makes rental property with positive cash flow especially inviting to younger retirees.

The Power of Leverage

Are there investment real estate properties that you might buy for the $50,000 you've inherited or managed to save? Not many. The need to borrow large amounts of money in order to make a purchase is one of the fear factors that keep many prospective investors out of the real estate marketplace. But using borrowed money is standard practice and one of the most effective strategies for profitable real estate investment.

Here again, it's necessary to oversimplify the financial details of a story to illustrate the money-making concept of leverage. There aren't many $100,000 investment properties available in today's real estate marketplace, but the number makes the concept easier to understand.

> **LEARNING THE LANGUAGE**
>
> In the real estate marketplace, **leverage** refers to the use of mortgage financing that allows a relatively small amount of cash investment to purchase a property with the expectation that appreciation and inflation will create a disproportionately large return upon sale.

Joe Smith bought a house for $100,000. He invested $10,000 as a down payment and took out a mortgage for $90,000. He sold the house five years later for $150,000, paid off his mortgage, and put $50,000 "profit" into his bank account. Way to go, Joe! That's a return of 500 percent on your original $10,000 investment!

Well, not exactly. There's an essential aspect of leverage that's been left out: the cost of carrying the mortgage (the interest rate). Upside leverage is created when the cost of borrowing money is less than the free and clear return from the property. "Free and clear" means the cash-out number you get after all expenses, such as taxes, maintenance, and selling costs, are deducted.

Joe Smith made a substantial return on his investment because he was using the power of OPM (other people's money) to increase the base upon which his investment would grow. In the real estate marketplace, the smaller your down payment, the greater your leverage and, therefore, the greater the possibility of a phenomenal return on your investment capital as can be seen in the illustration below.

The $10,000 invested down payment allows the purchase of a $100,000 property. The percentage of inflation and appreciation then affects the entire $100,000. So your $10,000 is growing just as though it were $100,000. This works as long as the cost of borrowing the $90,000 is less than the rising value of the property.

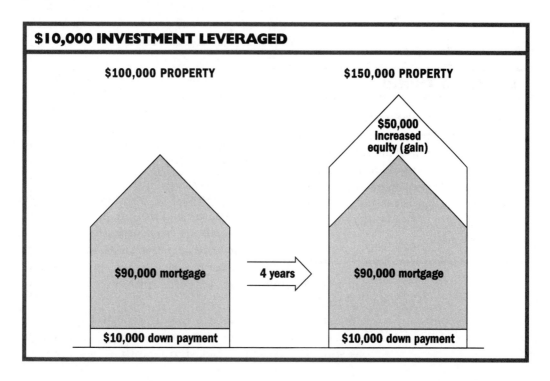

$10,000 INVESTMENT LEVERAGED

$100,000 PROPERTY

$150,000 PROPERTY

$50,000 Increased equity (gain)

$90,000 mortgage

4 years

$90,000 mortgage

$10,000 down payment

$10,000 down payment

Although the situation occurs far less frequently in this country than elsewhere in the world, you can also lose money by using leverage in real estate investing. When interest rates are high and inflation and appreciation are low, the smaller your down payment, the more potential there is for serious financial pain. Let's create a worst-case scenario:

Jane Jones buys a $100,000 property with $10,000 down on an adjustable-rate mortgage. Rates go up during the first two-year term of the ARM, to increase the interest rate by two full points on almost $90,000. The increase in monthly mortgage payment is not quite covered by the rental income, so Ms. Jones finds herself in a negative cash flow situation. (She's putting in money each month just to make the necessary payments.) She decides to sell. But inflation has been held to a minimum and appreciation in the area has been negligible. Even if she sells at fair market value, the real estate broker's commission will wipe out most of the positive return. Therefore, she has paid more for the use of the borrowed money than she will make through the sale.

STOP AND THINK!

The key to using **leverage** is a mortgage interest rate that is lower than the probable rate of increase in the value of the property. Beware the opposite, however. High interest rates and slowly increasing real estate values can create **reverse leverage,** in which you are paying more for the use of the money than you are potentially making.

Just as positive leverage can easily bring a return of 500 percent or more on your down-payment investment, reverse leverage can wipe out 100 percent or more. Some sellers must actually bring cash to the closing to pay off the mortgage in a reverse-leverage situation. Whereas a small down payment increases the potential for huge returns from positive leverage, it also increases the risk of reverse leverage because the amount of debt being carried is great.

In good times, real estate leveraging has made many fortunes. Some investors refinance a property as soon as the value rises significantly. They take out the accessible cash and use it as a minimal down payment on another property. When those two properties rise in value, these investors refinance again and buy again, building their holdings from two houses to four or more. And as long as the economy keeps expanding and financing is available at good rates, they can continue to build their investment pyramids. This is absolutely legal. It's also risky because cash flow is seldom more than marginally positive—or sometimes negative—and a long vacancy in a unit can cause enough financial strain to force a quick sale to get cash out (which usually means a selling price at below fair market value).

Understanding leverage is one of the most essential keys to success in the investment real estate marketplace. Once you understand the principle, however, you can learn to use it in ways that will accomplish your investment goals while meeting your risk profile. Maybe that's a bit much to think about so early in this book. But keep reading. You won't get pat answers or works-every-time rules of thumb, but by the time you come to the end of Part I, you should have all the pieces in hand to put your own investment puzzle together and see positive results. Then you can choose your vehicles from Part II.

STOP AND THINK!

Personal-finance advisors and real estate professionals generally agree that you should not invest in real estate any amount of cash that you might need during the next three to five years. The advice is based upon the premise that a sale forced by narrow time constraints might not be profitable.

Limiting Risk

Risk is everywhere—crossing the street, getting married, having a child, taking a pill. Used to be, many people thought their money was risk-free in a "savings" bank. Then there was the savings-and-loan debacle of the 1980s, and the federal government had to bail out the banks. And people began to fear that perhaps their savings weren't "safe" after all. But there's a difference between "risk-free" and "safe."

Money in a savings account in a federally insured bank is considered safe. If the bank goes under, the government makes sure you'll get your money, up to the limits of its insurance. But that doesn't mean the account is risk-free. If the interest paid is less than the rate of inflation, you will, in fact, have less buying power; in other words, you'll lose money.

Investing in real estate has risks, to be sure, just as it has opportunities. The smart investor looks for ways to lower risk and risk factors. Throughout this book you'll read about real estate investment pitfalls and high-voltage situations; whenever possible, you'll get advice on how to avoid them, work around them, or work through them. Right now let's briefly look at the three main areas of risk in real estate investment.

THE ECONOMY. You may not have control over the national economy or even your local chamber of commerce, but you certainly can be sensitive to goings-on in your community.

MORTGAGE MONEY. You can't control the financial marketplace either, but you can search out the best terms and the cheapest money available. And you can make certain that your mortgage-loan agreement has no snares and does have safeguards for the borrower.

THE QUALITY OF YOUR INVESTMENT PROPERTY. You have complete control to choose or not to choose a property. To limit risk, you can get professional help, such as inspection services, accountants, lawyers, and buyer-brokers. (Read more about the people in the real estate marketplace in Chapter 5.) Most important, you have your own skills and knowledge, which you can sharpen at will.

KEEP IN MIND

- **Real estate is a local business** affected by the local economy and demographics.
- **Real estate can add balance, stability, and control** to your portfolio.
- **Real estate is considered a nonliquid asset.** The need to sell quickly to liquidate this asset will usually reduce its return.
- **How much investment real estate to include in one's wealth-building plan** is a matter of personal choice that should be governed by the investor's financial resources, goals, risk profile, skills, and knowledge.
- **Plus factors** in real estate investment are the hedge against inflation, the potential for appreciation, the power of leverage, positive cash flow, and tax advantages.

How This Book Can Help You Invest Profitably

"Knowledge is power."

Francis Bacon (1561–1626), British essayist

Real estate is defined in most dictionaries and textbooks as the land and everything attached to it. We literally live on it and in it. In fact, real estate is the only investment vehicle that everyone touches every day. It is so familiar that many of us forget that it is a commodity, an economic "good," like soybeans or precious metals. Like other goods, it has a value that responds to the forces of supply and demand. (See Chapter 6 for more about supply and demand.)

The familiarity of real estate has positive and negative effects. For people just starting out with a few thousand dollars to invest, real property is often a comfortable and appealing investment because it lacks that sense of distance and strangeness associated with moneymaking opportunities that are far removed from everyday life, such as the stock market. Real estate as an investment vehicle doesn't exist in a boardroom in Chicago, with parts of it scattered across the nation and sometimes even in foreign nations. Instead, your investment could be whole and complete quite near where you live, maybe even just down the street!

As a moneymaking opportunity, real estate doesn't seem cerebral, scary, complexly structured, and totally under someone else's control. It's a let's-keep-it-in-the-family type of investment. But that sense of comfort and easy familiarity actually increases the investment risk for some property buyers, especially newcomers to the marketplace.

Because they see real estate everywhere in their everyday lives, some rookies forget that buying and managing investment property is a business, and a competitive business at that. They dash into the marketplace equipped only with homebuying experience, and sometimes not even with that. Sometimes they are enticed into the marketplace by no-cash-down, get-rich-quick, tape-and-seminar salespeople who promise a surefire formula for success on the road to riches.

Unlike an experiment in chemistry class or a bicycle that needs assembly, the outcome of a real estate venture cannot be determined or predicted by a formula or a procedure. That's why the vast majority of those "surefire" programs full of formulas and procedures simply don't work as a means of building financial security and wealth. In the real estate marketplace, a buyer who is proceeding step-by-step in a formula program will almost certainly encounter obstacles that are not written in that particular script. And so it follows that in most cases the "program" will not include solutions to the problems or answers to the puzzles. Sometimes, following someone else's "works-every-time" program can even lead to significant financial loss because of overpaying for the property or overcommitting to rehabilitation and underestimating its costs.

"But wait!" you say. "With all the computer programs and information available nowadays, why can't someone come up with a good program that really will work in the real estate investment marketplace—a program where you can key in the specific data for your deal?"

The answer is simple: because real estate investment is not a science. There are indeed elements of both mathematics and science in many areas of the marketplace, but in that same marketplace, there are also human beings, money, goals

---

LEARNING THE LANGUAGE

Metes and bounds: a method of describing land by recording boundary lines, terminal points, their angles, and degrees of latitude and longitude. Originally, *metes* referred to distance and *bounds* referred to direction. Today, the words are used together when referring to a legal description of property. Metes and bounds set each piece of property in the world apart from every other one.

and motivations, and the unique metes and bounds of each and every piece of real property.

The process of making a profitable real estate investment is more like playing in a football game than doing a scientific procedure or following the instructions in an assembly process. You simply can't count on proceeding step-by-step because the steps and strategies in the real estate process are not always predictable and sometimes not even logical. The old cliché that no two deals are alike is true because no two pieces of property are alike, no two buyers and sellers are alike, and the financial elements of no two deals are alike. Every transaction has obstacles, differences of opinion, and adjustments. Elements in the transfer of property ownership can change right up to the final whistle at the closing table (when the ink is still drying on the last required signature).

Just as it's very difficult to buy a piece of property without some understanding of the procedures required by real estate law, it's almost impossible to make a good deal without some flexibility, sensitivity to the goals of the other party, and insight into the workings of the marketplace. The person who is checking off steps in pursuit of a secret formula or method learned from a get-rich-in-real-estate program often misses clues to the seller's motivations and goals. Those clues might have determined a successful negotiating strategy. When rushing in on a wave of hype and a bit of newly learned general-marketplace information, the weekend seminar–trained neophyte might even fail to estimate the value of the prospective purchase within its local marketplace. If that happens, the best nothing-down bargain may turn out to be a pit into which the buyer pours money.

Why are all these words being spent to discuss investor training programs that promise a formula or method for success? Because those programs are advertised widely and appeal to a great many people;

> ### LEARNING THE LANGUAGE
>
> **Closing table** is literally the table upon which the closing is enacted. The closing of a real estate sale or purchase is the final procedure in which documents are executed and recorded, the sale is completed, and ownership passes from seller to buyer.

because they don't work for the vast majority; and because it's important you understand that this book is not one of them. Before you decide to buy investment real estate, you must put aside ideas like: *Get Rick Quick! Easy Method! Works-Every-Time Strategy!*

There is money to be made in real estate, but as an investment vehicle, it is not quick, easy, or surefire. Success is definitely related to knowledge and understanding of the marketplace. There are indeed methods, procedures, and strategies that work and they will increase your chances for significant profit, but each decision and each move must be judged for its appropriateness to the particular circumstances of a particular transaction.

But how can a new investor make such judgments?

First, you must take the time to understand the what, where, why, when, and how of the real estate marketplace. Once *you* understand these working elements, you won't be shackled to a guru's formula or method. You'll be able to make your own decisions in response to the elements of your particular deal. Your understanding and judgment will guide you in each and every venture, no matter what the type or size of the investment.

Does that sound like a dream goal to you? A too-good-to-be-true tactic to increase your odds for making money? Well, it's not too good to be true. It's the goal of every smart real estate investor. *And helping you to achieve it is the goal of this book.*

Taking the time to learn the concepts that govern the real estate investment marketplace may seem like an imposing and distasteful chore when you have some money in hand and opportunity seems to be beckoning. But it's neither as difficult nor as boring as you may think. If you keep reading, you're going to experience one "ah-ha, now I understand" insight after another. The financial return on your reading time may be the best investment you'll ever make.

The Power of a Particular Place

What makes van Gogh's *Sunflowers* worth millions of dollars? After all, it's just a piece of canvas rather heavily loaded with paint. There are lots of copies. And, heaven knows, there are millions of other flower paintings in the world.

The answer is simple: There is only one original painting (it is unique) and owning it is considered very desirable (there is a demand). These same elements determine the value of real estate.

Each parcel of real property is unique because it is the only place on the earth defined by that particular set of metes and bounds. The degree of demand for a particular property is determined by many factors, but most important among them is its unique location. Let's take a minute to look at how the singularity of every piece of property influences its value.

> **STOP AND THINK!**
>
> Don't ever accept: "This building is exactly like that one; it's just in another spot. They're worth the same money." Location (not size, style, or construction) is the primary determinant of value in the real estate marketplace.

There's No Place Like It

Every piece of real estate is land, a particular piece of the earth. Its surface can be staked and walked upon, and its ownership extends theoretically downward to the center of the earth and upward to the limits of the atmosphere. When you buy real estate, therefore, you buy not only what you see but what's under the land and above it.

Ownership of the earth beneath the boundaries of your parcel of land is the basis for mineral-rights laws, not to mention the making of a goodly number of millionaires in gold, oil, and other deeply buried desirables. Toxic elements beneath the soil, however, can destroy value. Looking in the opposite direction, ownership of airspace above a parcel of land allows for condominium law where you hold title to the airspace between designated walls in the building and an undivided interest in the building itself and the land upon

Title in real estate has nothing to do with the name of a book or song. It is the legal evidence that one has right of possession to the land. Title is conveyed from one party to another by a document called a deed. It is correct to say either, "Title to the property will close on January 15" or "We will take title to the property on January 15."

which it stands. (See Chapter 13 for more about condominium ownership.)

In every state, there are laws governing the sale and purchase of each unique piece of real property. You can learn them or you can hire professionals (real estate brokers, title insurance companies, or lawyers) to take your transaction through to closing according to the state and local laws that apply to it. That's the procedural part of transferring title to each piece of land. And getting it done is relatively easy. Before it can happen, however, there must be a contract of sale with a named purchase price.

Determining the purchase price that makes the property a good investment is not so easy. It requires knowledge not only of all aspects of the particular property but also of the unique marketplace in which it is being sold.

Demand Drives Up Price

The ageless law of supply and demand governs every marketplace in your life. It goes like this:

■ **If supply exceeds demand, prices fall.**
■ **If demand exceeds supply, prices rise.**

Supply and demand determine value in the real estate marketplace just as they determine the price of household goods, groceries, oil, or any other commodity sold in the world. To be in demand, a property must be desirable to buyers. The more desirable it is to buyers (the more in demand), the more likely it is to be profitable to the seller. Every investment purchase therefore should be based upon a sound understanding of the elements that influence the desirability of and demand for a particular type of property in a particular location. Coupled with supply, these factors determine value in the real estate marketplace. (See Chapter 6 for more on marketplace factors.)

Some of the specific factors that influence supply and demand in the real estate marketplace are the same as those that influence the value of other kinds of investments: national and even international economic trends, the pace of new construction, and the price of materials, for example. But in the real estate marketplace, local factors have greater influence than they do in other investment vehicles.

Real estate remains a local business because the "product" is fixed. (Land and buildings cannot be moved to areas of higher demand to increase their value.) Most of the economic statistics and information published in national newspapers and broadcast on radio and television are based on nationwide figures. Because we live in a huge nation whose overall economic profile contains many diverse economic pockets, you cannot rely solely on national statistics to make judgments on your local real estate marketplace. In other words, what's being touted as a great economy in most of the nation may be a dismal economy in your investment area, or your local economy may be hot while most of the nation is sluggish.

"Hot tips" in real estate are more like a *Dick's Picks* sheet at the track than a *Wall Street Week* recommendation for a stock purchase. Information about the top horse and his or her competitors at Churchill Downs, Kentucky, will probably increase the likelihood of your picking a winner but it will have little, if any, bearing on opportunities at tracks in Florida, New York, or Texas. Real estate buy, hold, or sell tips, therefore, cannot be broadcast nationwide like stock market tips. Like the handicapper at the racecourse who studies first how each horse has performed in comparison with the other horses in that race and then factors in the weather, the post position, and the jockey, the real estate investor must first compare each prospective purchase with similar properties in the local area and then factor in local sociological and economic trends. There is no "hot tip" that will be appropriate everywhere in the nation.

By now you're probably convinced that you can't get real estate investment help by flipping to a particular television channel or by attending a get-rich-quick seminar. You know that you'll have to make your own decisions about what constitutes a good investment in the real estate marketplace. Perhaps you can imagine yourself with all your investment money in hand standing alone in a huge marketplace. A little scary, isn't it? Are you perhaps thinking about closing this book and going back to the study and contemplation of which mutual fund should get your money? Don't!

Learning to deal in the real estate marketplace is not as difficult as it may sound. Remember, you will most likely invest ncar where you live. Becoming familiar with the local economy means reading the morning paper a little more carefully and listening with a critical and discerning ear to the social talk on the golf course, around the watercooler at work, or at backyard barbecues. And there's a lot more about what to watch for and how to make evaluations in Chapter 6.

It's a Game without a League

The mechanics of dealing in the real estate marketplace are not the only obstacle to success. There's yet another reason why many prospective real estate investors quit before they've begun to succeed. Investing in real estate is a game where experience and training are not prerequisites for playing. You might say it's a game without a league because only the price tags on properties of interest limit who can compete against whom. A first-time buyer might be competing for a particular property with an investor who currently owns six other properties and who has bought and sold several-times-six properties in his career. Or a rookie might find himself or herself negotiating with a seller who makes a very comfortable living buying and selling similar properties.

How bad is that? Imagine that you've been invited to play a little flag football on a Sunday afternoon. You gather a team of friends and go out to the park dressed in jeans and T-shirts with like-colored flags in your back pockets. When you get there, you find yourself facing the New England Patriots in full uniform.

And that's not all. You notice that the field is not exactly level. You're going to have to run uphill to score a touchdown. Even if you know all the rules of football, the odds are against you.

Is that picture scary or what? Never mind the mutual funds, now you're ready to take your investment cache and run down to your neighborhood bank for a nice, safe CD!

Well, that might be a bit of an overreaction to a frightening fantasy. Stock market trading, mutual funds, even certificates of deposit all have a place in a good financial plan, but so does real estate investment. Reading this book may not get you ready to take on the real estate equivalent of the Patriots but it will equip you with most of the knowledge possessed by pros and semipros who are dealing in smaller properties priced at under two million dollars. In fact, when you finish, you may have better market savvy than many of them.

> **"He that will not sail till all dangers are over must never put to sea."**
>
> Thomas Fuller (1654–1734), *Gnomologia*, 1792, No. 2352

What This Book Will Do for You

So there are no surefire formulas and there are no quick picks or 100-percent predictions for your local marketplace. Well then, what can this book do to help you put real estate on your road to wealth? Let's take a look at what's to come.

The Concepts
Part I, "A Foundation to Build Upon," contains the nuts and bolts material you absolutely must know to function profitably in the marketplace. But this is more than a book of facts, rules, and procedures.

Chapters 3 and 4 will focus on you as a player (you could be your own worst enemy, you know) and Chapter 5 will cover all the other players as they relate to you, the buyer or seller. Evaluating property, making good judgments, negotiating, and protecting yourself legally are covered in Chapters 6, 7, and 8, with financing and taxes discussed in Chapters 9 and 10.

The Investment Vehicles

Part II, "Choosing the Right Investment," gets right down to what to buy and how to do it. It will discuss the eight investment vehicles most appropriate for beginners: single-family houses, multi-family houses, condos and co-ops, mixed-use buildings, vacation-area properties, small apartment buildings, land and subdivision, and real estate investment trusts REITs). Among the investment factors covered in these chapters will be:

- **What's available**
- **The plus points of the investment vehicle**
- **The risk factors**
- **Where to find properties**
- **How to pick a good one**
- **Management and tax tips**

Chapter 18, "But Can You Make a Living at It?" is a bonus—an entirely new chapter for this third edition, and a reason to keep this book on your shelf "just in case." It takes real estate out of the "investment" category in your life and moves it to "career." Can you do it? Will it be secure enough? This chapter answers lots of questions you may have as making a living in real estate becomes an increasingly viable opportunity for many.

The Boxes

Throughout the book, you'll find highlighted or boxed material to help you access information more easily. You've already encountered all four categories of material but here's an overview for the rest of the book.

Learning the Language is the definitions box. In addition to its rules, procedures, and challenges, the real estate marketplace has a language all its own (words or definitions you'd never find in a pocket dictionary). Because you'll miss much of what's going on if you don't know these words as they apply to the real estate marketplace, they are defined at appropriate points in the text.

Defining these words in context when you first encounter them eliminates the need for a glossary at the end of the book. In your reading or in your dealings in the marketplace, whenever you come across a word you don't understand, check for it in the index. You'll find it listed alphabetically, along with the page number where it's defined.

Stop and Think! is the "Don't miss this!" box. It deals with essential information, pitfalls, and warnings. You should stop, take notice, and think about what you read in these sidebars. These boxes will help to keep you out of trouble.

Digging Deeper tells you where to go for more information. It might list books, magazine articles, professional associations, organizations offering help, government agencies, etc. Wherever possible, it will include addresses, phone numbers, and Web sites.

Keep in Mind boxes are placed at the end of each chapter to summarize and reiterate the main points of the chapter. They list what you might consider "Lessons Learned."

Food for Thought is also scattered into each chapter in the form of quotations in the margins. The words may be thought provoking, insightful, or maybe just good for a laugh. The speaker of the quotation might be anyone from an ancient Greek philosopher to a living real estate tycoon or even a world-class figure who has nothing to do with real estate but something important to say that applies just about everywhere.

On Your Mark, Get Set, . . .

So are you ready to suit up for a moneymaking game in the real estate marketplace? Not so fast!

What you really need right now are a comfortable chair and a good reading lamp. Think of *Making Money in Real Estate* as a one-volume training manual or perhaps a football game playbook that tells you what the pros have learned by trial and error. This is the time for training your mind. You'll get plenty of hands-on experience when you actually enter the marketplace.

Will the mental training be worth the effort? Well, you'll have a much better chance of winning in the investment real estate marketplace than you would playing flag football against the Patriots. Odds are that you'll close the book and put reading it right up there on your list of "The Best Moneymaking Things I Ever Did."

KEEP IN MIND

- **There is no get-rich-quick, easy-method,** works-every-time program in the investment real estate marketplace.
- **Location and local economic factors** are important in determining property value.
- **Every piece of real estate is unique.**
- **A real estate investment decision** should be based on the specifics of the property in question and the elements of the particular deal being negotiated.

Are You the Real Estate Type?

"The self-explorer, whether he wants to or not, becomes the explorer of everything else."
Elias Canetti (1905–1994), writer and Nobel Prize winner

With a few exceptions, the road to wealth in investment real estate is a hands-on enterprise. It is management intensive, as the textbooks say. Traveling it successfully requires knowledge, skill, time, and work. It also requires self-knowledge. This is an investment field where you must gauge your own strengths and weaknesses as accurately as you must weigh the pros and cons of the investment itself. Because of those requirements, certain character traits can increase the odds for success, satisfaction, and peace of mind.

Are you the real estate type? Will you fit in at the negotiating table? Can you identify and compete for properties that will rise in value? Will your management style attract competent and reliable employees? Steady tenants? Are you likely to take your profits from the sale of one property and enthusiastically look for two others? Is there that spark of entrepreneurial spirit in you?

Only you can look at yourself and answer those questions. But to do so effectively, you must have some criteria to help make your judgments. In real estate investing, ten personality characteristics are most likely to contribute to success. Alphabetically, they are:

1. Assertiveness

2. Attention to detail

3. Awareness

4. Creativity

5. Initiative

6. **Perseverance**
7. **Rational judgment**
8. **Self-confidence**
9. **Strategic planning**
10. **Tact**

Are you overwhelmed? That's some list of character traits. But don't fret, there's hardly a saint to be found in the real estate marketplace. No one is or could be exemplary in all of these characteristics, all of the time. Rather than try to rate yourself in each category separately, consider all ten as elements of the real estate investor paradigm. Every individual stands taller in some areas than in others. The question is how you stack up when you consider the ten qualities as a whole.

In this chapter, each of these characteristics will be discussed in terms of its importance in the real estate marketplace. As you read, ask yourself: Do I see this in my personality? Can it be developed if necessary? Would I feel comfortable relying on this characteristic?

Again, remember that no one situation is likely to require all ten characteristics at full capacity. But each character trait will be called upon many times in your real estate investment career. In Part II, the amount of demand on these traits will be rated for each of the starter investment vehicles. Right now let's survey the ten character traits.

Assertiveness: The "Find Out Why and Do Something" Trait

Imagine this: You find a run-down 11-room Victorian in a neighborhood of otherwise well-kept houses two blocks away from the commercial district of the town. Several of the houses have obviously been converted to multifamily units. You know a restaurateur in the next town who wants to open a satellite to his very successful place. The renovation needed to create a restaurant on the ground level and three one-bedroom apartments on the second and third floors would be relatively easy. The prospect of a long-term, high-rent commercial lease plus three apartment leases sends you to the town hall to check on zoning restrictions in the area. The clerk at the zoning board office tells you that your idea is absolutely impossible. That street is zoned residential.

What do you do? The assertive person does not take "No, that's impossible" for an answer. He or she asks, "Why?" or "Why not?" and sets out to find the answers. With the research gathered in hand, the assertive person steps forward to make the case. It doesn't matter whether that "case" is for a zoning variance or simply for a refund on an appliance or lumber purchase that was defective, the demand on character is pretty much the same. This personality trait is the opposite of passive acceptance or the "Wadda ya gonna do?" attitude.

Webster's Collegiate Dictionary defines the word *assertive* as "disposed to or characterized by bold or confident assertion." *Bold* and *confident* are the key words here, but be careful not to confuse assertiveness with outward aggression. Being assertive does not mean being combative.

Assertiveness is sometimes used interchangeably with aggressiveness when the pros talk about what contributes to success in the real estate marketplace. This pairing holds true when aggressiveness means "marked by driving forceful energy or initiative," but it does not hold true if aggressiveness means "tending toward or exhibiting aggression" or "marked by combative readiness." Anyone in the real estate marketplace ready to fight or with the proverbial chip on his or her shoulder is prone to failures not only in negotiating but also in dealing with the many support people (who are described in Chapter 5) who are involved in every deal.

LEARNING THE LANGUAGE

Zoning laws divide a municipality or county into areas (zones). Within each zone, the laws specify the type of real estate that can be built there and its usage. If property owners wish to make improvements or changes not allowed by these laws, they can apply to the **zoning board of appeals** for a variance. A **variance** changes a portion of the zoning law for one particular property without changing the laws that apply to the entire zone. See Chapter 5 for more about the zoning board.

Attention to Detail: It's the Sum of the Parts

Every great real estate deal is the coming together of myriad tiny parts, like the compressed carbon molecules that make a sparkling diamond. The person who is to succeed in making those great deals must be attentive to every part.

The scope of attention required is both broad and high. Here are just a few everyday moments in the real estate marketplace when attention to detail might make a difference.

- **Attentive buyer to home inspector:** "Was that muddy brown streak on the outside of the foundation actually a termite tunnel?"

- **Inattentive buyer (thinking):** "The contract had a date by which the inspection had to be completed and acted upon by the buyer. Now, when was it? Yesterday? Well, they probably didn't really mean yesterday, did they?"

- **Attentive buyer to mortgage broker:** "What was that in the mortgage about a new interest rate to be determined in five years? Who will set that rate?"

- **Seller to buyer who had better be attentive:** "Oh, by the way, we forgot to mention that there's a buried oil tank in the backyard. But don't worry; the environmental protection guys don't know a thing about it."

- **Inattentive owner speaking to tenant:** "There's a $50 penalty because you're three weeks late with your rent." Tenant in reply: "Hey, there's nothing in this lease that says I have to pay a penalty. You want me out of here? I'll get out!"

Real estate investors deal with local property laws, tax laws, and contract laws. Owning property

---

STOP AND THINK!

"Do it yourself" can be disastrous in real estate because you may not know which details need attention in each of the many facets of a deal. Pay for the protection of professional help. Use property inspectors, get several estimates for repairs, use an attorney for contract review before you sign (or insert an attorney-review clause in the contract), have an accountant check out the cash flow, and use a real estate agent to do a comparative market analysis. See Chapter 5 for more about the folks who can watch out for details.

requires knowledge of building structure and maintenance. It requires management and accounting skills, and it brings up financing and insurance questions. How can you possibly pay attention to all the details of all those issues?

You can't, but you must. The attention to detail required of a real estate investor is similar to that required by a good project manager in a large corporation. You must assign qualified people to check on potential problem areas and you must monitor their work.

Too much attention to detail can also be a stumbling block in a real estate deal. Sometimes a buyer or seller will get so focused on a particular detail (it might be anything from some loose shingles on the roof to the proposed date for the closing) that the whole process of purchase and sale comes to a halt. The most successful investors step back to get some perspective on how that stumbling-block detail fits into the whole picture. This type of situation is a good example of why rational thought must govern emotional response when you are investing in the real estate marketplace. You can find more about the need to keep your head in control instead of your heart in the section titled "Rational Judgment" later in this chapter.

Awareness: The "What's Really Happening Here" Trait

Maybe you know a coworker who seems to go through life in a plastic bubble. He or she can work away quietly on a given project while everyone within sight or sound is bustling over rumors of a hostile takeover. If someone were to yell "FIRE!" this person might look up and say, "Where's everyone running to?" Guaranteed: Your unaware coworker would not succeed in the real estate investment marketplace. Let's look at the types of awareness every investor needs.

> **"Take nothing on its looks; take everything on evidence."**
>
> Charles Dickens (1812–1870),
> *Great Expectations*

Awareness of Events

Because real estate responds most strongly to local economic and demographic trends, it is absolutely essential that the real estate investor be aware of what is going on in the area where he or she intends to invest. That's why virtually all experts agree that the best place to get started is in your own neighborhood or town.

An aware personality predisposes you to read and listen to the local news and then put the pieces together for an understanding of what is happening behind the scenes. For example, let's say that Steven Lee, a man of Chinese heritage, wins the mayoral election. He has been campaigning for better police protection in neighborhood commercial areas. The aware investor might start looking for residential rental properties in areas of the city that are zoned for commercial use. (These properties are usually less expensive than those in areas zoned for residential use only. Increased safety, however, would make these rental apartments more desirable, and therefore more likely to bring higher rents.)

Some extra time might be spent exploring purchase opportunities in areas where the Chinese population is large, acknowledging the fact that it's the nature of politicians in general to return favors to those who elected them. If Mr. Lee is like them and is successful during his term as mayor and is reelected, it's not unlikely that all property values in those "safer" sections of town would increase.

Awareness of Physical Surroundings

The successful investor should also have the ability to observe and understand the physical environment surrounding a piece of property under consideration. The scope of this demand for awareness is huge. Think about questions such as:

- What is the type and value of the properties that make up the neighborhood?
- What are the pros and cons of the size, shape, and terrain of the lot?
- What are the traffic patterns in town?

Here we're talking about the observation of details that directly affect profit potential. For example, let's say a small, six-unit apartment building is for sale. A potential investor walking through the neighborhood would be assured by curtains and cats in the windows, flowerpots on the fire escapes, and tricycles in the vestibules. But streets littered with empty bottles, food wrappers, cigarette butts, and drug paraphernalia would set off mental warning bells. The aware investor would also look for bus or subway stops and the availability of parking. He or she would probably make several visits to the site at different times of the day to gauge noise and traffic.

Or let's say you're considering a handyman special in a suburban area. You think all the repairs can easily be done within your budget and skills, until you notice a strange gathering of gnats over a particularly green area of the lawn. When you walk out to the spot, you find soggy, smelly earth—an almost certain indication of septic-tank problems that could make your purchase unprofitable.

Awareness of Motivations

If you go into a real estate transaction knowing only your own motivations and goals, you'll know very little of what's making (or not making) the deal. The aware investor tries to find out why the seller is selling. As negotiations proceed, it's important to assess the goals of the other side, the pressures that influence their moves, and how they try to pressure you (often an indication of their own fears and concerns). Pop psychology calls this skill "being aware of where they're coming from" but it's more than that. You also have to be aware of where they're trying to go.

Needless to say it's important to be aware of your own motivations and goals and to bear in mind that every single person involved in the deal has some motivation, even if it's only to fill the job requirements that allow for a salary. Speaking of earning a living, remember that it makes little difference whether real estate agents pledge loyalty to you or the seller; their

> **"If you know the enemy and know yourself you need not fear the results of a hundred battles."**
>
> Tz'u-Hsi, Chinese dowager empress

primary motivator is to earn a commission on a transaction, regardless of which party fares better in the deal.

Creativity: The Art in Real Estate

Creativity as a required character trait for real estate investors? Most people would say this is stretching it, maybe a little like requiring sensitivity for traffic cops. But there are two kinds of creativity that can make or break the success of an investment property choice: imagination and problem solving.

Imagination as a Property Finder

Imagination is one of the strongest aids to finding bargain properties with potential for excellent return on the investment. Think about these situations:

- A developer looks at a piece of raw land littered with debris, crossed by creeks and gullies, and in some areas blocked by virtually impassable vines and brambles. He sees it with gently curving roads, upscale homes, and beautiful landscaping.
- Four young investor-partners look at an abandoned factory building and, rather than unused industrial space, they see the potential for residential space, perhaps a condominium community. They see plenty of parking, space for a pool and tennis courts, elevator shafts already in place, and a sound brick structure.
- A couple about to retire looks at a 100-plus-year-old dilapidated house and sees a historic restoration bed-and-breakfast inn. They see an excellent location near the town green, a welcoming front porch, and irreplaceable detail in the moldings, doors, and fireplaces.
- A middle-management executive looks at a large 1930s in-town house and sees a four-unit, multifamily investment property that would bring in a steady stream of extra income each month. He sees zoning for multifamily use already in place in a residential

neighborhood, large rooms and wide staircases, and the possibility of managing the property himself.

The imaginative creativity required in the real estate marketplace is the ability to look beyond the immediate limitations of what one sees. For example, any Realtor will tell you that dirt and disrepair increase time on the market and decrease the probable selling price even in otherwise very desirable properties. Why? Because most people cannot see beyond surface appearances. The investor who judges a property by its location and soundness and then can imagine its appeal when all the clutter has been removed often gets a bargain.

> **LEARNING THE LANGUAGE**
>
> **Raw land** is land in its natural state. It has not been cleared or subdivided into building lots. Paved streets, curbing, sidewalks, water, sewers, electricity, telephones, and television cable are not available, except perhaps at the current road frontage.

I Never Thought of That!

Creativity in real estate can also mean the ability to see many different ways to solve the same problem. It sometimes means thinking unconventionally to come up with a new way to use a piece of land or change the functional use of a building. Or perhaps seeing that a room formerly used as a bedroom might function better as a kitchen or dining room. Sometimes it simply means doing repairs more efficiently for less money.

This problem-solving creativity can save the day when you're negotiating a price. The art of the deal is very often centered in finding ways to make a lower price appealing to the seller or finding ways to get some extras thrown in for the higher price the buyer must pay. Changing the closing date, deciding who will fix what, extending leases, and working out purchase-money financing are just a few examples of negotiating with creativity. (See Chapter 7 for more about negotiating.)

> **STOP AND THINK!**
>
> If someone comes to you with a "creative" real estate deal that seems too good to be true, it probably is. The best deals must be ferreted out, usually in territory that is very familiar. Be extremely suspicious of all get-rich-quick package deals.

Initiative: The "Make Something Happen" Trait

The real estate road to wealth is not for passive people who wait for something to happen and then react to it. No one will come knocking on your door with some land to sell. (If they do, it's likely to be a scam.) If you really want to make money in the real estate marketplace, you, the investor, must take the initiative and go out to find property. Then you must estimate market value, calculate cash flow, and make the first offer.

Initiative is also an essential character trait in resolving the many problem situations that can come up in the marketplace. For example, if owners assume that there are no property-management problems unless told otherwise, they put themselves at the disadvantage of reacting and responding to complaints instead of heading them off. By the time someone actually complains, tempers are often ready to flare and the mood can be combative.

In contrast, the manager with initiative will often take a proactive approach that anticipates problems, finds ways to keep them from happening, and moves the day-to-day operations forward toward the goals that have been set. Changes can be made gradually, everyone is happier, and happy tenants tend to stay longer (and pay their rent).

Sometimes initiative means going an extra mile or two to make something happen the way you want it to. Take applying for a zoning variance. The investor with initiative will anticipate the concerns and objections of the owners of neighboring property. Rather than argue points at a zoning board meeting, he or she might call on every owner within the distance specified by zoning law as having an interest in the variance. Hoping to allay fears and win support, the investor will work on a one-to-one basis, showing the plans and explaining their effect on the neighborhood to each owner who is willing to listen. It's a big expenditure of time and effort but it can mean the difference between success and failure.

Perseverance: The "Stay With It" Trait

In the real estate marketplace, some of the most costly words an investor can speak are "I give up" or "I quit." Stick-to-it and don't-take-no-for-an-answer attitudes are essential. But that perseverance must be tempered by the reality of facts and numbers and by rational judgment.

Don't Quit

Whether it be land development or a renovation, unfinished real estate projects are rarely profitable. Folks just don't like to buy work in progress—or if they do, they want a bargain-basement price. To be successful, therefore, the real estate investor must be willing to keep on going to the end of a project. For example, once an exterior wall is torn down, the renovation must go forward even in the face of delays and disappointments.

There are limits to perseverance as a plus factor, however. When actual costs are far in excess of estimates, you may have to weigh cutting your losses against an escalating negative cash flow. For example, adding central air-conditioning to a four-plex is certainly an idea to enhance market value. But if costs are running close to double the original estimate by the time that only the two units on the first floor are air-conditioned, completing the second floor will continue to increase the cost. It will then take a lot longer than anticipated before the additional rent from centrally air-conditioned units will even approach paying off the cost of installation. At this point, it may be best to stop the work. You can still get higher rents on the two units that have been air-conditioned but a "half air-conditioned house" will not have the additional market value you were anticipating for a quick sale.

Persevering beyond limits set by rational judgment can turn into just plain stubbornness. And stubbornness can lose almost as much money in the marketplace as quitting. It's important to be committed to your investment, but commitment must always be sup-

> "The difference between perseverance and obstinacy is that one often comes from a strong will, and the other from a strong won't."
>
> Henry Ward Beecher (1813–1887), American clergyman

ported by careful evaluation. Don't let pride push you into "pushing on" when a strategic retreat would cut your losses.

Don't Take No for an Answer

In addition to both the physical drive and the determination to complete projects, there is another kind of persevering mental attitude that adds to success in the marketplace. It prompts the investor to return to knock again at a closed door, to get beyond the administrative assistant who says, "That's against office policy," and to make another offer to the seller who says, "I won't take a penny less." This character trait will be useful in

- negotiating successfully;
- doing the detective work often required to get answers to your questions;
- finding investment property not listed with Realtors;
- dealing with local officials, such as planning and zoning boards, buildings inspectors, and tax assessors;
- dealing with tenants and property managers; and
- dealing with banks and other sources of mortgage financing.

Rational Judgment: The "Lead with Your Head, Not Your Heart" Trait

For everyone involved in the homebuying process, love is a factor—a factor that actually belongs in the deal. When you're hunting for a place to call your own, a prospective purchase really should tug at your emotions, at least a little. "Home" must hold some promise of comfort and happiness. Personal residences that are bought strictly by the numbers (without the sense of loving the place) often see For Sale signs on the front lawn again within just a few years. But love should *not* be a factor in purchasing investment real estate.

In fact, emotion of any kind should not play a role in your decision to buy. You must be very careful not to judge a property by the standards that would make you personally comfortable. Instead, base your investment property selection on an analysis of market value versus purchase price, structure and condition, income and cash flow, and probable appreciation.

Numbers rather than feelings should also rule in managing your investment property. Remember, as an investor you are in business to make money. Choosing tenants because "they seem nice," or overlooking contractual agreements, such as consistently allowing the rent to be late, will ultimately undermine your success.

Finally, proposed expansion, renovation, and repairs to existing buildings, and improvements to raw land should always be carefully examined to be certain they will meet current building codes and to estimate how much the dollar outlay is likely to return in property appreciation and increased income (rents, for example). Your aesthetic sense may cry out to add a front porch, a brick walkway, and well-trimmed yews to the front of your three-unit multifamily property. But among the questions you must ask are:

- Will tenants pay a little more rent because of the improvements?
- Are the improvements needed to bring the property's appearance up to the standards of the neighborhood?
- Are the improvements likely to increase the market value of the property when you sell it? By how much?

The character trait of rational judgment will sometimes make demands on yet another trait: patience. To repeat: Real estate is a long-term investment. The decision to sell must be based not on whim or convenience but on a careful evaluation of market values

---

LEARNING THE LANGUAGE

Buildings inspectors are members of the municipal buildings department, which enforces compliance with the local building codes.

Building codes set out minimum standards for construction in order to preserve, protect, and promote the public health, safety, and welfare. If you build new, add on, or renovate, you will be required to comply with the local building codes. Your work will be inspected by a local buildings inspector.

> **"It is not enough to be busy—the question is, what are we busy about?"**
>
> Henry David Thoreau (1817–1862), American philosopher

and conditions. Often the investor must wait patiently for appreciation and changes in the local economy before putting the property on the market, liquidating the investment, and taking the profit.

Self-Confidence: The Bedrock upon Which Everything Is Built

In the homebuying marketplace, Realtors shiver when a buyer wants to bring his or her relatives or friends to see a property before making an offer. These pseudo-inspectors usually come with the idea that they should "help" by finding *something* to warn the buyer about. Often it takes a good deal of homebuyer self-confidence to acknowledge these well-meaning "you-better-watch-out-fors" and yet base the purchase on his or her own evaluation of the property and how it meets personal needs, goals, preferences, and financial limitations.

In the category of self-confidence, investment real estate is *exactly* like homebuying. When choosing each investment property, you should listen to all the comments and evaluations of professionals and friends, weigh and judge their merit, and in the end make the decision yourself, factoring in your goals, abilities, and resources. This takes an immense amount of self-confidence. But without it, you could spend untold hours chasing after "perfect properties" while bouncing from one bit of advice to another. And you could lose out on many opportunities.

Self-confidence is also required for property improvement and property management. Just about every day, there are decisions that must be made and plans that must be implemented. Whatever the task or the challenge, you must believe that you can do it or that you can find and hire the professional help that you will need. If you don't have this confidence in yourself, your investment property will suffer from innumerable delays.

Strategic Planning:
It's a Small Business After All

Lack of long-range planning is one of the most frequent mistakes among neophytes in the real estate investment marketplace. It seems to be a big enough job just to buy a property, get financing, and find tenants. Few people new to the marketplace want to think about a plan for operations, future maintenance, improvements, and potential sale. But if you don't spend the time to set goals and work toward them, you lose some of the essential criteria for making profitable decisions. You may be working hard without knowing what you are working for!

Ask most successful real estate investors where they want to be financially in five years and they can tell you their plans pretty specifically. But their strategies are not limited to setting long-term investment goals and working toward them. They often spend time planning negotiating strategies. They develop strategies for dealing with late-paying tenants. They have a plan for presentation long before they submit their subdivision drawings to the local planning or zoning board. They might develop three alternate options in a strategy to get the best deal on financing.

In short, the real estate investor must have a business outlook. Plans are made, evaluated, revised, and remade as time passes. Among the types of questions the planning investor most frequently asks are:

- How can we do this project better, faster, cheaper, safer?
- How can we use this amount of money most effectively?
- Do we hire more people to get this job done faster or a few good people to get it done better?
- What will be the tax implications of this purchase, improvement or sale?

DIGGING DEEPER

Remember that you must handle the paperwork and the recordkeeping of your real estate investments as a business. *Taming the Paper Tiger at Work* by Barbara Hemphill (Dearborn Trade Publishing) will help you with setting up a working system.

Tact: The "Speak Softly and Carry a Big Stick" Trait

Antisocial types rarely make a killing in the real estate marketplace. Dealing in property means dealing with people. And dealing effectively with people is a major factor in investor success. In addition to interacting with individuals from the many professions involved in finding, buying, taking title to, and selling your investment real estate (all discussed in Chapter 5), you'll most often need the ability to be tactful in three situations:

1. Negotiating price and terms

2. Managing rental property

3. Applying for a zoning variance

The dictionary definition of tact is "a keen sense of what to do or say in order to maintain good relations with others or avoid offense." Tact for the real estate investor, however, goes a little further. In addition to maintaining good relations and avoiding offense, an investor's tactful communication usually tries to move the situation in question closer to his or her goal. Tact is an essential factor in a real estate investor's strategy for success.

The opposite of tact is temper. A flash-fire temper is one of the most detrimental personality traits in the real estate marketplace. If you slam your fist on the table, raise your voice, use profanity, insult your seller, or cut off a telephone conversation, you have lost ground, ground maybe never to be regained. If you have a quick temper, acknowledge it and use agents to do your negotiating or management in your stead.

DIGGING DEEPER

Concerned about your ability to be tactful in a negotiating situation? Try reading an old classic that is still among the best available advice: *Getting to Yes: Negotiating Agreement without Giving In* by Roger Fisher and William Ury (Penguin Books).

Are You Right for Real Estate?

So, what do you think? Do you score somewhere over a 5 on a scale of 1 to 10 in all these traits? If you've read this far, you probably do (or else you're working on self-enhancement at a phenomenal pace and might just come from behind to win by a head).

But hold on! You're still not ready to start investing. Even if you're a perfect real estate type, there's yet another question. Are you willing to spend the time and do the work required on this road to wealth? That's covered in the next chapter.

KEEP IN MIND

- **Real estate investment is not for everyone.**
- **Ten important character traits** for success are: assertiveness, attention to detail, awareness, creativity, initiative, perseverance, rational judgment, self-confidence, strategic planning, and tact.
- **If you go into a real estate transaction knowing only your own motivations and goals,** you'll know very little of what's making (or not making) the deal. The aware investor tries to find out why the seller is selling.
- **Successful real estate investment demands** the ability to look beyond what you actually see.
- **The real estate road to wealth is not for passive people** who wait for something to happen and then react to it.

How Much Time, Work, and Money?

"In order that people may be happy in their work, these three things are needed: They must be fit for it; they must not do too much of it; and they must have a sense of success in it."

W. H. Auden (1907–1973), Anglo-American poet

Chapter 4

Have you glanced at Part II yet? Are you impatient with all this conceptual stuff and itching to get started with a nice moneymaking investment? Are you starting to read the real estate classifieds and driving around prospective neighborhoods?

These things are all good. You're demonstrating genuine interest, and that's an essential for success. But don't rush out with cash in hand and sign anything that looks like an offer form or you could be very sorry. There's a reason for all this prep work.

Working through the concepts and questions of these essential foundation chapters will help you to define the size and nature of the investment vehicles that will be most appropriate for you. The character-trait profile in Chapter 3 is an important part of that picture, but still only a part. For an overall view, you must also understand the tools of the real estate trade: time, work, and money. Their requirements and limitations will have just as much influence upon your opportunities as your inherent character traits.

Studying to get an understanding of the marketplace before investing in real estate is difficult and sometimes tedious work. Nowhere is that work more important to success (both initially and long term) than in grasping the demands made by each type of investment and assessing your ability to meet them.

The theory here is obvious: The best real estate investment plan will match the time, money, and skills that you have available with the time, money, and skills required by an investment vehicle. This chapter gives you an overview of the time, work, and money requirements in the real estate marketplace; Part II discusses those requirements as they apply to each type of investment vehicle.

It's a Matter of Time

There are two aspects of time to be considered when investing in real estate: *holding time* and *working time*. Both apply in some degree to every investment vehicle. But the variables of "How much?" and "What kind?" are wide, sometimes even within the same vehicle type.

Holding Time

Time is a factor in all financial investments and returns. In just about every real estate investment deal, there is a significant lapse of time between purchase and sale. Let's call it holding time. During the holding time for a piece of property, the money you invested in it cannot be used for any other purpose. In simplest terms, it cannot earn compound interest as it would on deposit in a bank.

Getting compound interest on your money—for example, in a certificate of deposit—is one of the simplest and safest forms of investment. Comparing your earnings in a compound interest situation with your profit from the sale of a property is an excellent awareness jolt for the effects of time on the use of money. Many people forget that both holding time and the possible alternative uses for the investment capital are important factors in real estate investment. To demonstrate this point, let's look at two fictitious examples that would almost certainly never

LEARNING THE LANGUAGE

Interest is money charged or paid for the use of money (called the **principal**). **Compound interest** is interest paid on accumulated interest as well as on the principal.

happen in today's marketplace because virtually everyone uses the leveraging power of borrowed money. These demonstration numbers, however, make crystal clear the need to factor in the limitation that holding time puts on the possible uses of your investment capital.

You buy a piece of land for $100,000 cash, hold it for two years, and sell it for $115,000. Expenses aside, your gross profit is $15,000, or a 15 percent return. Or you put that same $100,000 into an investment that pays 5 percent per year compounded. In two years, you will have $110,200, or a 10.2 percent return. In this example of a short-term sale, you have been compensated with better earnings for the fact that your real estate investment was nonliquid. However, taxes and purchase/sale costs have not been factored in, so the return is not really as good as the gross figures indicate.

In a more likely situation, you buy a piece of land for $100,000 cash, hold it for ten years, and sell it for $150,000. Expenses aside, your gross profit is $50,000, or a 50 percent return. If you put that same $100,000 into an investment that pays 5 percent per year compounded, in ten years, you will have $162,900, or a 62.9 percent return. In this case, your return would have been better in the more liquid investment. Not much of a return in either example, however, because the effects of inflation have not been considered.

Obviously, numbers can be added and "bent" in many ways. Though unreal in today's marketplace,

---

STOP AND THINK!

Never calculate your expected profit simply by counting dollars. You must ask how much cash you will have invested and how long you must hold the property before the anticipated selling price can be achieved. Remember: You want a better return than you could get by investing that same amount of money in a more liquid investment.

these numbers are being used to demonstrate that it's not the dollar amount you make on a real estate sale that really determines how well you did with the investment. It's the profit relative to the dollar amount you invested over the length of the holding time. In this example, on a $100,000 cash investment, a return of $15,000 in two years is better than a return of $50,000 over ten years.

But now consider the outcome if that same $100,000 property was purchased with an investment of $10,000 and a mortgage of $90,000. The $10,000 investment then earns $15,000 in two years and $50,000 in ten years. That's the power of leverage. Of course, you have to deduct carrying costs and taxes, but the picture gets even brighter if, instead of land, the investment is a rental unit that provides income to cover costs, with tax benefits to sweeten the pie. (See Chapter 10 for more about the sweeteners.)

Optimal holding time varies from one category of property to another and from one property to another within the same category. Some types of property, such as the fixer-upper, usually demand the shortest possible holding time because they require high expenditures and intensive working time while producing no income until they are sold. Land, on the other hand, is usually held for long periods of time because it requires little or no working time and only property taxes as expenditures. Some investment vehicles—small apartment buildings, for example—are held for long periods of time, not because the real estate is appreciating significantly but because the annual net rental income is excellent.

Much has been written about the time-value-of-money factor in making a good investment choice, both in real estate and other investments. You can get into some complex numerical calculations here, or you can simply be aware of the time factor whenever you

---

LEARNING THE LANGUAGE

Fixer-upper is real estate slang for a property in need of cleaning and cosmetic repair. **Renovation** (which means to make new again) implies a more extensive project, including replacement of dated appliances and perhaps some working systems. **Rehabilitation** (which means to make livable again) can border on rebuilding.

choose a real estate investment and call in professional help (an accountant or a real estate counselor, for example) if holding time becomes a critical issue in profit potential. Whether long or short holding time is more appealing to you depends on how it balances with three other factors: working time, work requirements, and money.

Working Time

Working time is the amount of your time that you must devote to a real estate investment. What you are doing to enhance your investment position, however, may or may not seem like work. Investor working time may be walking open land on a brisk autumn day or talking about what's being built in your hometown while on a ski lift at Mount Snow. At the other end of the spectrum, working time can mean cleaning out debris after a delinquent tenant leaves in the dead of night, being chained to the computer on a sunny Saturday afternoon to enter accounting data, or sitting for hours awaiting your turn before the planning board only to have your hearing postponed until the next scheduled meeting.

Because only a small percentage of investors consider real estate their primary occupation, choosing an investment vehicle that has working-time demands that fit the time you have available is extremely important. Some investments, such as a multifamily rental property, demand only a few hours a month throughout the year. Other investments, such as a renovation, demand full-time attention, but only for a relatively short period of time (sometimes just weeks, rather than months). Some investments, such as condominium apartments, have virtually no time demands.

To avoid undue stress in your life, fit your real estate investments to your schedule, not your schedule to the investments. For example, a teacher who has every summer off may become interested in foreclosures and renovations. A physician who works very long hours may choose to buy a block of condominium apartments. A retired couple might buy a multifamily house

> ## "I must govern the clock, not be governed by it."
>
> Golda Meir (1898–1978), Israeli political leader

in which they occupy a unit. (See Part II for more about the working time required for each type of property.)

If your time is very limited, you can also consider hiring professionals to put in some of the required time, or investing indirectly through a real estate investment trust or mutual fund. Don't even imagine that you will be totally free of time commitments, however. Delegating all responsibility would mean losing contact with your investment, and that is dangerous indeed. If you do plan to hire professionals, remember to factor the cost of help into your estimates of cash flow and return on your investment.

The Question of Work

Do you prefer work to empty hours? You can find plenty of it in the real estate investment marketplace. All kinds. There's something here for the cerebral person who likes clean hands; something for the work-boots, mud, and sawdust type. Are you gregarious? There's something here for you, with plenty of opportunity for getting together with other

---

DIGGING DEEPER

Is the information sharing and camaraderie of getting together with other investors important to you? There are investors' associations in most states and in many local areas. Or you can start one in your area. For more information contact:

National Real Estate Investors Association
525 West 5th Street
Suite 230
Covington, KY 41011
888-762-7342
http://www.nationalreia.com

To find an affiliated local group, use the state-by-state search function on the Web site.

---

investors, talking with tenants and managers, and listening and looking for property tips while socializing. Are you a control freak? There's nothing like property ownership to put you in control.

But work should not overwhelm you. If it does, you will soon learn to hate it, and that emotional response will cut deeply into your likelihood for success. It is important therefore to evaluate the work demands of a real estate investment. Try to choose something with requirements that are at least somewhat familiar and not distasteful. If you enjoy the work you must do, the burden is light. Often it doesn't even feel like work.

As we discussed under "Working Time," the first question to ask when evaluating work demands is: How much working time is required? The second question is: Can I do the kind of work required? If your answer is no, you can still hire someone else to do the work while you supervise. Just remember to factor in the cost of help.

There are essentially four different kinds of work for the real estate investor:

1. Property search and selection

2. Maintenance

3. Management

4. Recordkeeping

Let's look at the requirements of each of them. While reading, consider if you would do this type of work yourself or hire someone to do it. Remember, the more you can do yourself, the more profitable your investment will be. In effect, you will be paid for your time and work.

Property Search and Selection

Finding appropriate and potentially profitable investment properties requires knowledge of all the basic principles of the real estate marketplace. Equally important, it also requires up-to-the-minute familiarity with the local area, its economy, demographics, and real estate laws and customary procedures.

If you hire a buyer broker (an agent contracted by and working in the best interests of the buyer) to do this work for you, don't give up control or research completely. The agent may be committed to you—in fact, you may even become best of friends—but remember that he or she is earning a living by selecting and selling property. In the vast majority of cases, the agent doesn't earn a commission (get paid) unless a deal is made. Sometimes the desire to get paid generates pressure to make the deal.

Also remember that your real estate agent is not actually making the investment and not putting up a significant down payment in the hopes of making more money. It's your money and your commitment. Even if someone else does the hunting and finding of property, you should make the decisions as to the quality of the investment and its appropriateness for your needs and goals. (See Chapter 5 for more about buyer brokers.)

LEARNING THE LANGUAGE
Down payment is the cash portion of the purchase price paid by the buyer from his own funds when the remainder of the purchase price is financed. The smaller the down payment, the greater the risk for the lender.

Maintenance

The care and improvement of investment property requires knowledge of building construction, working systems, and local building codes. It also requires that you are familiar with local contractors. With some types of work, such as electrical work, plumbing, and heating, local ordinances prevent you from doing repair or renovation yourself by requiring that a licensed contractor do the work.

Even when you can do certain projects yourself, such as adding a deck or porch, you must apply for a building permit, and your work will be inspected by the buildings inspector. For interior or exterior fix-up not requiring a building permit (painting or window replacement, for example), you can do the work yourself or hire someone. Even if you hire help, however, your knowledge of materials and workmanship will usually guarantee you better work and value for your dollar.

Management

Taking charge of investment property requires most of the same management skills that make for success in any business. In fact, there are now college majors in real estate management.

To increase the profit potential of your investment property, you must be able to set policy (such as how to choose new tenants) and see that your policies are adhered to. You must be able to select and supervise hired personnel. You must be able to settle disputes (between tenants, for example, or between the superintendent and tenants) and you must be able to make financial decisions that will affect income and expenditures (such as when to raise rents or when to do roof repairs).

In some instances, you may be required to plan for change or expansion (the conversion of a small apartment building to condominiums, for example, or the subdivision of land). And perhaps most important, you must decide when to sell and for how much.

Recordkeeping

Recordkeeping is the sit-down work of the real estate marketplace. Sometimes it even feels confining when you'd rather be out with a hammer or a paintbrush. And it's a lot more complicated than adding and subtracting and keeping track of accounts receivable and accounts payable.

Real estate recordkeeping requires knowledge of tax and property laws. It includes the necessity of collecting, sorting, and storing all the bits and pieces of paper that prove what you did and didn't do to or with the property. It means keeping track of names, addresses, phone numbers, and e-mail addresses for workers, tenants, insurance agents, buildings inspectors, etc. It means keeping track of service providers such as electricity, heating oil, municipal water and sewerage services, and refuse removal. You get the idea.

Even if you hire someone to do the job of recordkeeping for you, you must supervise rather closely because quite often lost papers mean lost money. Not to mention that money has been known to disappear when the owner isn't paying attention.

Why Work?

The work required in owning investment property is a put-off for some people. But for others, it is a main attraction. There is a sense of satisfaction in working for yourself and in watching the value of a property grow. There is the reward of keeping tenants satisfied and collecting the rents on time. There is a sense of control over changes and decisions. There is the comfortable feeling that many hours have been filled, profitably.

And it's almost never boring.

It's About Money

Research conducted by social scientists shows that creative, profitable work may indeed contribute to well-being, self-satisfaction, pride, and happiness. But in the end, the vast majority of real estate investors buy property to make money. And money is the core of the investment apple. You need it to get started, you need it to keep going, and you want to take away as much as possible when the investment is sold. There's an entire chapter on mort-

---

STOP AND THINK!

Beware the carnival barkers who shout about "nothing-down deals!" It is possible to buy real estate with little or no cash down payment, but there's usually a reason for the deal. Consider these situations:

- The seller is desperate and agrees to hold a mortgage for the entire purchase price. (Ask: *Why is he desperate?*)
- The property is in an urban renewal area with financing supported by state and local government, lenders, and charitable organizations. (Ask: *Can I be certain that the area will experience "renewal"?*)
- The property is owned and being sold by a bank after foreclosure. (Ask: *Is the asking price really the fair market value?*)
- An "angel" agrees to help with the financing for a share in the profits when the property is sold. (Ask: *Will there be enough left after splitting the profits to make the ownership effort worthwhile?*)

gage financing (Chapter 9), so at this point let's talk about how money can affect your investment choices.

Start-up Cash

Yes, it's true; there are ways to buy investment property with no down payment. (You'll find them in Chapter 9.) But most real estate investments are just that: investments—you put in money with the expectation of getting more money out in return. How much start-up cash you need depends on the type of investment, the price of the property, and the financing that can be arranged.

For newcomers to the marketplace, it's important to remember that the required down payment is not the total amount of cash that will be needed. You must prepare for mortgage-application fees, closing costs, and title insurance, and you should have some money left over for repairs and unexpected expenses.

In addition to those start-up costs common to all real estate transactions, some investment vehicles require considerably more cash. As previously mentioned, a renovation is heavy on up-front money for materials and labor. For a conversion of an apartment building to a condominium community, considerable money will be required for legal fees. If you create a subdivision on your land, you will need cash to pay for planning by civil engineers, drawings by surveyors, environmental testing and compliance, and legal help for presentations to the planning board.

On the other hand, some investment vehicles make only small demands for extra start-up cash. If you buy an occupied multifamily house, small apartment building, or mixed-use commercial/residential building, you will need minimal additional start-up cash and you will begin collecting rents immediately. Condominium

> ### LEARNING THE LANGUAGE
>
> In the real estate world, **subdivision** means the breaking up of a single parcel of land into smaller parcels (lots). It is done by applying for approval to the local governmental commission (usually the planning board or zoning board). To obtain approval you must file a map describing the subdivision, along with other required information on the proposed use of the land and how the new usage will affect the surrounding areas. The creation of a condominium community is called a **one-lot subdivision.**

and co-op purchases sometimes require owners' association dues in advance, but there are few other cash needs. In Part II, you'll find more about how each investment vehicle makes demands on start-up cash.

Cash Flow

Cash flow was introduced in Chapter 1, but let's look at the box below to see how it works. The example uses numbers for a very small mixed-use building with one commercial tenant on the first floor and two residential tenants on the second.

When considering a purchase, look at the cash flow on a monthly basis as well as on an annual basis and keep in mind the state of the local economy. In an area where unemployment is low and the occupancy rate

---

HOW CASH FLOW WORKS

Using easy-to-work numbers, here's an example of how the elements to be considered in cash flow come together.

Rental income:

Gross income, two residential units:	$ 12,000
Gross income, one commercial unit:	16,000
Total annual gross income	**$28,000**

Operating expenses:

Property taxes	$ 4,000
Insurance	1,500
Maintenance	4,500
Total operating expenses	**$10,000**

Debt service:

Interest payments	$ 12,000
Principal payments	1,000
Total debt service	**$13,000**

Income ($28,000) minus expenditures ($23,000) equals a positive cash flow of $5,000 for the year.

---

for housing is high, there will most likely be a low vacancy rate in most rental properties. This will tend to stabilize the monthly cash flow figures and increase the annual positive cash flow. In an area where the vacancy rate is high, however, monthly cash flow will be more uneven and might even be negative in some months. Be sure you can financially tolerate the vacancy of some units. There's more about cash flow in the individual investment vehicle chapters of Part II.

Like working time, positive cash flow can be rare in some investment vehicles, notably land and renovations. With others, particularly small apartment buildings and multifamily houses, it can be a motivation for purchase.

That brings us back to the planning questions: Why are you buying real estate? What is more important to you: long-term appreciation or monthly income? To help you evaluate these questions and the time and work factors that will accommodate your needs and goals, there's a personal evaluation worksheet on page 66. But before getting to that, let's look at Uncle Sam's role in the earning power of your real estate investment dollar, and let's give a nod to your friendly local tax collector.

Taxes

There are two kinds of taxes that affect real estate: local assessments for property taxation and federal income-tax laws. Needless to say, taxation is a huge topic, so huge that writings about it fill whole libraries. Chapter 10 is an introduction to the basics of real estate taxation. Then in Part II, taxes are considered as they apply specifically to each of the investment vehicles discussed. Right now, let's go over some general issues.

LEARNING THE LANGUAGE

A **mill** is one tenth of one cent. A town's **mill rate** is the expression of its tax rate. For example, if a town's tax rate is 3.5 mills per dollar of assessed valuation, its mill rate is 3.5 (.0035 on each dollar, 35 cents on $100, and $3.50 on $1,000). To figure the taxes on a property assessed at $100,000, you multiply the mill rate (.0035) by the assessed valuation ($100,000) to get an annual tax of $350 (a dream in today's economy!).

In the real estate world, **depreciation** means the decrease in value of buildings and other improvements because of deterioration or obsolescence. For tax purposes, **depreciable life** means the number of years used to determine the length of the time over which depreciation tax deductions can be taken.

All real property can be taxed by local government. Usually "local government" means the municipality and/or the county. Each property is assessed for value and then taxed at the established mill rate for the given tax year.

It doesn't take a university degree to realize that the cost of holding real estate in a town with a low tax rate and low property assessments will be less than the cost of holding real estate in a town with a high tax rate and high assessments. Local taxes therefore are a factor in virtually every purchase decision, but certainly not the only factor. It's possible that a high-tax community will be the more desirable for other reasons such as good schools or a growing trend to upscale neighborhoods.

While local assessments and taxes are cost and cash-flow factors to be considered before purchase, federal income-tax benefits can actually be a purchase motivating factor in real estate investment, even though they are not as favorable as they once were. Depreciation on buildings can lower the owner's annual income-tax payments. Property exchanges can delay the payment of capital-gains taxes when a property is sold and a similar property is purchased with the proceeds of the sale. Investment vacation homes have a whole set of tax laws that allow you to use your place for an annual getaway while still claiming substantial tax benefits.

Tools-of-the-Trade Evaluations

To help you decide the type of investment vehicle that suits your current needs and goals, you should measure the necessary tools of the real estate trade (time, work, and money) against your personal resources and goals whenever you are considering an entry into the real estate marketplace. Once you have focused upon a specific piece of property, you should subject it to a tools-of-the-trade evaluation before making a purchase. Use the worksheets on pages 66 and 67 to guide your evaluations.

KEEP IN MIND

- **Holding time and working time** should be factors in every decision to purchase investment property.
- **Investing in real estate** requires skills and knowledge in four areas: property search and selection, maintenance, management, and recordkeeping.
- **Start-up cash, cash flow, and taxes** all affect the feasibility of a purchase.
- **Before each search for an investment property,** evaluate your personal resources against the time, work, and money—the tools of the trade—that might be required.
- **Before each purchase of an investment property,** evaluate the demands of the particular property with regard to the three tools of the trade.

WORKSHEET: PERSONAL NEEDS AND GOALS

TIME

Holding Time. How long are you willing to hold an investment vehicle?

Working Time. How many hours per week are you willing to work at your investment vehicle?

WORK

How much personal knowledge and skill can you contribute to each of these work-demand areas?

Property Search and Selection.

Maintenance.

Management.

Recordkeeping.

MONEY

Start-up Cash. How much cash do you have available for start-up?
Can you get more if needed?
Cash Flow. Do you need positive cash flow?
How much?
If no, how much negative cash flow can you manage?
For how long?

TAXES

Depreciation. How much can depreciation of a property help you to lower your annual income-tax payments?

Other Tax Benefits. Are you willing to search out other tax benefits to make the investment more profitable?

WORKSHEET: PROPERTY EVALUATION

PROPERTY (full address and brief description)

PRICE (asking price and in parentheses your purchase-price goal)

TIME
Holding Time. How long do you anticipate holding this property? Note any important factors that might influence profitable time, such as completion of an interstate highway or a new corporate headquarters.

Working Time. How many hours per week of your time will this property require?

WORK
Property Expectation. Use techniques in Chapter 6 to estimate fair market value and future market value. Make notes on why you think the property will appreciate.

Maintenance. Note the maintenance requirements for this property. How will they be met?

Management. How much time and skill are needed to manage this property? What decisions might come up? Are there any plans for change?

Recordkeeping. What type of records must be kept? Rental information? Receipts for tax purposes? Plans for change? Soil tests? Who will keep the records?

MONEY
Start-up Cash. Is your start-up cash adequate for this property? Can you get additional cash if needed?

Cash Flow. Calculate anticipated cash flow as shown on page 62.

Taxes. What are current local property taxes? What federal tax benefits do you intend to claim on this property?

Who Are the Players?

"Everyone realizes that one can believe little of what people say about each other. But it is not so widely realized that even less can one trust what people say about themselves."

Rebecca West (1892–1983), British author

The very act of buying and selling anything requires another party. Make "anything" real estate and the requirements expand to include people working to protect the interests of the seller, people working to protect the interests of the buyer, people working for the interests of the community or town, and sometimes even people working in the interests of the state or nation.

To interact effectively with all the participants in each of your real estate investment deals you must have at least a minimal understanding of their jobs. What are they trying to do and why? How much should you trust each of them? How can you determine when trust is merited and when caution is the word of the day?

To begin answering these questions, let's meet the people you're likely to be dealing with. They will be introduced more or less as you might encounter them in the typical buying process.

Who's Who in the Marketplace

To exist, a market must have something of value to be traded and it must have traders (buyers and sellers). The investment real estate market has both valued goods and traders and also two extra complications: tenants and agents. The tenants can influence both buyers and sellers. The agents can represent and influence either buyers or sellers and sometimes both. Understanding the goals and concerns of these four marketplace players is your first step to successful negotiating.

Buyers and Sellers

There is no typical buyer or seller. People of widely different socioeconomic backgrounds and ethnic heritage invest in real estate. The only universal generalization that can be made about these traders is that each is in the marketplace to transact the business of buying or selling; understanding that universal motivation is an important key to success.

Wherever and whenever property is bought or sold, three questions are likely to influence negotiations for both the price and the terms of a sale. Consider them carefully during every transaction.

1. **What is the motivation to buy or sell?** Is a seller liquidating assets and leaving the real estate marketplace or moving on to another property or perhaps properties? Is a buyer looking for long-term income or for appreciation? If you know what your adversaries are seeking, you are in a stronger position to use their goals to help you move toward yours. (See Chapter 6 for more about this negotiating strategy.)

2. **What are the pressure points? Time? Money? Space? Location?** Pressures that push us in one direction or another are often quite different from our original motivations. Is a seller carrying two mortgages? Does a buyer need a place to live as well as an investment property? Try to find out exactly where the shoe is pinching.

3. **How long has there been a sustained effort to buy or sell?** The real estate marketplace makes tough demands on body and spirit. Both sellers and buyers often get tired of making the effort. People who have been at it for a while are more likely to deal.

Tenants

Tenants are as different from one to another as are buyers and sellers. They do, however, have at least one thing in common: All tenants are upset by the prospect of a change in ownership. Place a For Sale sign in front of the property where they're renting and the questions cascade: Can I stay if it's sold? Will the rent go up? Will the new landlord let me keep my pets? Will the maintenance work be done? Some of the answers are in the lease and some are not.

After their initial anxious response, tenants either accept the selling process and cooperate with the landlord or resist and make attempts to discourage prospective buyers. It's important that you, the prospective buyer, make contact with current tenants. (Questions to ask can be found in Chapters 12, 13, 14, and 15.) Try to get a sense of whether each tenant is supporting or sabotaging. Keep in mind that what you hear may be highly colored by anxiety and the desire to manipulate. Check and recheck for the facts.

LEARNING THE LANGUAGE

A **lease** is a legal document by which the owner of a property (called the **lessor** or landlord) gives the right of possession to another party (the **lessee** or tenant) for a specified period of time (the **term**) and for a specified amount of money (the **rent**). A lease should specify whether the tenancy and its agreements will survive a change of ownership or terminate with the property transfer.

A **lease with option to purchase** is an agreement in the lease by which the tenant is granted the right to purchase the property at a named price and terms. The option may be valid for the entire term of the lease or for only a portion of it.

In leases on commercial real estate, the responsibility for paying various expenses associated with the property is often designated by the type of lease.

- **Under a net lease,** the tenant pays all operating expenses (heat and electricity, for example) but not the real estate taxes or insurance.
- **Under a net net lease,** the tenant pays all operating expenses plus insurance premiums.
- **Under a triple net lease,** the tenant pays all operating expenses, real estate taxes, and insurance premiums. In some cases, the triple net lease commercial tenant may also be required to make the payments on the existing mortgage.

Real Estate Agents

Twenty-five years ago virtually all real estate agents represented sellers. Those among us who sometimes think about *the good ole days* remember that sellers' agents were friendly, courteous, and often very helpful to buyers. But in those days, everyone (buyers, sellers, and agents alike) knew the ancient Latin motto of the real estate marketplace: *caveat emptor* (let the buyer beware). The role of the agent in the marketplace has now changed significantly. (That does not mean, however, that buyers should ever stop being wary.)

Today, a real estate agent can represent either the seller *or* the buyer in a transaction, with the commission still to be paid out of the proceeds of the sale. Or, with the consent of both buyer and seller, the agent can represent both parties (called a *dual agent*), or neither party (called a *transactional agent*). In yet another current-day relationship in the marketplace, some buyers hire buyer brokers for a flat fee that is paid in addition or regardless of any commission to be paid from the proceeds of the sale.

The traditional commission on real estate transactions has been 6 percent on buildings and 10 percent on land sales but, by law, that figure is negotiable. It can even be a flat fee. In today's marketplace, commission is another item that must be agreed to before listing contracts are signed. A real estate commission can be whatever the broker and the parties agree to. It can also be split between the listing broker and the selling broker in any way that is agreed upon, but 50-50 is still the most prevalent division.

LEARNING THE LANGUAGE

Even though it's often seen in print with a lower case "r", **Realtor** is a proper noun. The word is a registered trademark of the **National Association of Realtors (NAR)** and can legally be used only by members of this trade group or to refer to them. Not every real estate agent is a Realtor. Realtor brokers and salespersons must conduct business according to the Code of Ethics of the NAR.

Both **real estate brokers and salespersons** must be licensed in the state in which they work. Only brokers, however, can assume an agency relationship with either a seller or a buyer. Licensed real estate salespersons act under the sponsorship and supervision of a broker. Both brokers and salespersons work with one another to show and sell investment property.

No matter whom they represent, all licensed real estate brokers and salespersons are required to state all known facts about a property accurately and honestly

---

DIGGING DEEPER

Founded in 1908, the **National Association of Realtors** is the nation's largest trade organization. Within it are over 1,700 state and local-area Boards of Realtors. You can get information on the Realtor Code of Ethics and Standards of Practice and/or file a problem complaint at any local Realtor Board office. For more information on the CRS, CCIM, and SIOR competency designations and other professional information about Realtors, visit http://www.realtor.org; for consumer information, including online searches for Realtors or for properties for sale by zip code, visit http://www.realtor.com.

> **National Association of Realtors (NAR)**
> **430 North Michigan Avenue**
> **Chicago, IL 60611-4087**
> **800-874-6500**
> **http://www.realtor.com http://www.realtor.org**

If you believe that a licensed real estate agent has broken the law or acted inappropriately (which might include racial or sexual discrimination), you can file a complaint with **your state's real estate commission.** The number is listed under state government agencies in the blue pages of your telephone book.

For more information about working with an agency that represents buyers exclusively and for referrals to agents in your area, contact:

> **The National Association of Exclusive Buyer**
>   **Agents (NAEBA)**
> **5415 Orlando Avenue, Suite 300**
> **Maitland, FL 32751**
> **800-986-2322**
> **http://www.naeba.org**

---

to the best of their knowledge. When a broker or sales-person is acting as the agent of a specific party (either seller or buyer), however, that party can also expect that the real estate agent will work in his or her best interests. That may mean advice on the fair market value of a particular property, background information on what's happening in the community, and help with negotiating strategies. Whether or not you choose to hire a broker or salesperson to act as your buyer agent, you should always remember that the agent's work is done and the advice is given with the hope of making the deal and thereby being paid a commission.

Theoretically, all licensed real estate brokers and salespersons can handle all types of real estate transactions, but in practice there is some degree of specialization. Generally, single-family houses, multifamily houses, and small-tract land sales for housing are handled by residential real estate agents associated with the brokers' offices found on every Main Street in America. Larger investment properties, such as apartment buildings, mixed-use buildings, commercial properties, and large tracts of land for both residential and commercial development, are usually handled by specially trained agents.

The National Association of Realtors encompasses two groups of these specialists, and each group awards a competency designation requiring both proven and varied experience and extensive study.

1. **CCIM** (Certified Commercial Investment Member) is conferred by the Commercial-Investment Real Estate Council.
2. **SIOR** designates membership in The Society of Industrial and Office Realtors.

If you see either the CCIM or the SIOR on your Realtor's card, you'll know that your agent is well versed in the complexities of investment real estate's bigger deals.

For beginners, however, the gateway into the investment real estate marketplace is usually through smaller residential properties and neither the CCIM nor the SIOR designations are needed for effective work by a Realtor. The NAR confers a **CRS** (Certified Residential Specialist) designation, which indicates both varied experience and the completion of specialized course work in residential sales.

Even more important than degrees and designations, however, is the commitment and competence of the individual real estate salesperson. Some of the best purchases in investment real estate have been put together by assertive agents who went beyond the usual requirements of their jobs. Unlike the homebuying marketplace where virtually every property listed with an agent is shared on the MLS (Multiple Listing Service) with every other Realtor, many investment properties are sold through open listings. Top agents in search of property for a customer often contact prospective sellers who perhaps have advertised their properties "by owner" at some time during the past six to twelve months or who formerly had a listing on the market that didn't sell and has expired.

In the investment marketplace, it's not at all unusual for a buyer to say to an agent, "I want a small motel with my living quarters on the premises," or "I'm looking for a liquor store with some residential units above it." When a search through the MLS records brings up little or nothing, the exceptional agent might go out looking for such a property, either by driving through promising areas of town or by searching through the town tax records. He or she then contacts the owners personally to ask if there is any interest in selling to a client who has expressed a desire to buy that type of property. The result is often a short-term open listing that enables the agent to show the property to his or her client.

As a beginner in the real estate investment marketplace, you should choose an agent early in your search for property. A good buyer's agent will advise and guide you regarding current property value and the potential for appreciation. He or she will also seek out prospective properties that you may not have found on your own and often will direct you to financing opportuni-

LEARNING THE LANGUAGE

MLS (Multiple Listing Service) handles the shared database of properties listed for sale by members of the local Board of Realtors. It supervises the entry of each listing into the Realtors' computer data bank. Realtors using the service agree to split the commission between the listing broker and the selling broker according to agreed-upon percentages.

An **open listing** is an agreement between a property owner and a real estate broker in which the owner agrees to pay a certain commission if the real estate agency sells the property at an acceptable price and terms. The owner keeps the right to sell the property without a broker and not pay any commission, and the right to enter into an open-listing agreement with any other broker. A seller can have concurrent open-listing agreements with each and every real estate agency in town.

An **exclusive-agency listing** names one real estate broker as the agent of the seller but reserves the owner's right to sell the property without the aid of a broker and not pay a commission. These listings are usually shared on the MLS.

An **exclusive right to sell listing** names one real estate broker to have the right to sell the property. During the term of the listing contract, that broker will collect a commission even if the owner sells the property to a relative. This is the most common type of listing on the residential MLS.

ties. Check for these characteristics in each agent that you work with:
- At least three years experience in real estate sales
- Full-time professional
- Local area resident with community knowledge and involvement
- Good listening ability; pays attention to what you are seeking and the limitations that you set for price and location
- Attention to detail in property inspections and contract terms
- Ethical commitment and trustworthiness.

Theoretically, the best way to find a "good agent" is through referral from another successful and experienced investor. But such investors are also your competitors and agent referrals are not as common as one would hope. If you have no one to advise you, watch the local newspapers. Many brokers advertise the names of their top agents each month. It is also a common practice to advertise the names of listing agents with the photos of their advertised properties. If such advertising is done in your area, make note of the names of agents who have listed properties similar to the type you are seeking. An agent with several listings in one type of real estate—let's say, multifamily houses— is likely to know the subspecialty well and therefore be more capable of giving good advice.

Appraisers

An appraiser is a real estate professional who is paid for his or her opinion of property value. Some investors never make a deal without an appraisal, others hear only about the appraiser who will be hired by the mortgage lender. (Bank appraisers will be discussed later.) Whether or not an appraiser could be helpful to your particular deal depends on your comfort level in estimating value and on the complexity of the property in question.

Many experienced investors make their own appraisals. (You'll learn how in Chapter 6.) They call in a professional appraiser only if some element of the deal, such as the best use for the property, raises questions that would affect profitability. In such cases, the purchase contract can be written subject to the appraisal.

When a written appraisal can make or break a deal, choosing an appraiser is an important decision. Until 1989 almost anyone could hang out an appraiser shingle, and most real estate brokers also called themselves appraisers. But the Financial Institutions Reform, Recovery & Enforcement Act created the USPAP (Uniform Standards of Professional Appraisal Practice). Today, state licensing is required for anyone wishing to

---

DIGGING DEEPER

Appraisers seem to have created more national trade organizations than any other real estate profession. Several of these groups support the **Appraisal Foundation,** a nonprofit educational organization that will provide information about the appraisal industry as a whole and about the various specialty groups. Links from its Web site to those of sponsoring organizations allow you to search online for appraisers in your area. Contact:

Appraisal Foundation
1029 Vermont Avenue, N.W.
Suite 900
Washington, DC 20005
202-347-7722
http://www.appraisalfoundation.org

---

act as a real estate appraiser and federal regulations are setting guidelines and making specialization designations. There are currently three levels of appraiser licensing using the following guidelines:

1. **State Licensed Appraisers** without certification may appraise noncomplex 1–4-unit residential transactions valued up to $1 million. More complex and nonresidential transactions are limited to properties under $250,000.
2. **State Certified Residential Appraisers** may appraise 1–4-unit residential transactions without regard to transaction value or complexity.
3. **State Certified General Appraisers** may appraise all types of real property.

As of January 1, 2008, qualification guidelines for state licensing will change but they will still be subject to the USPAP. You can contact the Appraisal Foundation for licensing and certification updates.

If you choose to use an appraiser, remember that you are paying for an opinion on the value of a piece of property. It's an educated, professional opinion to be sure, but still an *opinion*. There are no guarantees of estimated value in the real estate marketplace.

Choose an appraiser based on his or her license level, years of experience in the local marketplace, and, most important, experience in the type of real estate you are considering. To get this information, get a referral from another investor in the same type of property, if you know one, or simply interview the appraiser and ask the appropriate questions.

Working with the Purchase Contract

After you have found an investment property and agreed upon a price, you will enter into a purchase contract and meet another crew of real estate "helpers." If they do their jobs well, each will contribute to a successful closing. Let's do a brief survey of responsibilities.

Lawyers

In some areas of the country, particularly the Northeast, lawyers close title. Usually included in their fee are contract review, document preparation, title search, closing settlement accounting and funds disbursement, and the recording of the deed. Escrow monies can be held in the trust account of either the buyer's or seller's attorney or in the trust account of the real estate agent.

Once a purchase contract is fully executed, some states mandate a period (commonly three to five working days) for the opportunity of legal review before the agreement becomes binding. Other states neither require a legal review period nor the use of a lawyer to close title. But lawyers are a part of virtually every deal, even though you don't see them, because the contract forms with the blanks to be filled in that are used in real estate offices are composed by lawyers. Generally, these standardized documents are protective of the rights and interests of both sellers and buyers.

> **"Castles in the air are the only property you can own without the intervention of lawyers. Unfortunately there are no title deeds to them."**
>
> J. Feidor Rees, British writer

LEARNING THE LANGUAGE

Escrow monies are the good-faith deposits made by the buyer and held by a third party until the conditions and contingencies of a contract have been met.

An **abstract** (formally called an **abstract of title**) is a compilation and summary of all the recorded documents relating to a parcel of land. In most areas today, the abstract is being replaced by title insurance.

An **abstract attorney** reviews and summarizes the recorded documents relating to a parcel of land and may give an opinion as to the condition of the title.

A **cloud on the title** refers to an invalid encumbrance on a piece of real estate. If the encumbrance were valid, it would affect the rights of the owner. A claim against the property by a former owner who lost ownership rights in a tax foreclosure would be a cloud on the title.

A **quitclaim deed** is a release that removes a cloud on the title. The person who signs it (grantor) gives up any claim or interest in the property in question. Sometimes there is a financial settlement to get a claimant to sign a quitclaim deed. One of several heirs to a property might sign a quitclaim deed to his or her interest in the property.

Even if you live in a state where title companies, closing agents, or lender's representatives routinely close title, you can (and should) choose the protection afforded by a provision in your purchase contract for review by an attorney before the agreement becomes valid. To do so, simply use the clause shown in the "Stop and Think!" box.

Choose a local attorney who knows real estate law. You can arrange a flat fee for contract review or an hourly fee for representation if you anticipate any legal difficulties. (See Chapter 7 for more about the attorney's role in your contract.)

In addition to advising on the purchase contract and perhaps closing title, you may also need the help of a lawyer if you decide to subdivide a tract of land, convert a building from a single-family to a multifamily residence, convert a rental apartment building to a condominium community or co-op, or convert a residence into a mixed-use building.

Your Professional Property Inspector

> ## STOP AND THINK!
>
> If you want a few days to think about the terms of your contract and the opportunity to go over it with a lawyer of your choice who will have the power to change it or get you out of it, include the following sentence above your signature in your purchase contract:
> *This agreement is subject to review and approval as to form and content by an attorney of the buyer's choice. The attorney may rescind the contract for any reason before midnight (date).*

Soon after your purchase contract is fully executed, you should arrange for a professional property inspection. Most homebuyers today routinely include a home inspection clause in their purchase contracts, but many investors forget that the inspection contingency is also available to them. You can hire an inspection firm to evaluate a single-family house or a multifamily house. Even contracts to purchase condominium apartments, mixed-use buildings, and small apartment buildings can be subject to a working systems and structural inspection. Of course, one of the challenges is getting the tenants to cooperate. (There's more about inspection-contingency clauses in Chapter 7.)

Property inspection was a virtually unknown profession at mid-20th century. Today, however, the American Society of Home Inspectors, the largest of the trade groups in the field, has over 6,000 member firms in the United States. The cost of a professional inspection varies by area of the country and the size of the property to be inspected. The average inspection takes two to three hours, longer if the property is in need of extensive repair or is particularly large. Try to accompany the inspector throughout the inspection process; you'll learn a lot.

A professional inspector will test the working systems of the property, visually inspect the structure, and prepare a room-by-room written report. Inspectors will not take responsibility, however, for anything that cannot be inspected visually, such as the condition of plumbing within the walls. The inspector's printed report can often be used to reopen negotiations.

Choosing and working with an inspector is covered in Chapter 8. There's also a box on page 153 with a listing for the professional trade groups for property inspectors and their Web sites.

If you would prefer specialized inspections of such components as roofing, the foundation, or heating, plumbing, and electrical systems, you can make your purchase contract contingent upon inspection by professionals in each field. These inspections are

---

LEARNING THE LANGUAGE

In the real estate world, **to survey** means to use professional instruments to measure and determine the precise boundaries of land and sometimes its topography. A **survey** is the map or description that results from the process of surveying.

An **easement** is an interest in the land of another party that does not include possession of that land. A utility easement, for example, might allow an electric company to run high-tension wires over a section of your property. A shared drive along a property line might include an easement on each neighboring property that allows both owners to use the entire width of the driveway.

A **right-of-way** is the right to pass over land owned by someone else. It may be indicated by an easement or it may be a strip of land that is owned by the user. A railroad, for example, might have a right-of-way across a pasture.

An **encroachment** is a structure or a part of a structure that illegally intrudes on the land of another. If the business next door has a commercial sign that hangs over your property, that's an encroachment.

usually done by contractors and include estimates for doing the work. If you are considering a property in need of rehab, you may want to get at least three estimates for each anticipated job.

Surveyors

To help ensure good title and to avoid disputes with your neighbors, you'll want to have your property surveyed. (If you're getting a mortgage loan, the lender will require it.) Real estate agents and settlement agents will usually provide you with a listing of surveyors who work in the area.

In addition to the exact boundaries of the lot, a survey will usually show the precise location of any buildings or other improvements, such as a driveway or parking lot on the site, and may indicate other physical features, such as a pond or a stone wall. It will also show the location of any easements or rights-of-way and the existence of any encroachments from adjacent properties. (The corner of a neighbor's garage that extends over the property boundary is an encroachment.)

The Settlement Agent

In areas where lawyers do not close title, the settlement agent (sometimes called the closing agent or escrow agent) is a third party with no personal interest in the transaction who collects the necessary paperwork, prepares the documents, does the accounting, makes necessary disbursements, oversees the closing procedure, and records the title transfer and other necessary documents. Sometimes settlement agents also hold the escrow funds. The settlement agent in your area may be your title insurance company, an abstract attorney, your mortgage lender, or sometimes even the listing real estate broker.

The Title-Insurance Company

Most experts recommend title insurance and most mortgage lenders require it. Title insurance is a guarantee against loss because of a dispute over ownership. It does not guarantee that you will always own a property, but rather that your legal costs will be covered if there is a suit over title and that you will be compensated for your loss if your title is found to be invalid, defective, or inaccurate.

Insuring title begins with a search of public records regarding the property in question. If there are no clouds on the title, the title-insurance company will agree to issue both owner's and lender's insurance. Sometimes the search will turn up potential problems that can be eliminated by a quitclaim deed, and sometimes the title company will insure a title even though there are questions in the search material. For example, let's say that an old gravel road once crossed the corner of the property you are considering. It was a legal road shown on the deed as a right-of-way but the road was, in fact, eliminated long ago. Today, there is a subdivision of houses in its path nearby. In this case, the paper road might be noted in the title insurance as an exception or it might be completely disregarded.

Title insurance to protect the lender is issued in the amount of the mortgage and decreases as the principal is paid off. Owner's title insurance often, but not necessarily, covers the full purchase price. It remains in effect as long as ownership is held. The buyer usually pays for both policies with a one-time fee due at the closing. (There is usually a reduction in cost when both types of policies are purchased simultaneously.)

Unless the title-insurance company is also your settlement agent, it's unlikely that you'll ever meet a real person involved in your search. Most title insurance is procured through lenders, attorneys, or closing agents, but you have the option of shopping for it and choosing your own company. Title-insurance companies are regulated by state law, but in most states,

DIGGING DEEPER

American Land Title Association (ALTA), the trade organization for the title-insurance industry, offers an online search for title-insurance companies working in your local area. They will also send you printed material about protecting your interests in real estate.

American Land Title Association
1828 L Street N.W., Suite 705
Washington, DC 20036
202-296-3671
http://www.alta.org

there is enough variability in rates to make shopping worthwhile.

The Figures in Financing

Chapter 9 is devoted to getting the money to buy the property you want, so at this point let's just do the introductions to some important people in the lending business. In your hunt for money, however, you should always be aware that your real estate agent is an excellent point of contact with the lending community of your local area.

Lending Institutions

Just about every known lender in your area will have an office full of mortgage representatives, sometimes called loan originators. Their job is to sell (and explain) their products (the types of mortgages available and the terms). They help applicants fill out the paperwork and they collect the application fees. Many mortgage reps work in the field and will come to your home to sell their loans. In some instances, you can apply by phone or on the Internet and may never meet the mortgage rep from your lender.

Mortgage Brokers

Virtually unheard of before 1980, the mortgage broker is one of the hot real estate careers of the new millennium. They now originate approximately half of the home and small-investment mortgage loans in the United States.

Why the big change in 25 years? Well, after most of the savings and loan institutions (S&Ls) went belly-up in the late '80s, mortgage lending became a national business. The potential sources for your mortgage money are no longer restricted to your hometown or even your home state. Mortgage brokers hunt in the huge national money marketplace.

In the same way that real estate brokers find buyers and sellers and bring them together to make a deal, the goal of a mortgage broker is to find a ready, willing, and able borrower and a ready, willing, and able lender and bring them together. Mortgage brokers do not lend the money for mortgage loans, they process them. Processing includes:

- Qualifying the buyers (determining if they can afford the payments on the loan)
- Taking the application
- Preparing the loan documents
- Arranging for lender inspections and appraisals
- Transmitting completed forms to the lender
- Recording and documenting the completed transaction according to local laws (which may include the voluntary lien on the property that the mortgage papers represent).

Once you have closed on your purchase using a mortgage broker, you will make your mortgage payments directly to the lender, with no further contact with the mortgage broker. So why bother with the broker? Why not go directly to the lender? You can. Brokers, however, are valuable when you need unusual financing (for example, a particularly large loan on a seaside hotel or a loan on a unique property such as a lighthouse) or when you are shopping for the best rate and terms.

Mortgage brokers, like real estate brokers, usually don't get paid unless they put a deal together. When they place loans with institutional lenders, the lender pays them a certain percentage of the loan value, expressed in basis points (a basis point is 0.001, or one-tenth of 1 percent of the face value of the loan). Some mortgage brokers also collect a one-time service fee from the borrower.

Mortgage Bankers

Mortgage bankers do very much the same work as mortgage brokers, but they usually keep in contact with the borrowers by servicing their loans. Generally, servicing a loan means collecting payments, paying

---

LEARNING THE LANGUAGE

A **lien** (rhymes with bean) is a creditor's claim against property. It can be voluntary, such as a mortgage, or involuntary, such as a mechanic's lien placed by an unpaid plumber. All liens are encumbrances, but not all encumbrances are liens.

DIGGING DEEPER

For more information on what a mortgage broker can do for you and referrals to brokers in your local area, contact the national trade organization at:

National Association of Mortgage Brokers
8201 Greensboro Drive, Suite 300
McLean, VA 22102
703-610-9009
http://www.namb.org

To learn more about mortgage bankers and the current real estate climate and financing, contact:

Mortgage Bankers Association of America
1919 Pennsylvania Avenue, N.W.
Washington, DC 20006-3404
202-557-2700
http://www.mbaa.org

---

property taxes when the lender holds tax escrow, following up on delinquent payments, and supplying the borrower with interest and principal payment data for tax purposes.

Mortgage bankers may actually lend the face value of the loan at its inception, but that mortgage is generally sold into the secondary mortgage market soon afterward. Many borrowers, however, never know who actually holds their mortgage because their point of contact remains with the mortgage banker.

The chief advantage of dealing with a mortgage banker is the wide base of opportunity for sources of money, including insurance companies, credit unions, and pension funds. Qualification guidelines for these loans may be less stringent than among the traditional lenders accessible to the average investor. (See Chapter 9 for more about qualification guidelines.)

Mortgage Underwriters

It is unlikely that you will ever meet a mortgage underwriter professionally. But his or her work will decide between the "approved" or "declined" stamp on your mortgage application.

Loan underwriters evaluate borrower applications to determine if the loan is a prudent investment. They're especially attentive to property appraisals and credit reports. If you want to incline them toward "approved," make their work easier by being careful that all the necessary paperwork is collected and in order.

Bank Appraisers

Because the lender's level of risk in making a loan is largely determined by the value of the property to be mortgaged, virtually every mortgage loan requires the work of an appraiser hired by the lender. Some appraisers are independent contractors hired one job at a time. Others are full-time employees of the bank. In either case, their task is to assign a realistic current market value to the piece of property in question.

The lender's appraiser will be sent out to inspect the property after your mortgage application is filed. Odds are you will never meet this professional. But if you have information that might favorably influence the appraisal (such as information about another property nearby that sold at a price higher than yours, records showing the income generated by the property, a particularly good professional inspection report, or architectural drawings for intended renovations), make an appointment to be present when the appraiser arrives and give him or her the printed information. Be pleasant at this meeting, but don't try to find out what the appraiser thinks. You won't be told.

Government Inspectors

If you are using government-sponsored financing (FHA and VA loans are the most common but there are also some state loan programs available), you can expect that government representatives will also inspect your property. Organizations that support mortgages often have minimum construction and maintenance standards that must be met. If the building does not meet those standards, the seller is sometimes required to do the repairs before the loan can be made. In some special programs, however, the buyer can borrow additional cash to make the repairs. (This will be covered further in Chapter 9.)

You should also anticipate inspectors from the local, state, and national governments if you are renovating a historic property or if you are working with state and local programs to provide public housing. Scheduling these inspections is often almost as much of a problem as complying with the regulations.

Men and Women About Town

It's not all over when it's over. When you walk away from the closing table with the keys in your pocket and the survey in hand, you're not ending, you're just beginning. You've got work ahead of you and many more real estate people in your life. Let's meet some of those who work for your government.

The Tax Assessor

Now, here's someone most people *never* want to meet. But if you are a property owner in the United States, some contact is virtually inevitable. Real estate taxes can be levied by:

- **States**
- **Counties**
- **Cities, towns, and villages**
- **School districts**
- **Drainage districts**
- **Water supply districts**
- **Sanitary sewer districts**
- **Park, forest preserve, and recreational districts**

If you feel that an error has been made in the tax assessment for your property (it's too high in comparison with the assessments for neighboring properties, for example), you may contest the assessment by presenting your case to a local board of appeal or board of

LEARNING THE LANGUAGE

Real estate in the United States is taxed **ad valorem.** That's Latin for "according to value." The job of the tax assessor in each taxing district is to determine the fair market value of each property.

Grandfathered is a real estate term that refers to laws that allow the continuation of the use of a building that met building standards and laws when it was built but does not conform to current codes and standards. In other words, the building predates the law.

tax review. If you do not get satisfaction, protests or further appeals regarding tax assessments can ultimately be taken to court.

In addition to the general (*ad valorem*) real estate tax, special assessments can also be made by any of the tax bodies listed previously. These special assessments usually fund public improvements that directly affect private property. Some examples are paved streets, curbs, sidewalks, storm sewers, and streetlighting. When their properties directly benefit from the improvements, property owners are often required to contribute toward paying for the work. Special assessments are valid taxes, and if unpaid, they become a lien on the property.

Before buying investment property, you should always make a trip to the local tax assessor's office. Ask when the last general reassessment took place. Is another scheduled in the near future? Or does the tax assessment on each property change with each change of ownership? Ask if any improvements that involve special assessments are planned for the area in which you intend to buy. Sewers? Streetlighting?

Special assessments or a general tax reassessment can give your positive cash flow a good punch in the belly. If special assessments have been levied, try to get the seller to pay them off in full before you take title.

Buildings Inspector

In some cities, rental property is inspected at regular intervals for compliance with building codes and health standards. Often, an even more thorough inspection of the property is done whenever ownership changes hands. Repair and upgrade requirements are not uncommon.

The Boy Scout motto *"Be prepared!"* is the best advice in this department. Stop and talk with the folks in your town's buildings department. Ask what the standards are for rental housing if the town does a change-of-ownership inspection and what changes or upgrades are most often required. Then add the estimated costs for these improvements to your projected cost of purchase or negotiate with the seller to have them done before you take title.

In addition to inspecting for structural soundness and the good working order of electrical, heating, and plumbing systems, buildings inspectors today may check for hazardous materials. Among those materials currently on inspection lists are asbestos, lead-based paint, radon, urea-formaldehyde insulation, carbon monoxide, electromagnetic fields, and underground fuel storage tanks.

If you are renovating, rehabilitating, or adding on to an existing property, you will meet the buildings inspector repeatedly as he or she checks for code compliance and gives (or withholds) the necessary approvals. If you are engaged in new construction on a land investment, you will also get to know your local buildings inspectors. They are required to inspect new construction at predetermined stages and unless they give their stamps of approval, work on the building will not be allowed to continue.

> ### STOP AND THINK!
>
> Be especially careful if you are buying a very old investment property with many grandfathered systems. In some municipalities, a change of ownership wipes out the allowances made for the age of the building and you could be required to bring either structural elements or working systems (or both) up to code. You could be buying a major renovation project that could prove to be extremely expensive. Ask at the buildings department what the local policy is regarding change of ownership and grandfathered rental property.

Environmental Inspector

The environmental inspector is a relatively new professional in the real estate marketplace. These inspectors were rare everywhere until the last 20 years of the 20th century and, even now, not all municipalities employ their own environmental engineers (or environmental inspectors). To compensate for municipal vacancies, these inspectors are sometimes called in from the county and state level. You will meet them most often if you are developing land.

In the early 1990s, the Environmental Protection Agency (EPA) began requiring environmental inspections in some real estate transactions. Many municipalities throughout the country have followed suit. It's a good idea to check out environmental protection and inspection laws in your community before you buy.

The environmental inspector looks at property for contaminated soil, air, or water and for the presence of hazardous substances used in construction. If you are developing land with the intention of using septic systems for waste disposal, you will be required to test the soil for drainage and composition.

Planning and Zoning Boards

Planning and zoning boards were already mentioned in Chapter 3. Because no nationwide or statewide zoning ordinances exist, the responsibility for planning and maintaining community growth rests with local government. These powers are conferred by state enabling acts.

Compliance with zoning laws is generally enforced through the use of permits. Landowners are required to obtain zoning permits before they can apply for building permits. Without zoning board approval, there can be no new development. An appointed position on the local zoning board therefore is a position of power in the community.

A Word About Tact

Dealing in the real estate marketplace involves dealing with people as well as property. When dealings occur among people, the most aggressive players don't always win and an aggressive plan isn't necessarily the stronger plan. There is often more power in the art of listening well and being willing and able to compromise than there is in the act of pounding the table to drive your point home.

The word *neighbor* has special meaning in this business because what you do with your property affects your neighbors, and vice versa. Yes, real estate investment is definitely a competitive game, but it is also a game where an awareness of the needs and goals of other people on the field can often enhance the likelihood of success (not to mention lower your blood pressure, provide more opportunities for laughter, and bring back smiles and greetings when you walk down the street). After all, you may well want to do business with the same people again, or have to do so.

KEEP IN MIND

- **It's essential that you,** the buyer, understand the roles of the other people involved in your deal.
- **Real estate agents** can work for the seller, the buyer, or both at the same time, but they always work in hopes of putting together a deal that will earn them a commission.
- **You can make your real estate purchase** contract contingent upon the review and acceptance of an attorney of your choice.
- **In addition to local lending institutions,** you can search for financing through a mortgage broker or a mortgage banker, and on the Internet.
- **Stop by the tax assessor's office** before you make an offer on a property.
- **Walk and talk softly,** even if you are carrying a big stick.

What Makes a Good Deal?

"Sometimes your best investments are the ones you don't make."

Donald Trump, *The Art of the Deal*

Chapter 6

Imagine this, if you will: You're hot on the trail of your first investment property and your pulse is pounding hard and fast.

Stop! It's time to slow down and call in your brain. Take all the time you need to check and compare the character trait profile that you did in Chapter 3 with the demands on ownership made by this type of property. (The demands of each type are considered in Part II.) If you find that you have a good and workable match, take the next step.

No, the next step is *not* "make an offer." After you check the appropriateness of your character to the demands of this type of investment vehicle, you should carefully consider the time, work, and money demands of this particular property.

"OK," you say, "then if everything fits perfectly with the resources at hand, it's a go! Right?"

Not exactly, or at least not yet.

Whenever you find a property that looks good, feels right, and just seems to call out to you, the real estate game gets exciting. You're about to make a big move. You think you can win at this. The warm-up is over and you're anxious to make a deal.

Right then a DANGER sign should pop up in your head. It's a time when emotion, competition, and the drive to win can overwhelm your rational judgment. You can get so caught up in getting what you want that you forget what you started out to get. Remember, the name of the game is investment real estate. You are in it to make a profit. Of all the questions appropriate to choosing property, this is the most important: *Will it make money?*

Moneymaking can take several forms. Your goal might be short-term or long-term profit. Or perhaps cash flow could be more important to you than capital gains. Creating a tax shelter might be an added incentive to buy. No matter what your goals, however, two factors will play an important role in your decisions: property value and potential for appreciation.

Because neither of these two essential considerations can be determined exactly, predicting profit in investment real estate is never an exact science, very much like predicting economic trends. Property value is influenced by many factors, including the ever-present law of supply and demand. Appreciation is influenced

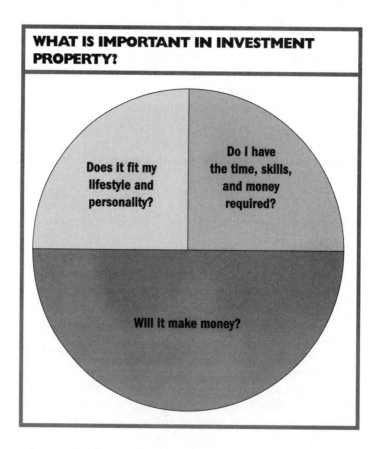

WHAT IS IMPORTANT IN INVESTMENT PROPERTY?

Does it fit my lifestyle and personality?

Do I have the time, skills, and money required?

Will it make money?

by future events, some of which are beyond the buyer's control. The decision to invest in real property therefore must rely on both knowledge and judgment. This chapter is all about giving you the tools you'll need to develop profit-conscious judgment.

The Importance of Fair Market Value

You (and everyone else in the world) want to go through life thinking that you're shopping wisely and getting a good deal. Realizing that you paid too much for a car can leave you with a cramped feeling in your stomach. Thinking that you paid too much for a piece of investment real estate can leave you with. . . Well, let your imagination run wild!

So how can you tell what your prospective property is worth? Some experts say value is determined by the deal. On the other hand, how can you make a deal without some idea of value? Investors new to the marketplace often confuse fair market value and market price. (Be sure to read **Learning the Language** below carefully.) The goal of savvy investors is to estimate fair market value accurately and then negotiate a deal at a market price below that estimate.

Negotiating strategies for getting a good market price will be discussed in the next chapter. Right now, let's work on getting as accurate an estimate of property value as possible. To estimate market value, you can call upon the same methods and tools that professional appraisers use. (Appraisers were introduced in Chapter 5.) The three most commonly used appraisal techniques are *market data, replacement cost,* and *income analysis.* It's possible to use all three methods when appraising some properties,

---

LEARNING THE LANGUAGE

The concept of **fair market value** is commonly explained as the highest price a ready, willing, and able buyer is likely to pay and the lowest price a ready, willing, and able seller is likely to accept. Fair market value is always an estimate. It is the *probable* price based upon the assumption that both the buyer and the seller are fully informed and that the property has been on the market for a reasonable period of time.

Market price is the actual amount that a property brings in a given market. Market price may be lower, higher, or right at the fair market value estimate.

but in other cases only one or two methods will be appropriate. Let's look at them.

The Market-Data Method

The market-data method of appraisal (also called the sales-comparison method) is the one most widely used for estimating market value in single-family and two- to four-unit multifamily houses. It is essentially the same procedure that is used by real estate agents to help home sellers set asking and probable selling prices. Listing agents call it a *comparative market analysis* or CMA.

A market-data estimate of value is obtained by comparing the property in question with similar properties (called comparables) that have recently been sold. As each sold property is compared to the subject property, adjustments are made for differences in location, physical features and amenities, time on the market, and any changes in local economic conditions.

In today's marketplace, the market information necessary to do a comparative market analysis is readily available by computer from data stored in Realtors' files. With a few clicks of the mouse, you can access data on everything from room size to taxes, and the asking prices, actual selling prices, and time on the market of just about everything in town that has been sold through real estate agents. If you are working with a buyer's agent, or even a neutral transactional agent, you can (and should) ask your salesperson to use this method to estimate the fair market value of the property under consideration before making your first offer.

Without the help of Realtors' sales data (if you are looking at a property being sold by the owner, for example), it is somewhat more difficult to do a market data valuation, but certainly not impossible. You will have to spend some time at the town hall. The tax assessor's

---

LEARNING THE LANGUAGE

Comparables are properties sold during the past six months to a year that are similar to the subject property in style, size, age, and condition. Location is an important factor in the reliability of a given comparable property as a market value estimator. The closer and more similar the location to that of the subject property, the more likely market value will be similar.

office stores information (including the selling price) on every property in town as public record. With perhaps a little help from the town clerk, you can collect data regarding recent sales in the areas of town that are of interest. Once you have the selling prices of several properties similar to the one you are considering, you can compare physical features and amenities as recorded in the tax assessment records. What you won't be able to get, however, is time-on-the-market data, which might have made a significant difference in the prices the sellers were willing to accept. (The longer the time on the market, the more likely the sellers are to reduce their selling price.)

The Replacement-Cost Method

To appraise by the replacement-cost method, you assume that the property can be reproduced or replaced and you estimate that cost. Except in those cases where historic preservation is a factor, almost all investors calculate cost estimates for replacement with the assumption that current materials, tools, and technology will be used to build a similar property. Only rarely does an investor consider doing cost estimates for reproducing an older property exactly, thereby keeping both the benefits and drawbacks of its age.

The replacement-cost method is usually employed when there are few similar properties in the area, thus making a CMA difficult. It is also employed when there is no expected income from the property. For example, a quick-turn-around fixer-upper that might be located in a mixed-use area, in an area of custom-built homes, or on a country road would qualify neither for a CMA nor an income analysis appraisal of value.

There are five steps to appraising value by the replacement-cost method. Let's go through them as though you were considering the

---

LEARNING THE LANGUAGE

Highest and best use in the real estate marketplace refers to the most profitable single use to which a property can be committed or to the use most likely to be in demand in the near future. This theoretic use must be allowed by zoning laws, financially feasible, physically possible (you can't put a parking lot on the side of a cliff), and of maximum benefit to the community. If any of your investment activity takes you before a zoning board, you are likely to hear the term *highest and best use* frequently.

purchase of a particular property: a four-unit multi-family house that is 40 years old. (There's a summary of the steps in the box on page 101.)

1. Estimate the value of the land. In theory, land does not wear out so it is not considered depreciable. In actuality, however, its value is affected by the local economy, by its surroundings, and by its use. Get some insight into value by looking at land assessments at the tax collector's office. Keep in mind, however, that assessments are not always made at 100 percent of current value, not always up-to-date, and not always accurate. In addition, the tax assessor values the land as it is presently being used. For purposes of a replacement-cost appraisal, you should value the land at its highest and best use.

Try to envision the land as vacant and available for its highest and best use. For example, let's say the four-unit multifamily house was located in an area that had experienced commercial development. Would the land be more valuable with a multistory parking garage on it? Or would it be more valuable if you converted the house to professional office space for local doctors, lawyers, and other consultant-type businesses? You might poke around in the tax collector's office to get the land assessments for similar lots that have already been put to other uses. If there is still vacant land in the area, you can also ask your real estate agent about the going rate for lots (sometimes expressed as dollars per front foot).

Even if you have no intention of changing the use to which the land is put, try to value it at its highest and best use. That potential will definitely affect the value of the property when you finally sell it. Keep in mind, however, that the current use may well be the highest and best. If you are having trouble with this concept, engage the help of your real estate agent. You can even ask to talk with the broker or office manager or, in a large firm, with a commercial specialist.

2. Estimate the current cost of replacing the structure with a similar one. Professional appraisers have several meth-

ESTIMATING PROPERTY VALUE: REPLACEMENT-COST METHOD

Subject property: 40-year-old, four-unit multifamily house
These five steps are explained on pages 100–103.

Step 1: Value of the land	$ 60,000
Step 2: Current replacement cost	$ 200,000
Step 3: Estimated accrued depreciation	$ 133,320
Step 4: Replacement cost	$ 200,000
Depreciation	−133,320
Estimated value of the building	**$ 66,680**
Step 5: Value of land	$ 60,000
Value of building	+66,680
Estimated total property value	**$126,680**

ods available for estimating replacement or reproduction costs. If you hire one, he or she should explain to you the methods used and give you a breakdown of how the figures were arrived at. For your purposes of estimating value, the square-foot method will give you the working figures you'll need.

First you will need the cost per square foot of recently built comparable structures. (Your real estate agent can help you obtain these figures or you can survey some local builders.) Next you will need to know the number of square feet of living space in the current structure. This information is often included on the listing data sheet. If not, you can buy a 50-foot tape measure and actually measure the foundation. Then multiply the square feet in the foundation by the number of stories in the living area. Once you have the number of square feet in the subject property, multiply that figure by the current building cost per square foot to obtain the approximate cost of building a replacement structure.

3. Estimate the amount of accrued depreciation. For a ballpark figure, you can use the *straight-line method* of calculating depreciation (sometimes called the *economic-life method*). In this type of valuation, depreciation is assumed to occur at a steady rate over the building's entire economic life (the period during which the building is likely to remain useful for the purpose for which it was built). Remember that these figures are for the building only. Land is not considered depreciable. To calculate the annual depreciation, the building's cost is divided by the number of years of its expected life.

For example, let's say our four-unit multifamily house has a replacement cost of $200,000 and an economic life of 60 years. It will depreciate $3,333 per year. Because we know it's 40 years old, we can calculate the depreciated value of the building to be $66,680. (Rate of depreciation per year times age equals accrued depreciation, or $3,333 times 40 equals $133,320.)

4. Deduct the estimated accrued depreciation (Step 3) from the estimated replacement cost (Step 2) to get the estimated depreciated value of the building. In this example, $200,000 minus $133,320 equals $66,680.

5. Add the estimated land value (Step 1) to the depreciated value of the building to arrive at the estimated value of the property.

Physical deterioration refers to the effects of time and use. It may be curable or incurable. Curable problems

---

STOP AND THINK!

Do *not* base your negotiating or your profit projections solely on your estimate of depreciated value. The straight-line method of calculating depreciation is the least complex but also the least precise. For more reliable information, you will need to consider all age-related aspects of the property. Appraisers look at physical deterioration, functional obsolescence, and external obsolescence.

are those that, when repaired, will increase property value in an amount equal to or greater than the cost of the repairs. (Exterior painting is a good example.) Incurable problems are those for which repair costs will exceed the added value to the property. (Repair to a cracked and buckling foundation is a good example.)

Functional obsolescence refers to outmoded or unacceptable physical design features. It, too, can be curable or incurable. If the feature (old bathroom fixtures) can be remedied without cost that exceeds increased value, the obsolescence is curable. If the feature (adding central heating) would require a greater expenditure than the potential added property value, the obsolescence is considered incurable and reduces the market value of the property.

External or economic obsolescence refers to negative factors *not* intrinsic to the property and beyond the control of the owners. Generally, such factors concern changes in the character of the neighborhood or the local economy. For example, a property's value would be diminished by proximity to a new waste-treatment plant or by its location in a neighborhood that had become known for drug dealing. Unless the use for the land could be changed, the property value of an old-fashioned, soda-fountain/greasy-spoon restaurant now situated between a McDonald's and a Burger King would suffer from economic obsolescence. So would an office-supply store or any small-business building in a town that had been decimated by the exodus of a major corporation. External obsolescence is always incurable because the owner cannot remedy the problem.

If the economic useful life method of calculating depreciation brings the figure for your deal into the questionable range (you would make a profit only if everything comes out just as you have estimated), consider hiring an appraiser or real estate consultant or counselor before going further. These professionals will factor in the intangibles of function and use. (For more about real estate counselors, see page 113).

The Income-Analysis Method

The income-analysis method of appraisal relates the value of investment property to the income it is likely to produce. For purposes of the beginning investor (you're not ready to buy Mall of America yet), two techniques can be applied: the *gross rent multiplier* or the *capitalization rate*. Both depend upon gathering data for similar properties in the area. A comparison can be found in the box below.

GROSS RENT MULTIPLIER (GRM). This method is most often used for appraising single-family investment houses or two- to four-unit multifamily houses. An appropriate sales price for the subject property is calculated using its probable monthly rental income as a comparison factor against the monthly rental income and actual sales prices of comparable properties that have recently been sold in the area. It is a determinant of value as a factor of income.

Let's look at an example of how to get the GRM. First, take the recent selling price of a comparable property and determine the amount of monthly rent from that property. Let's just say that the recent selling price of a comparable property was $100,000 and the monthly rental income is $750. Then divide 100,000 by 750 and you will get a GRM of 133.3.

Repeat this calculation with three or four other comparable properties to get the typical gross rent multiplier for the local area. (Your real estate agent can help you get this information.) Once you have the average gross rent multiplier for the area, take the fair market monthly rent for the property you are considering and multiply it by the GRM. The answer you get will be the estimated market value. In the $100,000 example property, this multiplication comes out to $99,975. So our estimating method

---

ESTIMATING PROPERTY VALUE: INCOME-ANALYSIS METHOD

Gross Rent Multiplier

1. Monthly gross rent	$ 1,200
2. GRM for area	× 129.5
3. Estimated property value	$155,400

Capitalization Rate

1. Net operating income	$ 12,000
2. Capitalization rate for area	÷ .077
3. Estimated property value	$155,844

gives us a value that is off by 25 dollars but you get the idea, right?

CAPITALIZATION RATE. This is the method of estimating property value typically used for large investments, such as apartment complexes, shopping centers, and office buildings, but it can be applied by the small investor to mixed-use buildings and multi-family houses. In this method, the estimated market value of the property is calculated from the expected return (yield) that is typically being generated by investments in similar properties in the area. It presumes that you can get information on selling price and net operating income for comparable properties. Your real estate agent can help you obtain this data, but keep in mind that the figures provided on a listing are not guaranteed to be accurate.

> **LEARNING THE LANGUAGE**
>
> **NOI (net operating income)** is the annual effective gross income minus all operating expenses. Typical operating expenses include:
> - Management fees
> - Accounting and legal fees
> - Property taxes
> - Insurance
> - Maintenance
> - Utilities provided (heat, electricity, water, cable TV, etc.)
>
> Debt service (mortgage and interest payments) and depreciation are not included when calculating the NOI.

Let's go through the steps in applying the capitalization method to an investment property that you are considering:

1. **Calculate the potential annual gross income** (the total amount of income if all the units are rented and rent is paid at the prevailing rental rate for that size unit for all 12 months of the year). When considering an investment property, it's important to check that the current rents being charged in the subject property are in fact typical of area rental rates for the size of unit in question. Also include any other income from vending machines, laundry machines, and fees for special use of common areas, parking, garage, or storage-space rentals.

2. **Deduct for vacancies and nonpayment of rent** and come up with a figure that is the *effective gross income.* Your real estate agent can help you get vacancy rates in the area, and you can ask the seller for rental records for the past two or three years.

3. **Deduct the annual operating expenses** from the effective gross income to come up with **net operating income (NOI).**

4. **Determine the capitalization rate for the area** by gathering sales price and rental income for comparable buildings. (Your real estate agent can help you get this information.) To calculate a property's capitalization rate divide the NOI by the sales price of the building. For example: an NOI of $12,000 divided by a sales price of $155,000 equals a capitalization rate of .077. Compare several properties in the area to come up with the average capitalization rate for your type of property.

5. **To estimate the value of the property under consideration,** take its NOI and divide it by the capitalization rate for the area. In this case, the calculations come up with $155,844.15 so the estimate is $844.15 higher than the actual price. That's why we call this "estimated" value!

The Numbers Game

Look at the calculations in the boxes on pages 101 and 104. Using three different methods, the result is three different estimates of value. How do you know which is right? Well, there is no "right" answer. Remember we are trying to estimate value. In these three examples, two of the methods come out quite close in price. The other, based upon replacement costs, assigns a lower value to the property. What should you pay? Start your negotiations below the lowest value. You can use your appraisal work to help convince the seller.

When appraisers apply all three methods to a property evaluation, they routinely get three different answers. In the appraisal profession, the process of combining all the available information to come up with an appraised valuation is called reconciliation. Because an "average" figure just won't do, reconciliation is the art of the job. The appraiser must know which method is most appropriate for the type of property being evaluated and give more weight to that figure while also factoring in the information provided by the other methods.

The job of the appraiser is to arrive at current value. You, as an investor, want to know if this investment property will be profitable, so your job is more complex. You must consider all the data that an appraiser can provide, plus the effects of mortgaging (debt service), the potential for appreciation, and the appropriateness of the investment to your investment capital and your skills, lifestyle, and personality.

Always tap the skills and resources of your real estate agent when working on market evaluations. The agent has abundant data available that will allow you to use appraisal methods either to do your own valuations or to check against the valuations of the appraiser you hire. Remember always that an appraisal is an estimate of current fair market value. There are never any guarantees.

The Importance of Future Market Value

Unless you are buying a property primarily for its current positive cash flow and projected future cash flow and intend to hold it indefinitely, you should consider probable holding time and the potential for appreciation before you make your first offer. Current value is only one face of the moneymaking real estate coin. It determines how much money you must bring to the closing table. Future value is the other face of the coin and every bit as important. It determines how much money you will take away from the closing table when you sell.

But estimating the future worth of a piece of property is more easily said than done. For one thing, crystal balls don't work—and if they did, their owners would be unlikely to share the insights. So we can't know what's going to happen. We can only look at what is known and make judgments (and sometimes educated guesses) as to what we *think* will happen.

> **"Where profit is, loss hides nearby."**
>
> Japanese proverb

To complicate matters still more, many of the factors that affect real estate value are beyond the control of the property owner. That makes choosing the property that will appreciate an art. And like most art, it is dependent at least a little on luck. With that in mind, let's look at some of the most important factors in determining future value.

Location! Location! Location!

Where a property is located is certainly not the only thing that determines its value, but it's the only thing that absolutely cannot be changed. You can add buildings or subdivide ownership of the land, but the spot on the face of the earth is still the same. What can change and what will affect value are the economics and demographics surrounding the property.

We've already discussed highest and best use as a factor in determining current worth. It also helps to determine future appreciation because a "highest and best use" that is not now feasible—either physically, legally, or economically—may indeed become a possibility in the future.

As an example, let's consider an early 20th century Victorian house that currently has two large residential rental units. It's located in an area zoned for multifamily residential properties but on a street that is only one block away from the commercial center of the town. With current zoning, the property is at its highest and best use. But if the local economy is good and there is a demand for professional office space in the area, the zoning might be changed to allow for mixed use. Some of the multifamily buildings can then be converted to professional office space, childcare facilities, or small shops.

The property will generate more rental income and therefore become more valuable if it is converted to professional offices or a combination of shops and offices. The zoning change eliminates the legal barrier to the change of use. The cost of conversion becomes economically feasible because the rent from the professional office units will support the cost of renovations and still yield a positive cash flow. Thus, the property can appreciate significantly if the use of the land is changed.

Both the character and the value of neighboring properties also significantly affect the worth of real estate. The appraisal principle of conformity states that value is created when a property is in harmony with its surroundings. The white elephant (a single-family house on a street of older multifamily houses, for example, or a residential property in a commercial area) loses value because it is unlike the real estate that surrounds it. Significant appreciation is unlikely unless the character of the neighborhood changes or the land becomes so valuable for another use that it becomes financially feasible to tear down the building and replace it with a building of another kind.

Even in areas where the type of property is homogeneous, the worth of surrounding properties affects each individual property. Appraisers call this principle progression and regression. Stated simply in terms of a single-family house, the value of the smallest and plainest house in a neighborhood rises to approach the value of the larger, finer houses (progression). The value of a very large and fine house in a neighborhood of small and modest houses falls toward the top of the price range of the smaller houses (regression). In a neighborhood of larger and more luxurious houses, therefore, a small fixer-upper is likely to have a greater potential for appreciation than a large fixer-upper or a house with an addition in a neighborhood of smaller and simpler houses.

Beyond what already exists, value can be increased or decreased by future events. This is called the principle of anticipation. News that a major corporation will establish its national headquarters in a nearby town can dramatically increase residential real estate values. News that, sometime in the next ten years, a new interstate will bisect a well-established neighborhood can not only diminish the value of all the houses but can also make some properties extremely difficult to sell. For maximum appreciation on your investment property, you must do your homework in the zoning

> ## "Nothing succeeds like address."
>
> Fran Lebowitz, American journalist

> ### STOP AND THINK!
>
> Don't act on the assumption that a town's master plan or its zoning laws are carved in stone. They can be rewritten to accommodate changing community needs or changes in the local economy.

office (find out what's currently planned) and you must know local news and rumors (learn what's happening) before you buy anything.

What Makes a Property More Valuable?

A property appreciates when demand for that type of structure in a particular or similar location exceeds supply. For the real estate investor, correctly anticipating an increase in demand can mean significant profit. Let's take condominium investment for an example. In the late 1980s in most areas of the nation, condominiums were overbuilt (supply exceeded demand) and prices plummeted. That made them a poor investment, right?

Not exactly. In some areas, smart investors realized that there was or soon would be a shortage of rental housing. Condo apartments might not be selling well to homebuyers, but they were in demand by renters. The ability to purchase the units at low prices enabled investors to rent them with positive cash flow. Rents even went up in those areas where multifamily housing units were not being built fast enough to meet the growing demand. As aging baby boomers began to sell off their big nests and seek less maintenance-intensive housing, some of these condo communities began to increase in their appeal. These empty nesters and the growing number of single-parent families and single-person households increased demand on condominium units. Many condo communities began to appreciate again. Investors who anticipated the need for shared-space housing made money.

A property also increases in value when it provides amenities that have appeal. Choosing the right "extras" in a rehab or fixer-upper (central air-conditioning or new kitchen appliances, for example) can boost appreciation beyond the cost of the improvements if the location and the demand for that type of real estate will support the added cost. Increased amenities, however, cannot overcome poor location or inadequate demand.

Buying for maximum appreciation can sometimes be a matter of watching fad and fashion. What areas of a community are considered the "in" neighborhoods in which to live? Be aware that this desirable status can change with something as small as a change in the school district lines. The rehab of many neighborhood properties by independent investors or home-

> ### LEARNING THE LANGUAGE
>
> **Shared-space housing** is a late 20th century term for both condominium communities and co-operative apartment buildings. Private living space is not shared; each unit is being held independently. The "shared space" refers to common elements used by all of the owners or residents. It can include areas such as hallways, elevators, recreation facilities, and parking.

owners (sometimes called gentrification) can change what was a depreciating area into one of the fastest appreciating areas in town (both for sales and rentals).

Will Success Spoil Everything?

Sometimes success boosts appreciation. Healthy positive cash flow in a well-maintained and well-managed property usually makes the property more desirable to other investors and therefore worth more. But sometimes, success stimulates competition that, in the end, can actually bring value down.

Let's go back to the Victorian house to be converted to professional office units. The higher positive cash flow represents such a good return on the money invested that other investors follow suit and begin to buy up the two- and three-unit houses on the street. One conversion follows another and soon there is more professional office space available than there are professionals in need of space. Units stand empty, rents do not keep pace with inflation and increasing expenses, and property values begin to fall.

Real estate investors are drawn to the smell of money. Success with a particular type of investment can cause

> ## LEARNING THE LANGUAGE
>
> The **law of increasing and diminishing returns** holds that improvements will increase property value only to the maximum for that location and land use. Adding a second garage to the only house in the neighborhood that doesn't have one will increase its worth both in renting and selling. Adding a swimming pool to a small apartment complex already rented to capacity at the maximum going rate for the area will increase neither the rents nor the selling price. If money spent on improvements increases the income or the value of the property, it is an example of increasing returns. When money spent on improvements does not increase income or value, it is an example of diminishing returns.

overinvestment or overbuilding (remember the condo craze), which can result in the up-and-down swings of a particular marketplace. When considering the potential appreciation of a property, consider whether the property is at the beginning of a trend, in the midst of it, or near the peak. The midst is least risky; the beginning has the most potential for profit but is also the least certain; the peak may look like a sure thing but later turn out to be a loss.

Chance and Change

Just like life, there's an awful lot in the real estate marketplace that is totally beyond the control of mere humans. Both land and buildings are subject to the effects of natural phenomena, such as earthquakes, floods, hurricanes, tornadoes, mud slides, lightning strikes, and forest fires. When a disaster strikes a property that you own, it's important to keep your head in control of your emotions. Check insurance coverage, evaluate repair or rebuilding costs, and try to anticipate value when recovery is complete. Sometimes appreciation is significant when every building in the area has the shiny new face that results from necessary cleanup and rebuilding.

On the other hand, the time immediately after a natural disaster is often a bargain-hunting investor's paradise. After a hurricane, for example, many owners are willing to sell their vacation properties rather than face rebuilding. An offer that would have been flatly refused before the storm now looks appealing to the property owner. If you buy and do the necessary fix-up and then the property appreciates rapidly, people will say you are lucky. Sometimes luck is being ready for the effects of chance.

Change is even more certain than chance in the marketplace. Over time, communities, neighborhoods, and buildings respond to wear and tear and to shifts in demographics and the economy. Such changes can either boost appreciation or bring on depreciation. Anticipating the direction of change often requires something of a sixth sense. Remember, however, that accuracy is tremendously enhanced by knowledge of the local area (its geography, demographics, economy, and, not least of all, its spirit).

The flexible and creative investor can sometimes profit from a change in the neighborhood by responding appropriately to the developing needs of the community. A city mansion built in 1920, for example, can be converted to studio and one-bedroom condo-

> ## "Chance governs all."
>
> John Milton (1608–1674), British poet

> ## "Change is constant."
>
> Benjamin Disraeli (1804–1881), British prime minister and author

---

DIGGING DEEPER

Established as a separate trade organization in 1953, real estate counselors today are affiliated with the National Association of Realtors as the **Counselors of Real Estate (CRE).** The CRE is a by-invitation-only membership organization for leading real-property advisors who hold senior positions in their organizations and meet other criteria. The organization offers a program of strategic consultation and alternative dispute resolution. The organization's Web site features an online search function for Counselors of Real Estate in local areas as well as market news and abstracts of articles in the CRE's quarterly publication. Issues of the publication can be ordered online.

Counselors of Real Estate
430 North Michigan Avenue
Chicago, IL 60611
312-329-8427
http://www.cre.org

miniums or rental apartments. This change of use would answer the need for urban housing by singles. A small residential apartment building might be changed into a mixed-use building to accommodate a much-appreciated convenience store in the neighborhood. An abandoned school building might be an excellent project for redesign and rehabilitation into housing for the elderly. And of course, the most classic example of real estate change: A farm might be turned into a development of single-family homes as the circle of the acceptable-commute-to-work spreads farther and farther beyond the city or surrounds the building of a new industrial or research "park."

Better Than a Crystal Ball

Anticipating the future is never easy and never foolproof. But you can learn much by becoming familiar with the past. To get a better idea of where a town or neighborhood is going, find out where it's been. Most local libraries have records of local history. Look back at old newspapers and photographs. Go to the zoning board office and do some detective work. What was the zoning 10, 20, or 30 years ago? The changes that have occurred can give you an indication of where things seem to be heading and why.

It's also very helpful to become aware of current local politics. It's a fact of life that not all local government is free from corruption. Money and gifts sometimes change hands under the table. Do certain builders and developers in the town get preferential treatment over investors or homeowners when they ask for a variance or subdivision approval? Does the buildings inspector look more closely at some construction work than at others? Long before you are ready to make an investment purchase, start attending zoning and planning board meetings. You will gather valuable information about your town that may well help you identify prime investment areas.

For all your investment purchases, tap the knowledge and resources of your Realtor and the firm with which he or she works. If you want a professional opinion of current market value beyond what you and your Realtor can estimate, hire a professional appraiser. If you still want more information regarding the possibilities of appreciation or the effects of change in the use of the land, hire a specialist real estate consultant or counselor.

Many large investors, developers, and corporations hire real estate consultants to do market analysis, feasibility studies, highest-and-best-use studies, and even lease negotiations. Like appraisers, these real estate professionals do not sell real estate. They are paid a fee (either an hourly rate or a flat fee) for their time and effort. Although they generally work with large projects, they can also serve the small investor just as an architect who usually specializes in large public buildings can serve an individual or couple by designing a home.

KEEP IN MIND

- **You invest in real estate** to make money, and each investment should be evaluated as to its moneymaking potential before you buy.
- **Market data on the sale of comparable properties** can help you estimate fair market value for a prospective purchase.
- **Three additional methods of estimating the worth of property are:** replacement cost, the gross rent multiplier, and capitalization rate of return.
- **Appreciation depends** upon many factors, some of which are beyond the owner's control.
- **The single most important advantage** an independent investor can have is an insider's knowledge of the local area (geographic, demographic, and economic).

How to Improve Your Negotiating

"Negotiation is a basic means of getting what you want from others."

Roger Fisher and William Ury, *Getting to Yes*

Once you've spotted a possible good deal, you'll want to transform it from possibility to reality by persuading the owner to sell—sell, that is, at a price and terms that are acceptable to you. Now, it would be nice if the owner would see the deal from exactly your perspective. But that almost never happens, so you must negotiate an agreement that is recorded in a written contract and executed by all parties involved in the transaction.

In most cases, you'll be using a printed contract form with the blanks filled in to present your offers and to respond to the seller's counteroffers. It's important therefore that you understand the elements of a real estate contract (covered in the next chapter) before you begin your negotiations and that you are prepared to get help on contract review from an attorney. (Choose one with a large proportion of his or her practice in real estate.)

But the art of negotiating goes far beyond filling in the blanks on a printed contract form. In the real estate marketplace, as in almost every other aspect of human life, it's the art of getting as much as possible while giving up as little as possible. Toddlers negotiate their bedtimes. Teens negotiate for freedom. Husbands and wives . . . Well, you can finish that sentence.

Some individuals seem to have a real talent for negotiating, and it's quite natural that the rest of us occasionally feel a twinge of inadequacy when we watch them at work. But not feeling especially talented in the field shouldn't relegate you to accepting whatever someone else offers. Negotiating skills can be learned, especially real estate negotiating skills. You've probably already had a few training runs in homebuying and selling. Keep those experiences in mind as you focus on the concepts and procedures in this chapter. Then increase your self-confidence (and your chances of coming out ahead) by paying special attention to the tips and strategies that have been added at important points.

What Can Be Negotiated?

There's a lot more to negotiating an investment real estate deal than asking the question: What's the price I have to pay? In fact, sometimes how the money is to be paid (to whom and when) is almost as important as the purchase price. Financing is almost always a factor. Sometimes occupancy and closing date can make or break a deal. Adding the right contingencies can protect your position as a buyer and sometimes even make the actual selling price lower than the price on the contract. So let's begin this chapter with a list of the most commonly negotiated factors in an investment-property purchase.

The Price

Let's get a bit arty with this all-money factor. If negotiating could be depicted as a seascape, price would have to be the lighthouse. It's what your eye is drawn to, what you look at first even though the painter has rendered storm clouds in the sky and waves crashing on the rocks. Without good focus on the lighthouse, there will be no painting—or at least not a painting you are likely to buy.

Be aware, however, that the price printed in the purchase contract does not represent all of your expenditures. By negotiating away other costs, such as repairs or improvements, title insurance, mortgage points, closing costs, and transfer taxes, you can significantly reduce the amount you must pay to take possession and begin to use the property.

Closing Date

How soon title will pass from seller to buyer is often a factor that can change the price a seller is willing to accept or a buyer is willing to pay. A seller who is anxious to close will often agree to a lower price in return for a quick closing because negative cash flow is painful or because he or she needs to liquidate the property to use the cash elsewhere. On the other hand, a buyer who must liquidate other assets to raise cash for the purchase (by selling another piece of property, for example) might be willing to pay a slightly higher price in return for a delayed closing.

Occupancy

When you buy a home, you can usually move in right after the closing. That's not always the case in the investment marketplace. Because leases can survive a change in ownership, the right to occupy may not coincide with the passing of title. If you wish to occupy a unit in a multifamily house or a small apartment building, you can negotiate for the vacancy and the seller can negotiate with the tenant for a settlement on the remaining time on the lease (often a cash payment).

Sometimes, however, holdover leases are a plus. In a slow rental market, a seller might hold out for a higher price when all units are rented, especially if current rents are at or near the going market price.

Fixtures and Chattel

What stays with the property and what doesn't is almost always a factor in negotiations. In vacation property and some rental property, for example, furnishings might be included. In commercial or mixed-use property, refrigeration equipment, shelving, window treatments, or even carpeting may become a point of negotiation.

LEARNING THE LANGUAGE

Fixtures are items of property that are attached to the real estate (for example, installed wall-unit air conditioners; chandeliers; shades and blinds; installed wall-to-wall carpeting; sinks, tubs, and showers; and installed appliances such as water heaters, dishwashers, stoves, and wall ovens). Unless specific exception is made in the purchase contract, fixtures usually pass to the new owner.

Chattel is personal property not attached to the real estate (for example, furniture; curtains, draperies, and decorative window treatments; appliances, such as a washing machine, dryer, or refrigerator; yard-maintenance equipment; and in commercial buildings, display shelving and refrigerated cases). Unless specifically included in the purchase contract, chattel does not pass to the new owner.

Asking for these "extras" is usually best done as negotiations draw to a close and the seller becomes more firm on price. The negotiating strength for the buyer is that, psychologically and financially, the seller usually prefers to give up some "things" rather than to give way on money. Getting those "things" can save the buyer significant out-of-pocket expenditures.

Property Transfer Costs, Residuals, and Closing Costs

Local custom usually determines who pays transfer taxes, but in fact, the item is negotiable. The payment for a title search and title insurance is also negotiable. Unpaid back rents, back taxes, the oil or propane remaining in a tank, the balance on water, sewer, and sidewalk assessments or other special assessments, the real estate commission, and even the fees charged by closing agents can all be a part of contract negotiations. With careful attention to these details, a buyer can lower his out-of-pocket expenditures even when the seller is standing firm on selling price.

Financing

Seller financing occurs more commonly in investment real estate than in homebuying. When a seller is willing to hold a mortgage, the amount of the down payment, the interest rate, the type of mortgage, and the term for repayment can all influence the deal. Even when a first mortgage loan is to be obtained from a conventional lender, many sellers can be persuaded to carry a second mortgage or a short-term note in return for the buyer's agreement to pay a slightly higher price. Sometimes who pays mortgage points and other up-front charges for obtaining financing can also be negotiated.

Contingencies

Mortgage and property inspection contingencies are commonly included in real estate contracts. (There's more about the phrasing of these clauses in Chapter 8.) Other common contingencies, however, are specific to the type of property being purchased. The purchase of raw land, for example, is often contingent upon acceptable results from soil and environmental tests for contamination, hazardous materials, percolation (see box on page 152), and drainage. If the results are unacceptable for the intended land use, the property becomes virtually worthless, at least to that particular buyer.

For an investor who has plans for a residential development on a parcel of land, the purchase contract is often contingent upon subdivision approval by the local planning board. This contingency is a negotiating point on price because approval will positively affect the value of the property. (Who pays for the work involved in doing

---

LEARNING THE LANGUAGE

The term **mortgage points** refers to fees that lenders charge borrowers in advance of obtaining their loans. One point is 1 percent of the amount to be borrowed (the **face value** of the mortgage). For example, two points on a $100,000 loan is $2,000. In this example, because you must pay $2,000 to obtain the $100,000 loan, you are actually getting $98,000. However, you will repay $100,000. In the financial arena, this is called **discounting.**

A **contingency** in a real estate contract is a clause that creates a condition or conditions that must be satisfied before the contract is binding. For example, a mortgage contingency means the buyer must be able to get financing or the contract will become void and deposit monies returned.

tests and getting approval is also negotiable.) Such contingencies can cause long delays before closing is possible.

Sometimes a purchase is contingent upon certain repairs or improvements being completed. The buyer may actually offer to pay a higher price if the improvements are to be completed by the seller. With such a contingency for improvements, the buyer effectively mortgages the cost of the improvements over the entire term of the loan and increases the base price of the property for tax purposes. (There's more about base price in Chapter 9.) Out-of-pocket expenditures upon purchase are thereby decreased and the federal income tax due when the property is eventually sold may be lower.

To use improvement contingencies as a negotiating tool for a lower purchase price, a buyer might make a low first offer that includes the contingency that certain improvements be made. The seller, when making a counteroffer that is lower than the original asking price, usually refuses the contingency for improvements to be made before closing, pointing out that the improvements will increase property value. The buyer, with a return bid that is still below market value and also below the figure mentioned in the seller's counteroffer, can agree to delete the contingency for improvements if the new lower price bid is acceptable to the seller.

This could go on for a while. The seller says, "No, your price is too low, but at $XXX,XXX I'll throw in this improvement." The buyer says, "OK, I'll take that improvement but I'm only willing to increase my price to $XXX,XXX." And so it continues, each party giving and taking a bit at a time. In a good deal, both parties usually feel a bit squeezed.

Another buyer tactic is to begin with a lowball offer without mentioning improvements. In subsequent negotiating rounds, add the improvement contingencies. This can be done by making a significant increase in your offer while throwing in all the improvements you want in that one round of bidding. Or you can make a more modest increase in your offering price and throw in some of the improvements you want, waiting for yet another round to add more.

The rolling of repairs and improvements into the purchase price is a particularly effective negotiating tool if the seller has well-established connections with independent building contractors who will do the repairs at a lower price than they might quote to a new owner. Be certain to stipulate in the contract, however, that all repair work and improvements must meet with the satisfaction of the buyer. You do want quality work!

That's All Folks!

No, it's not! Don't let anyone convince you that you've reached the end of the list of negotiable items. It's true that there are certain "customary and usual" practices in real estate, but in fact everything and anything is negotiable. As you become more experienced in the investment marketplace, you'll learn more and more ways to make a good deal.

Your All-Important Warm-up Steps

The key steps in a successful real estate negotiation usually occur *before* the first offer is made, and they depend heavily on thinking rather than on talking. Knowledge is power throughout the real estate marketplace, but when negotiating, knowledge must be combined with careful timing. Before a word is spoken or a stroke of the pen made, a power stash of negotiating chips must be collected for use at the right time.

For both the seasoned professional and the neophyte, the strength-building exercises for good negotiating are the same: investigate, evaluate, and prioritize. Do them!

Investigate: Find Out More Than They Want You to Know

The market history of a piece of property can affect the price you will have to pay for it. Some of the relevant

> **"Think before thou speakest."**
>
> Miguel de Cervantes (1547–1616), *Don Quixote de la Mancha*

". . . chance favors the prepared mind."

Louis Pasteur (1822–1895), French chemist

data is in full view on the real estate listing sheet. More power-giving information is usually available from your Realtor's computer files or from his or her working knowledge of the local marketplace. And finally, the local municipal records office might just provide you with some big negotiating chips. Seek out the answers to these questions:

- **How long has the property been on the market with the current listing?** This is easy information to come by. Most listings are dated. The longer the on-the-market time, the more likely price can be negotiated downward.

- **Has the property been listed with other brokers prior to this listing?** Your Realtor will either go into computer records for this information or contact the local Board of Realtors. Now you are checking the accuracy of time-on-the-market information because listings with previous brokers do not show up on the current listing sheet. If you find that several other brokers have attempted to sell this property unsuccessfully, ask yourself: *Why?*

- **Have there been any price reductions?** This information is easy to get for current listings. But dig deeper. You want to know what the asking price was on each of the previous listings, if there have been any.

STOP AND THINK!

If your snooping brings out the information that the listing is about to expire, don't assume that you can approach the owner and make a price-reduction deal by cutting out payment of the real estate broker's commission. Most listing agreements contain a clause that extends commission payment responsibility for several months to a year beyond the listing expiration date when a buyer who has been shown the property returns later to buy it. If you try this sneaky tactic, you can end up losing a lawsuit that will cost both you and the seller many thousands of dollars more than you thought you were saving.

- **Have there been any other changes to the listing information?** Price reductions are not the only indications of an anxious seller. Improvements might have been made to the property, seller help with financing may be offered, or a bonus may be offered to the selling agent.
- **Have there been any offers?** Your agent may not be able to tell you what those offers were, but he or she can tell you how many. (Sometimes, "The offer was about $XXX,XXX," does slip out.) A property with several refused offers indicates a tough seller, but don't despair. Time wears away even granite. Sometimes an offering price that was refused six months ago will look better on your offering date because of the simple passage of time or maybe the change of season. Being the first offer on a property that has been on the market for six months or more with no offers usually gives the buyer a strong negotiating position. Being the first offer on a property that is relatively new to the marketplace puts the buyer in the weakest negotiating position.
- **Why is the seller selling?** Accurate information about seller motivation is rarely recorded on the listing sheet, but most agents can make a soft probe. Remember, however, that the answer you get may not be the whole truth. Sellers do not want to reveal a weak position. You can augment your snooping by checking at the local courthouse or records office to determine if there are foreclosure proceedings in process or if any liens have been placed against the property.
- **How long has the seller owned the property?** You can get information on the seller's date of purchase from municipal real estate records (open to the public). A particularly short holding time may indicate a seller in trouble (perhaps unable to meet the carrying costs). Or a short holding time may indicate that the seller got a real bargain and is looking for a quick and profitable turnaround. Or there may be some serious problem with the property. A longer holding time (ten years or more) usually means that

the seller has built up considerable equity. There may be a chance here for some seller financing.

■ **How much did the seller originally pay for the property?** Purchase price is recorded in transfer-tax records. It may take a little digging, but getting this figure could be the proverbial ace-up-the-sleeve in your negotiating game. Just as in poker, don't let anyone know what you know until you are ready to play the card.

■ **What's happening in the neighborhood?** If you haven't already done it, stop by the planning board office to check for zoning changes or variances, proposed roads, or newly approved construction in the area. You also should have been following the local news concerning the area for several months before buying property there. If you haven't, spend an afternoon getting caught up with newspapers in the local library or on the Internet.

Evaluate: Define the Parameters of the Negotiating Field

When negotiating to buy a piece of real estate, just about the worst thing you can do is pick an offering price out of the blue and see where it takes you. But that's exactly what a lot of beginners do and it often leads to paying too much or to failed negotiations because the seller is insulted and takes on an antagonistic

---

LEARNING THE LANGUAGE

Buyer's market refers to a market condition where there are more properties for sale than there are interested buyers. It's often referred to as a slow market. The buyer usually has more negotiating power.

Seller's market refers to a market condition where there are more interested buyers than there are properties for sale. It's often referred to as a fast or hot market. The seller usually has more negotiating power, and time is often a factor in the deal.

---

attitude toward the buyer. It's extremely important to set out negotiating limits and to make a plan for working within those limits. Ask yourself the following questions:

- **What's the probable fair market value of the property?** We talked about estimating this figure in Chapter 6. If you are working with a buyer's agent, he or she also may be able to help you by using computer programs available in the broker's office.

- **What's the pace of the marketplace?** Your agent can help you answer this question with data regarding average time on the market for the type of property you are considering. In a fast market, you may want to respond quickly at each step of the negotiating process. In a slow market, you can use time as a negotiating tool by "considering" each step and increasing seller anxiety through forced waiting.

- **What's my "steal it" deal?** Write down exactly what you ideally, but realistically, would like to pay for the property and the best terms you can imagine. But this won't be your first offer. Your first offer should be lower than your steal-it figure.

- **What's my top dollar?** Review the property evaluation numbers discussed in Chapter 6. What's the top price you can pay and still maintain positive cash flow? What's the top price you can pay and still meet your profit plans? (Negative cash flow doesn't always mean an unprofitable investment.) Write down your top dollar and what you want included at that price on the same sheet of paper as your steal-it deal.

By doing the evaluation stage of your preparation exercises, you set end limits (highest and lowest prices) to your negotiating. Your fair market value analysis will give you a point of reference and keep you from making a gross financial error.

Your awareness of market pace will help you evaluate what the

---

STOP AND THINK!

Never reveal your "steal it" or "top dollar" information to anyone concerned in the deal. That includes your agent and your lawyer. Successful negotiation depends upon the other party knowing only what you want them to know.

play on the field will be like before your negotiating game begins. How fast will movement be? Are slips and slides likely? Can you make an end run?

Prioritize: Decide What You Want *Most* and *Least*

It's said among real estate professionals that a good deal has been made when the buyer and seller are both smiling about their financial success or frowning about their financial pain at the closing table. Even in the all-pain situation, each party has gotten something they wanted and given up something that was expendable. The somewhat uncomfortable deal (for all involved parties) is the one where one party is smiling and one is frowning. Because of circumstances, insider knowledge, or experience in the marketplace, someone has won big and someone has lost badly.

All three situations commonly occur in the investment real estate marketplace and if you stay in it long enough, you'll probably experience them all. As a beginner, however, you especially want a good deal that feels good too. (If your first deal was a smile/frown deal and you discovered yourself to be a big loser, you probably would never invest in real estate again.)

In every good deal, you get something and you give up something. The goal is to get what's really important to you and to give up the "would be nice" items on your list. That implies, however, that you've made a list and prioritized it. Many people think: "I don't need to fuss with lists on paper. I have it all in my head." Wrong! Tension builds and many emotions come into play during the negotiating process. Making lists of your key objectives and tactics and the other paperwork you do to investigate and evaluate a property before you make the first offer will help to keep rational evaluation in the driver's seat of the deal. In other words, it will keep your head in control over pride, anger, intimidation, greed, retaliation, and the temptation to be caught up and carried along on a wave of buying enthusiasm.

PRIORITIZE YOUR NEGOTIATING CHIPS

Price	Rock bottom	Market value	Steal it!
	Essential	Important	Expendable
Closing date			
Fixtures			
Personal property			
Transfer taxes			
Residuals			
Closing costs			
Financing			
Contingencies			
Other			

So what should you prioritize? Everything. Look again at the section above titled "What Can Be Negotiated?" and use it as a starting point for making lists of what you want to achieve. (There's a sample worksheet on this page.) Depending on your individual negotiating style, the character of the deal, and the pace of the marketplace, you might start your bid for the property with a low offer that includes not only essentials, but also many expendables. As the negotiating proceeds and you make higher bids, you can give up items from the *Expendable* column while standing firm on those items from the *Essential* column and perhaps even adding items from the *Important* column.

Or you may start out with a simple offer that includes only your essential negotiables. Then as you increase your offer in response to each counteroffer, you can add from your *Important* column. As already mentioned, there is usually less objection from the seller to an additional negotiable item when the request has been accompanied by an offer of more money or a concession on closing date or financing.

The Process of Negotiating

No matter how much "help" you get or are offered from family, friends, your real estate agent, or your attorney, you (meaning everyone involved as a buyer if you are investing with partners) are essentially alone through the negotiating process. Advice may be plentiful, but no one knows your personal goals, skills, and financial situation as well as you do and no one will be as concerned with watching out for your best interests as you are.

That is not to say that you shouldn't listen to advice. You should. But assimilate it and then weigh it against your knowledge of yourself and your investment situation and goals. That said, let's go through the steps in a negotiation.

Determining the First Offer

The buyer is the initiator in almost every real estate negotiation. That means you will be asked to set the lowest limit on the selling price. The seller has already set the highest limit.

But where do you start? How do you determine if an offer will open the door to negotiations or cause the door to be slammed hard, if not permanently, in your face?

You can't know for sure. In fact, as you become an experienced negotiator, you'll almost certainly get a metaphorical door or two slammed in your face. It's part of the business.

Your objective with your first offer is to get the seller's attention and prompt him, her, or them to start thinking about what they have to sell, how much they will get for it, and when the transfer of title will take place. The offer should be less than you are willing to pay.

Your knowledge concerning the probable fair market value of the property, the pace of the marketplace, the length of time the property has been for sale, the seller's motivation for selling, and the seller's holding time and original purchase price will contribute to your choice of a first-offer figure. In a slow, buyer's market, with a property long on the market and somewhat overpriced, and a pressured seller, you can come in with a very low offer. (There have been successful negotiations that started at 50 percent or less of an asking price.) In a fast, seller's market, with a newly listed and fairly priced property, you may have to make your first offer close to the asking price in order to safeguard against getting shut out of further negotiations and allowing someone else's offer to seem more appealing. (In very hot markets, some investors start at 95 percent of the asking price, others offer the full asking price just to be sure they get the property.)

In red-hot markets (the suburbs of Washington, D.C. in 2005, for example) some brokers list properties at approximately fair market value and then take sealed bids that they fully expect to be higher than the asking price. All the bids are opened on a given date at a given time. This is a situation to be avoided. The buyer is giving up all negotiating power. The highest bid and the best terms will be chosen and the seller does the choosing. If you ever do get into this kind of bidding war and you happen to "win," be aware that there will (or should) be no further negotiation after the bid is accepted. So make sure you have everything you want written into the contract.

No matter what the tempo of the market is, however, you should always calculate your first offer based on your estimate of fair market value, not upon the asking price. Your challenge will be to get the seller to understand and accept your view of probable market value (that is, the price you want to pay).

STOP AND THINK!

Don't assume that a first offer should be a certain percentage (let's say 20 percent) below the asking price. The asking price is not an accurate gauge of market value. It is set by the seller with no restrictions from local government or trade groups.

Presenting the First Offer

Your first offer should always be in writing. This is easy if you are working with a real estate agent because they always seem to have a written offer form handy. Most of these "standard contracts" are written by lawyers with careful attention to the customary and usual real-property transfer procedures of the local area. It's important to remember, however, that there is really no such thing as a "standard contract." Every real estate purchase contract is an agreement between two parties over a unique piece of property. Every contract, therefore, is (and should be) unique. (You'll be able to test your particular contract against the guidelines set in the next chapter.)

Be wary also of using a *binder* or short-form contract, which is usually considered an agreement to go to contract. Under some circumstances, a binder might qualify as a binding contract and you will find yourself committed to a deal on which you thought you were only negotiating.

To protect yourself when making a written offer of any kind, be absolutely certain that you include an attorney-review clause above your signature. If you use this safeguard, you'll sleep well on the night when contracts are executed by both parties because you'll know that you still have several days to change your mind without penalty.

Negotiating without a real estate agent is more difficult. If you decide to do it face-to-face, take a written offer with you that covers all of the essential contract

---

STOP AND THINK!

Already mentioned in Chapter 5, an explanation of an attorney-review clause bears repeating. Attorney review is the ultimate escape contingency. To assure your ability to change your mind after a contract has been executed, be certain these words appear above your signature:

This agreement is subject to review and approval as to form and content by an attorney of the buyer's choice. The attorney may rescind the contract for any reason before midnight, [date].

Three to five working days is a common review period. Attorneys for both parties may agree to extend this period if there are problems that need resolution.

points (see Chapter 8). You can scratch out and write in changes as the negotiating proceeds, but be certain that you include an attorney-review clause above everyone's signature.

If both buyer and seller have e-mail and a real estate agent is not involved in the sale, your negotiating can be done electronically. This method offers the advantage of separation. No one will respond negatively to facial expressions or body language and the written-message medium will allow each involved party a "cooling off" time to think before responding. Be certain, however, that both parties accept the attorney-review clause.

The disadvantages of electronic negotiation include the possibility that buyers or sellers will miss a facial expression or some body language that may have indicated the other party's flexibility. Buyers or sellers may miss out on opportunities that a hunch or intuitive perception may have prompted. And, of course, there's always the possibility that one of the correspondents will hit the *send* button reflexively in anger, thus sending written words that probably should have been reconsidered.

When negotiating directly with sellers, try to avoid using the telephone. A slammed-down receiver can end negotiating almost before it begins. To start up again, you will have to deal with a lot of touchy-feely stuff like pride, stubbornness, and asking pardon, all of which can add a sour taste to every step.

When you make an offer through a real estate agent, you will be asked to accompany your signed written offer with an earnest-money check. The amount of this check is usually suggested to be $1,000 or more. Actually, there is no specified amount required; any-

---

LEARNING THE LANGUAGE

Earnest money (sometimes called **hand money** or **good faith money**) is the deposit given by the buyer upon signing an offer to purchase. It is usually held in escrow until closing. The amount of earnest money is usually a token $500 or $1000, but it can be any amount.

Escrow monies (sometimes called **deposit held in escrow**) is additional good faith money held by a neutral party until all contract contingencies are met, and often until closing. Many real estate agents urge buyers to put 10 percent of the purchase price into escrow. (This amount guarantees that there will be enough money to pay the commission if the buyer backs out.) The amount of the escrow deposit, however, can and should be determined by mutual agreement between the buyer and seller.

thing that seems appropriate will do. Once an agreement is reached and the purchase contract is signed by all parties, a larger deposit of "good faith" money is usually required. It is usually held in escrow until the closing. (This is the seller's assurance that the buyer is serious and will not walk away from the contract or hold the property off the market while looking for a better deal.) Most real estate agents will tell you that 10 percent of the purchase price is required as an escrow deposit. In fact, the amount to be held in escrow is negotiable. Any figure that is acceptable to both buyer and seller can be written into the contract.

The Counteroffer

Once the initial offer is presented, the seller can respond by

■ **accepting the offer as written,**

■ **rejecting the offer and refusing to negotiate, or**

■ **making a counteroffer.**

If your first offer is accepted as written, check your estimates of market value again. You may be paying too much. (This is why an attorney review clause is a strong tool. It can get you out of a deal without questions or challenges.) On the other hand, you may have hit the seller at a perfect moment (for you) and be very lucky indeed.

If you are still worried that you are paying too much, you also will be able to use your inspection contingencies to renegotiate price if the professional property inspection turns up structural defects or working systems in need of repair or replacement. (You'll find the wording for a buyer-protective inspection contingency in Chapter 8.)

If the offer is rejected with a refusal to negotiate, don't despair. The seller is merely telling you that the first offering price is too low. Often sellers do not want to open negotiations to a first offer that they consider too far below their expected selling price. (They think the possibility of "meeting in the middle somewhere" is too skewed to the buyer's side.)

To continue negotiations after a flat *"no"* from the seller, recheck your market-value estimates and your expected purchase price, then make a higher "first offer." It's a rare seller who won't respond at that point.

If the seller responds to your offer by making a counteroffer with a lower asking price, your negotiations have begun in earnest. Along with the lower asking price might be a new suggested closing date, a holding back of some fixtures, or an objection to some of the contingencies in the contract. You have now entered the give-and-take stage of negotiations.

Give Something/Get Something

After the initial offer and counteroffer, negotiations may settle down quite quickly and fully executed contracts can be had in just a few days. Or negotiating can go on for days, weeks, sometimes even months. It is important to remember, therefore, that you should never reveal all of your cards in any given round. Hold something back for later rounds. (You can always make another request or give up something to get something during the attorney-review period.)

Bear in mind that all negotiating is a trading process that goes: *You give me this and I'll give you that.* You should now use your prioritized list to give you an easy overview of your trading chips. As each round progresses, make notes on what seems important to the seller. Something on your *Expendable* list may be on the

---

DIGGING DEEPER

One way to increase your negotiating power is to convince the seller that you've done your homework. Gather written documentation to support your position. This might include a comparative market analysis, zoning information, calculations on rate of return, projections for economic growth or recession in the area, a list of repairs needed, information regarding similar properties to be built or renovated in the neighborhood, etc.

Do not present this information at the outset of negotiations. Instead release it gradually to support your offer as you come closer to your estimated buying price.

"The wise learn many things from their enemies."

Aristophanes (circa 448–380 B.C.), Greek playwright

seller's *Essential* list. If you spot it, you have a valuable chip. If the situation is reversed (seller's *Expendable* is your *Essential*), you won't have to pay or give up much for it.

Seven Secrets Every Good Negotiator Knows

After all this, there's still something more. Besides knowledge of negotiating concepts and the negotiating process, besides knowledge of the real estate marketplace and the property to be purchased, another key to successful negotiating is attitude. How a buyer regards negotiations can make a tremendous difference in success (a difference often measurable in dollars). Let's look at some points to remember.

Take Every Word Seriously

Who wants to read all that tiny print in a contract? You do, and carefully. It spells out what you are bargaining over.

Besides reading carefully, listen carefully to what the agent reports to you during each round of negotiations. Talk that seems unimportant to the casual listener may indeed hold clues to a seller's motivation, stress, or goals. You are in a high-stakes game; engage your brain while listening.

Don't Assume

It's very important that you don't project your own perspective onto the seller. Instead, try to put yourself in the seller's place and consider the deal from that viewpoint. Test out as many possibilities for seller motivation as you can imagine, but don't pick and stay with any particular one as the "right" answer. Work only with facts and information that you are given or discover. Basing decisions upon guesses can lead you down a path that may actually take you away from the meeting of the minds you are seeking.

Don't assume that other people are doing what you would have done or what you would like them to do.

Question your real estate agent about how and when the offer was presented. If the deal seems to be dragging or there has been no response from the seller, ask your agent to follow up. This watchful pressure is especially important when two agents from separate brokerage firms are involved.

Don't assume that everything actually is as it appears. Employ professionals to check structure, condition, zoning compliance, financial records, and marketable title.

Ask For What You Want

This seems almost too simple to need saying. Many beginners negotiate right to signing, however, hoping all along that things will turn their way while never actually asking for what they want. If you think the building needs a new entranceway, ask for it somewhere near your final offer. You may not get it, but you may get a price concession. Then again, you may get a new entranceway. If you would prefer some creative seller financing, ask for it. If the seller says, "No, I can't possibly do that," you can still go to a bank.

If you do ask for something and the reply is, "Of course, that's included," get it in writing. Don't let sellers or real estate agents intimidate you with a condescending look that says: Everybody knows that! A good line to use is, "Well, because we all agree, there's no reason why we shouldn't put it into the contract."

Object to What You Don't Want

If a clause in the contract bothers you, speak up. Never wave it away as insignificant. The worst attitude you can have is: *I don't want to be a bother.* Be a bother! This is your money and no one will watch over it as well as you.

Think Before You Speak

You don't have to respond instantly to a counteroffer or even to a question. "Let me think about it" can buy you strategic time.

You can always defer to another person who is buying with you, your attorney, your accountant, or even a relative who is lending you some of the down payment, as a third party who must be consulted before an answer is made. This strategy allows you to leave with dignity when a negotiating scene has become heated and then to reenter when emotions have cooled.

Never Say Never

Many a buyer and seller have regretted saying, "I'll never. . . ." Just as bad is the statement, "This is my final offer." If you can be persuaded to change your mind for a thousand dollars or so, you'll have to eat crow. And because you have already folded once, you'll lose negotiating power if contingencies come up later that change the character of the deal.

Remember, real estate may deal with huge pieces of land and buildings and large amounts of money, but each deal is put together in many, many small pieces. Changing one small item can lead to a domino effect that changes the whole deal. Try to avoid all over-reaching adverbs like *never, always, only,* and *absolutely.* When you make an offer or, in fact, any statement in the negotiation process, try to leave yourself some space to move about, to qualify.

Keep Your Temper Cool

Remember that negotiating for a piece of investment real estate is a business deal. Emotional displays are rarely effective in the business arena. Losing you temper and expressing anger are signs of weakness that often indicate a lack of recourse or resources. If you feel your temper heating up, walk away.

Be courteous. The calm negotiator gets many more chances to make changes than the negotiator who pounds a fist on the table. In the negotiating situation, who knows, a smile could be worth a thousand dollars.

KEEP IN MIND

- **To learn the art of negotiating,** you must negotiate.
- **Virtually everything in a real estate purchase contract** is negotiable.
- **The key steps to a successful negotiation** take place before the first offer is made.
- **Attorney review** is the ultimate buyer protection contingency.
- **Negotiating** is a give something/get something process.
- **The seven secrets every good negotiator knows are:**
    1. **Take every word seriously.**
    2. **Don't assume.**
    3. **Ask for what you want.**
    4. **Object to what you don't want.**
    5. **Think before you speak.**
    6. **Never say never.**
    7. **Keep your temper cool.**

How to Get It in Writing

"A verbal contract isn't worth the paper it's written on."

Samuel Goldwyn (1879–1974), American filmmaker

Chapter 8

If you've had the experience of buying a home, you are surely familiar with the "standard" contract forms that real estate agents pull out as soon as you say you want to make an offer. That's fine as long as you realize that in fact there's no such thing as a standard contract. Every real estate transaction is unique. Each purchase contract is the written representation of the meeting of the minds between the buying party and the selling party. The standard printed contract form is just a good starting point.

But what is that starting point? What's in these standard contracts? Most nationally franchised real estate firms have contract forms written by the company's legal departments. Smaller, local firms may use a contract form based upon recommendations of the National Association of Realtors or they may have their own "office standard" written by local lawyers and tailored to the concerns of the local marketplace. Both national and local standard contracts generally include all the necessary elements to make an agreement legally binding after the blanks have been filled in with the specifics of each particular deal and after the printed contract has been executed by all concerned parties.

So you are sitting in a real estate broker's office after returning from a second inspection of an appealing property. You are anxious and excited at the same time. You want the property you've been looking at, but you also want the best possible deal. Is filling in the blanks on a printed contract form and then signing on the dotted line really the best way to make your offer and begin the negotiating process?

The answer is "yes, but . . ." *Yes*, the written offer is the best way to begin negotiations, *but* you'd better know what you're doing or you could find yourself stuck in deep and dirty mud. The written offer works best because every real estate deal has many different aspects (for example, the building, the land, the financing, the legal title, the date of closing, and possession). Standardized contracts cover all of these many facets of the deal.

It's important that every aspect of the transaction be committed to paper because each can affect value. Neither party should have the opportunity to say, "Oh, I never agreed to that!" when, in fact, the matter in question had been a subject of negotiation. On the other hand, you, as buyer, want a standardized contract to be modified in such a way as to protect your interests and allow you to exit the agreement if certain conditions cannot be met. So read this chapter carefully for an understanding of the purchase contract and some important tips on how to use it to protect your interests. And then proceed with care and caution.

Talk Is Cheap . . . and Unreliable

Making a deal to buy investment real estate is usually more complex than making a deal to buy a home. Things come up, such as tenants and their leases, perk tests, zoning and building code compliance, fixtures and chattel, down payment money, mortgages, and tax assessments. It's always a puzzle with many pieces. So why not discuss all this stuff verbally with the seller, along with the price, and then write up the contract when everything is settled? It would certainly be nice to avoid all that scratching out, hand printing in the margins and between the lines, initialing, and retyping.

Don't do it! People (both buyers and sellers, and sometimes even agents) forget what they've said or change their minds after they've said it. The only way to establish a starting point for all negotiations and then move the deal along toward a meeting of the minds is the written word.

The standardized contract that you fill in and sign with your first and every subsequent offer is not a purchase contract until it is signed by all the buyers and all the sellers, with every change initialed by all parties involved. You can be held to *do* nothing and you *get* nothing until everyone signs. For example, what if the seller signs but only after crossing out the price and writing in a figure that is $10,000 higher than your offer? Is there a contract? Absolutely not! Both parties must initial the change. Without those initials, the revised contract is only a counteroffer. That's the safety net of the real estate contract as a bilateral agreement.

The standardized purchase contract form, filled in with your unique information, is therefore the best vehicle for negotiating because it states clearly in writing everything you want to make known and are willing to do at any given point in the negotiations. Items can be added or deleted as the negotiations proceed, and everything can be subject to the approval of your legal counsel. Be sure to include an attorney-review clause in every real estate contract that you sign, as discussed in Chapter 7.

Like all advice, however, everything you've just read has an "except when" clause. The use of the printed contract form as a written offer works well if you are negotiating through a real estate agent. But what if you find a for-sale-by-owner property that you want to buy? Very few sellers or buyers have blank contract forms in their kitchen drawers. Without an agent, you have four working options for negotiating:

1. **You can hire a buyer broker and agree to pay** a flat fee for negotiating the sale and drawing up a contract.

> ## LEARNING THE LANGUAGE
>
> **Perk test** (percolation test) is a procedure by which a hole is dug on the property and water poured in to determine the capability of the soil to absorb liquid. It is important for new construction and for septic systems.
>
> **A bilateral contract** is a two-way agreement. Each party agrees to act in response to the action of the other. The seller agrees to sell and the buyer agrees to buy according to the terms of the contract. No real estate purchase contract is valid, therefore, unless both parties agree to every clause.

This fee does not have to be anywhere near the "customary and usual" commission.

2. **You can ask a buyer broker to approach the sellers** and get them to agree to pay a negotiated commission (again, it does not have to be a traditional percentage, often a flat fee works well) out of the proceeds of the sale.

3. **You can obtain a standardized contract form from your attorney,** fill it in, negotiate it, and make the agreement subject to attorney review.

4. **You can negotiate with a "binder"** that is subject to a purchase contract to be drawn up by your attorney and executed by all parties in the deal within a stated number of days.

What Makes a Contract a Contract?

You've probably noticed that the attorney-review clause has been mentioned several times in this book so far. It's one of your best safeguards. But attorneys are human, and humans are not always perfect, so don't expect your attorney to take on responsibility for your financial well-being. You should review the work of your attorney and ask questions whenever you're uncertain.

To do that, you must understand what factors make for a good contract and what pitfalls to avoid. Let's start with the essential elements that every contract must have.

In Writing

To be enforceable, every real estate purchase and sale contract must be in writing. Verbal agreements and good-faith handshakes in other kinds of businesses do sometimes hold up as contracts in court, but not in real estate. And bear in mind that the "in writing" mandate also applies to every change that is made after the agreement is set out on paper. Let's look at two examples:

John Buyer makes an offer. Joe Seller makes a counteroffer. John Buyer makes a second offer. On the phone with the real estate agent, Joe Seller agrees to accept that second offer. But the next morning, he changes his mind and wants *more* money. Does John Buyer have a deal? No. The real estate agent should have driven to Joe's house and gotten a signature as soon as the agreement was made. Or, in today's marketplace, the deal could have been secured by e-mail.

Betty Buyer and Suzy Seller agree on the sale of a condominium. A week after the contracts have been fully executed, Betty Buyer has her agent ask Suzy Seller if she will be leaving the washer and dryer. Suzy Seller says yes, she'll do that for an extra $200. Betty Buyer agrees to pay the extra at the closing. At the day-of-closing inspection, however, she notices that the washer and dryer are gone. Is there anything Betty Buyer can do? No. The real estate agent should have written up the appliance agreement as an addendum to the contract, with the date and the signatures of both parties on the page.

Throughout most of the 20th century, the necessity that all agreements and changes be in writing often posed problems, caused delays, and sometimes broke apart deals when negotiating with a seller who lived some distance from the property being sold. Today, however, there's no excuse for allowing an agreement to remain at the verbal stage. The problem is solved by the fax machine, e-mail,

---

STOP AND THINK!

Don't let anyone convince you that a **"short form"** or **"binder"** is better than a purchase contract. They might argue that the binder establishes the selling price, takes the property off the market, and allows you to "iron out the details" later. In fact, under some circumstances, a "binder" can stand up as a valid contract and commit you to a purchase, with no way out. If for some reason you must negotiate with this kind of incomplete contract, be certain that you print the following statement above your signature:

This agreement is subject to a purchase contract acceptable to both parties, to be drawn and fully executed by midnight, (date).

It's usually best to allow five business days.

and overnight delivery. Clauses or whole contracts can be transmitted electronically between the parties, and the returned electronic signatures are legally binding.

The Date

An undated contract is not legally enforceable. To be extra safe, the date of the original contract should be written on its first page. In addition, each party should include the date of signing adjacent to his or her signature.

The Identities of the Parties

The full name (including middle initials) of each person who is involved in the buying and selling of the property should be included in the contract and each identified as "buyer" or "seller." It's also a good idea to include the address of each, especially when the seller lives somewhere other than at the property being sold. If a business or corporation is one of the parties, it should be identified as such with its name and address stated (and in the case of the corporation, the state where it is incorporated).

Identification of the Property Being Sold

The street address is the most conventional way to identify property and it is legally acceptable. When dealing with a condominium, it is also essential to include the apartment number, and you may want to throw in the name of the condominium community. Rural property or raw land sometimes poses a problem because it has no street address. In this case, you can identify the property by tax block and lot number or by metes-and-bounds survey information.

The Purchase Price (a Consideration)

The full amount of the purchase price should be written in, no matter what financing arrangements have been made or promised. In cases where the price is to be determined by an appraisal, you can write "appraised value as determined by XYZ Appraisal Company" on the contract line for price. You can and should limit this amount by specifying a "not above" figure. In other words, you agree to purchase the property at the appraised figure unless that price is above a certain, specified amount, in which case you are no longer bound by contractual agreement.

The check that accompanies the written offer is the consideration that will validate the contract if the offer is accepted. The amount should be indicated in the purchase contract. As mentioned in Chapter 7, this consideration is called "earnest money" and is almost always held in escrow until the closing. Despite the fact that most real estate agents look for $1,000 or so, earnest money can actually be any amount.

> ### LEARNING THE LANGUAGE
>
> **A consideration** is anything of value (usually money) that one party gives to another in exchange for a promise or action (turning over title to a property, for example). For a real estate contract to be valid it must include a consideration.

A Date to Close Title

Where and when title will pass from one party to another is often changed by mutual agreement, but there must be a date and place named in the contract as a point of reference. If the date of closing and occupancy is an inherent part of the agreement, a clause should note that time is of the essence.

Signatures

Each person involved in the purchase and each person who currently holds title to the property must sign the contract agreement. A missing signature can invalidate it. When businesses or corporations are involved, be certain that the persons signing have full authority to do so.

Within the Limits of the Law

Everything agreed to in a real estate purchase contract must be legal. For example, a seller cannot include in the sale something he or she does not own, such as

---

LEARNING THE LANGUAGE

Time is of the essence is legal terminology for a clause that will bind one party to perform the actions agreed upon in the contract on or before a specified date in order to bind the other party to performance. Notice that time is of the essence can be served by either the buyer or seller to the other party. For example, if the buyer serves notice that time is of the essence and the seller cannot close and give occupancy by the contracted date, the buyer can walk away from the contract and have all deposit money returned. If the seller serves notice to the buyer and the buyer cannot perform, the seller is free to sell the property to another party. There would, however, most likely be a legal battle regarding who gets the escrow money.

Serving notice that time is of the essence is a strong-arm tactic that can sometimes backfire. Before you brandish this sword, talk with your attorney, both about alternative strategies and the possible repercussions if the other party is unable to perform on schedule.

---

the land beneath a navigable river or land to which he or she does not hold clear title. If a part of the contract agreement is outside the law, the entire contract may be void, or that specific part may be void, depending on the laws of the state.

All of the parties entering into a real estate purchase contract must be legally eligible to do so. For example, children (minors) and the mentally incompetent are generally excluded from eligibility.

Deal Breakers

Successful real estate investors, in fact successful persons in every aspect of life, rarely settle for the "minimum required" of anything. And so it is with the purchase contract. The eight contract elements we've just discussed are enough to make a valid and enforceable agreement of sale. But you'll surely want to address many more issues to protect your investment dollar, give yourself a way out if things don't go as anticipated, and increase your odds for a profitable purchase. Contingencies (defined in Chapter 7) protect your ability to get out of the contract unscathed if major problems come up. Let's look at those you do *not* want to do without.

The Mortgage Contingency

Unless you're working a cash deal (very rare in the real estate marketplace), you will want to make your contract contingent upon your ability to borrow some of the money you will need to meet the purchase price. The next chapter is devoted to financing for investment property, so at this point let's just review the written items that will protect your ability to get financing in the contract. Be sure you list as contingencies:

- **Your ability to get the maximum amount** of mortgage loan money that you will need to borrow
- **The type and term of the mortgage loan**
- **The maximum interest rate** you are willing to pay or a statement that you'll accept the prevailing rate
- **A specified period of time to apply for and get** a written commitment for the loan from a lending institution

---

DIGGING DEEPER

Some sources for finding a lawyer who really knows investment real estate include:

- **Your Realtor** or your local Board of Realtors—get at least three names of attorneys or firms actively working in investment real estate.
- **Other active investors**—members of investment clubs, family members, friends. Avoid taking suggestions from the seller.
- **Your mortgage broker** or mortgage banker—these professionals work with attorneys regularly.

STOP AND THINK!

If your willingness to buy is contingent upon a certain type of financing—an FHA program, for example, or a state- or community-supported loan—be certain that you include the name and terms of that program in your mortgage contingency. Simply indicating the amount of the loan is not enough. An aggressive agent might just find you that loan amount but at a higher interest rate, a shorter term, or with points and insurance fees. You may be unwilling or unable to pay on those terms. By specifying the type of mortgage financing in the contract, you let yourself out of the deal if you cannot get what you want.

or other mortgage-money source. This contingency should include a named date.

Along with the mortgage contingency, the part of the contract that defines how the purchase price will be paid should include an accounting of exactly where the money will come from and when it will change hands.

This financial summary includes:

- **The amount of the earnest money check** to be held in escrow until closing
- **The additional escrow money** to be paid by a certain date (usually from five days to two weeks after contracts are fully executed)
- **The amount of the first mortgage loan**
- **The amount of borrowed money** other than the first mortgage (this might include some seller financing)
- **The amount of gift money** to be deposited in the buyer's account by a prescribed date
- **Additional cash to be paid at closing**

The Inspection Contingency

Unlike diamonds or gold, which can be inspected and accurately evaluated by universally accepted standards, land will always include unknowns beneath its surface and buildings will always hide many secrets behind their walls. There will never be any guarantee that you are buying a perfect property (in fact, there is no perfect property).

Including a contingency for professional inspections in your contract, however, will enable you to feel some assurance that the agreed-upon cost of the property will not escalate because of necessary repairs that must be paid by you, after the closing and out-of-pocket. Real estate investors should not wonder whether or not to have inspections. Instead, they should ask who will do the inspections and how much time will be needed to get the inspections done and reported upon.

The seller or the seller's agent will certainly insist upon a cutoff date for the inspection contingency. Without a cutoff date, an unscrupulous buyer could

---

> ## STOP AND THINK!
>
> When working with inspection contingencies, don't allow preprinted wording in your contract that will give the seller an opportunity to remedy a problem *as he sees fit* and thereby hold you to contract fulfillment.
>
> Be absolutely certain that your contract is contingent upon inspection reports *"that in the sole judgment of the purchaser are deemed satisfactory."* In other words, if you don't like anything that the inspector points out, you can walk away from the contract and get all of your earnest money back. Or you can negotiate with the seller to repair the problems *to your satisfaction* before closing, or to lower the price enough to cover the cost of repairs.

cite some flaw discovered by a home inspector and back out of the contract the day before the closing. Be certain that the date named will allow you enough time to get all the inspections you will need. Ask your agent what is the typical time allowance for property inspections in the area. (Two to three weeks is not unheard of.) Or call local contractors and inspection firms before you buy and ask each how much time they require to do an inspection and prepare a report.

You can also have inspections done by specialty firms, such as termite exterminators, roofing contractors, radon remediators, environmental cleanup firms (for buried oil tanks), or lead-paint specialists. If you choose a series of such inspections, however, you will have to make many trips back to the property, you will have to pay each company individually, and you run the risk of hiring inspectors who might have an interest in selling you their repair or remediation services. The better (and ultimately more economical) approach is to hire a professional inspector who does nothing but inspections and does not provide any repair services.

Professional-inspection reports generally cover a property from top to bottom, including all the features mentioned in the box below. If a general inspection raises questions without providing answers (inspectors are not specialists), *then* you can call in consultants. Poor water pressure might prompt a call to a well-drilling and maintenance company, a sagging roofline might require a roofing specialist, and high numbers on the radon test will require an estimate for repairing the problem. You get the idea. It's like having a general physical exam and then being sent to specialists if there is evidence or suspicion of a specific problem.

Clear Title

It's included in most standardized contracts but check anyway to be sure that your purchase contract is contingent upon the seller being able to provide clear title to the property. Clear title is title without liens or

---

DIGGING DEEPER

It may help you to be aware, before the inspection date, of exactly what the inspector will be inspecting. Here's the basic list:

- **Land:** drainage, soil contamination, buried oil tank, septic tank, leaching fields or lines
- **Foundation:** cracks, buckling, water seepage, sump pump, pest infestation (termites, beetles, ants, rodents, bats, etc.)
- **Structure:** building-code compliance, carrying timbers or I beams, floors, settling, stairs, doorjambs, windows, insulation, chimney construction
- **Roof:** support system, venting, shingles, leaking, gutters, downspouts
- **Working systems:** potable water and adequate well pump if there is a private water system, furnace and/or heating system, air-conditioning, plumbing, waste disposal, electrical wiring, cooking systems

(gas, propane, electric), appliances (hot-water heater, laundry facilities if included)
- **Health hazards:** Radon, lead-based paint, asbestos, formaldehyde in the foam insulation (UFFI)

Your community's buildings department can provide you with information on local building codes. Your local or state public health department and environmental regulation department will help you answer health-related questions. For more information on lead-based paint, contact the **National Lead Information Center** by phone at 800-424-5323 or on its Web site (http://www.nsc.org/ehc/lead/nlic) where a specialist is available to answer questions Monday to Friday from 8:00 AM to 6:00 PM EST.

encumbrances. (This is sometimes called "marketable title.") When the seller signs the contract, there may well be mortgages (known as voluntary liens) or claims (involuntary liens) against the property. The clear-title contingency assures you that all such claims will be disposed of before title passes to you.

However, even the best of sellers' promises and assurances can be broken, either intentionally or unintentionally. Most lenders therefore also require title insurance to protect their interest against claims that might arise subsequent to the closing. Even if not required by the mortgage lender, you should seriously consider buying title insurance. (See Chapter 5 for more information about title insurance.)

Records Review

The major factor that differentiates investment real estate from homebuying is money—making it, that is. Income and operating costs are therefore essential elements of the deal. Your purchase contract should be contingent on your right to review all lease and rent records, tax-return schedules for the building, and all maintenance and operating-cost records for at least three years. The contract should be contingent upon your finding them satisfactory to your offer. (You will want to examine more than one year of records because numbers can easily be juggled for short periods of time.)

DIGGING DEEPER

One way to get the names of professional inspectors in your area is to contact one of the national professional associations in the field. With that list of names in hand, you can ask for feedback on individual agents from your real estate agent, real estate attorney, or mortgage broker, or from other investors you know.

The American Society of Home Inspectors (ASHI)
932 Lee Street, Suite 101
Des Plaines, IL 60016
800-743-2744
http://www.ASHI.com
This is the largest professional home-inspection trade association in the United States.

The National Institute of Building Inspectors (NIBI)
424 Vosseller Avenue
Bound Brook, NJ 08805
888-281-6424
http://www.NIBI.com
This organization trains and certifies professional inspectors.

The Association of Construction Inspectors
1224 N. Nokomis N.E.
Alexandria, MN 56308
320-763-7525
http://www.iami.org/aci
This association comprises inspectors for new construction or rehab.

"The only people who don't change their minds are incompetent or dead."

Everett Dirksen (1896–1969), American statesman

Occupancy

If you are buying multifamily rental property and intend to live in one of the units, it is essential that you make the availability of occupancy a contingency. Many leases survive a change of ownership and moving out a tenant may prove costly and difficult. Sellers, on the other hand, can usually persuade tenants to move with a monetary incentive for breaking the lease.

Feasibility

Some purchase contracts are contingent upon getting approval from local government agencies for new construction, change of zoning, or change of building usage. Percolation-test results satisfactory to the buyer are often a contingency in land purchases because results often determine the type of development possible and its costs.

When purchasing a multifamily house, include a contingency clause that assures the legality of multifamily use because some sellers have converted large old houses without zoning board or buildings department approval. If you intend to do such a conversion, you can make your contract contingent on obtaining municipal approvals before closing.

Perhaps you are buying a multifamily house with plans to rent the first level as office or commercial space and the upper levels as housing. You will need a contingency for zoning board approval of the change in use and the conversion of a residential property to a mixed-use property.

If you are planning to build upon raw land or change an existing structure and its use, it's also a good idea to include in the contract a contingency stating that your intended use is not prohibited by covenants, conditions, and restrictions in the deed (called CC&Rs). CC&Rs, sometimes called simply *deed restrictions,* remain with the property through all changes of ownership.

DIGGING DEEPER

Here are some records you may want to examine while looking through "the books" concerning your prospective investment property.

- Accounting and bookkeeping costs and procedures
- Licenses, permits, etc.
- Advertising for tenants
- Lighting fixtures
- Air-conditioning
- Management fees
- Appliances and equipment—inventory, service, and repair costs
- Parking area maintenance
- Assessments—tax, special, and condominium community if applicable
- Pest control
- Cleaning services—general and vacant unit refurbishing
- Plumbing maintenance and repair
- Electricity
- Pool service
- Exterior maintenance
- Real estate taxes
- Floor coverings
- Refuse removal
- Heat
- Replacement and maintenance reserve
- Insurance
- Security services
- Interior maintenance
- Sewer
- Janitorial service and supplies
- Water
- Landscaping and maintenance
- Window washing
- Legal services

More Buyer Protection

Contingencies are essentially escape clauses, declaring in writing: If this doesn't happen, the deal is off. You don't want to sign a contract without them. Beyond the *if/or else* agreements, however, you'll also want your purchase contract to set down in writing exactly what each party agrees to do or has the right to do. Remember, it's human nature to change one's mind, sometimes prompted by greed, sometimes by convenience, and sometimes just by forgetfulness.

Let's go through the most common buyer-protection clauses found in purchase contracts. Remember, however, that this list is not definitive. If you think of something that seems important to your deal, be sure to ask your attorney about it.

Money

It's not just your earnest money that you want to protect. Contract errors and omissions can cost you many thousands in legal fees, missed opportunities, or repairs. Check for these specifics.

- **Your right to choose the escrow company.** Determine who will hold your money and who will close title. These are power positions, and it's important to have them "on your side," if possible, or at least neutral.
- **Interest on the escrow funds.** Agree as to who gets it or how it will be split. Interest becomes an issue when the escrow deposit is in many thousands and/or the proposed closing date is many months away.
- **Disposition of outstanding monies.** Agree in writing how rents, assessments, taxes, and outstanding debts will be handled.
- **The real estate commission.** Record how much it will be and who will pay it.
- **Buyer or seller default.** Establish what will happen if one party cannot or will not fulfill the contract. Spell out the penalties specifically.
- **Right to assign.** Add the words "and/or assigns" after your name as the buyer. This gives you the power to sell the right to buy the property even before you close title. (It can happen in a hot market!) It also allows you to turn over the right to buy to your heirs.

The Property

Because there is always a delay between the signing of the purchase contract and the closing of title, things can happen. Include clauses in the contract to assure that you will be getting exactly the property you agreed to buy. These are the most common.

- **Maintenance.** Your contract should state that the property will be maintained until closing in the condition it was on the date of the purchase contract.
- **Broom-clean condition.** This term means that refuse and the seller's personal property will be removed from the premises before the closing.
- **Damage liability.** The seller should be responsible for repairs necessary because of fire, flood, wind, earth-

quake, act of war, or other disasters until title passes. Most contracts also include the requirement that the seller maintain insurance coverage to the date of closing.

- **What stays and what doesn't.** Two lists are required—exactly what remains with the property and exactly what does not. Among the items in question are appliances, lighting fixtures, window treatments, floor coverings, and furniture.

- **Day-of-closing inspection.** Every contract should give the buyer the right to inspect the property just before taking title to it. Bring a notepad and pencil, the contract itself, and a camera. If you find anything missing or objectionable, you can negotiate at the closing. Even if title closes, money can be withheld from the seller (held in escrow) until the problems are corrected.

> **STOP AND THINK!**
>
> If you want to be sure that you'll take title to the property in the same condition that it was on the day you signed the purchase contract, take pictures! (Be sure you use a camera that dates each photograph.) It's very difficult to prove damage or deterioration without visual evidence.

A Word About the Closing

Some buyers feel overwhelmed by all the fine print, numbers, and dotted lines requiring signatures or initials at the closing. In an effort to move things along, they tend to nod, smile, and sign their names whenever a paper is put in front of them. They turn complete control over to the closing agent. Don't do this!

The closing is your last chance to get the deal you thought you were getting. Read the document before you sign anything. Ask questions when you don't understand. Bring a pocket calculator and check the numbers. Many, many mistakes happen. Those that are especially costly occur when a payment due from the seller is charged as due from the buyer. (You're paying double!)

Once the ink is dry and everyone leaves the closing, the property is yours. But there remains one last detail: Ask the closing agent when the deed will be recorded. Then check the town records to be certain that it's done correctly. Your ownership interest is not fully protected until that deed is on file.

KEEP IN MIND

- **A purchase contract** signed by only the buyer is a written offer not a contract.
- **If the seller makes any change in the purchase contract** before signing, it is still not a contract but rather a counteroffer.
- **Get everything in writing.**
- **To be legally enforceable,** a purchase contract must contain the date, the identities of all parties, an identification of the property, the purchase price, a proposed date to close title, and the signatures of all parties involved in the transaction. The agreement must also be within the limits of the law.
- **Every purchase contract should spell out the contingencies** that must be met before the deal can be made. Be sure to allow plenty of time before contingency cutoff dates.

Where Can You Get the Money?

"Americans want action for their money. They are fascinated by its self-reproducing qualities if it's put to work."

Paula Nelson, U.S. business executive, *The Joy of Money*

What's the biggest factor that keeps people from entering the investment real estate marketplace? You guessed it: money. Nonparticipants standing at the gateway and staring in usually ask, "How can a regular person like me get started when every price tag has more zeros in it than my annual income?"

That question is the mark of the uninitiated. If you've read this far, you already know the answer: People seldom pay cash. They use other people's money. We call that financing.

Financing and the concept of leverage were discussed in Chapter 1. Now that you're actually about to buy something, however, you certainly want to know more about how to use leverage successfully. Welcome to the mortgage marketplace!

If you own your home, you've almost certainly been here before. But it's a huge and ever-changing field and you may not have taken to heart and memory every aspect of mortgage financing that you encountered in your homebuying experience. Just in case you didn't, there's a quick refresher course in the box on the following pages. Take a few minutes to review it, and refer back to it whenever the need arises.

Even if you are familiar with every term in the box, don't skip to the next chapter. Financing investment property starts with the principles of home financing—and builds. The rules are the same, and different.

Chapter 9

MORTGAGE BASICS IN A BOX

What Is a Mortgage?

to mortgage: to conditionally transfer or pledge real estate as security for repayment of a loan

a mortgage: the document used to create the mortgage lien that is an encumbrance against property for money owed

a mortgage loan: the money borrowed with a mortgage. In common usage, the loan is often called "a mortgage."

deed of trust, or trust deed: works like a mortgage and is often talked of as a mortgage but it is the financing instrument used in title-theory states (mostly in the West) where foreclosure can be swift and without legal entanglements. Title to the property is held in trust for the lender. When the loan is re-paid, title is transferred to the buyer/owner.

collateral: the property pledged as security for a mortgage loan.

term: the agreed-upon period of time until the loan is paid off.

amortization: the paying off of a mortgage loan through scheduled, equal monthly pay-ments of principal and interest.

foreclosure: a procedure in or out of court that will extinguish all ownership claim of the mortgagor (buyer/owner) in favor of the mortgagee (lender) in order to sell the property to satisfy the lien against it. Foreclosure proceedings are started when debt payment is not made as scheduled.

Who's Who

mortgagor: the borrower; the one who gives the mortgage as a pledge of repayment.

mortgagee: the lender; the one who holds the mortgage.

trustor: the borrower in a trust-deed state.

beneficiary: the lender in a trust-deed state.

trustee: the third party in a trust-deed state who holds title to the property until the loan is repaid.

The Money Borrowed

principal: the money that is borrowed; the amount of debt not including interest.

loan-to-value ratio: the relationship between the amount borrowed and the appraised value of the collateral real estate, expressed as a percentage.

certitude of performance: a lender's evaluation of how much risk is involved in making a loan.

equity: the amount of interest (cash value) an owner has in a property beyond all liens against it.

balance of the loan: the unpaid principal at any given point in time.

Interest

interest rate: the cost of borrowing money, usually expressed as an annual percentage of the principal.

annual percentage rate (APR): the actual rate of interest (includes fees and other factors) that must be paid. Federal truth-in-lending statutes require that lenders disclose the APR of every loan.

teaser rates: low initial rates to attract borrowers.

buydown: a cash payment to the lender from the seller, buyer, or a third party to persuade the lender to lower the interest rate to be charged in the early years of a loan.

cap: limitation on the amount of change allowed in a variable-rate loan. The interval cap sets the maximum interest rate change (up or down) that can be made on any rate-change date. (Two percentage points is common.) The life-of-the-loan cap sets the maximum the interest rate can increase or decrease from the initial rate over the entire life of a loan. (Six percentage points is common.)

Types of Mortgage Loans

fixed-rate mortgage: the rate of interest remains fixed for the entire term.

adjustable-rate mortgage (ARM): also called a variable-rate mortgage, the rate of interest can be changed at stated intervals over the term.

convertible: a loan that can be changed from adjustable to fixed-rate.

assumable: a clause in a mortgage agreement that allows the property to be sold with the buyer taking over (assuming) the seller's debt and mortgage terms.

FHA: a mortgage loan insured by the Federal Housing Administration.

VA: a mortgage loan guaranteed by the Department of Veterans Affairs

straight mortgage: an interest-only mortgage loan. The borrower makes regular interest payments and agrees to repay the principal upon maturity of the loan or upon sale.

balloon mortgage: interest and principal payments are made according to a schedule for amortization over a given number of years (usually a long term) but the entire remaining principal is due on a given date (usually short term). The large payment of balance due is called the balloon payment.

shared appreciation mortgage (SAM): a mortgage arrangement where the lender offers a lower interest rate and better terms in return for a percentage of the profit when the property is sold.

joint venture or participation financing: an arrangement between an entrepreneur and a lender in which the lender puts up all or part of the required cash in return for a share of the profits.

Common Clauses

due on sale (also called an alienation clause): a provision in the mortgage agreement stating that the entire principal balance is due and payable if ownership is transferred to another party. This clause prevents assumption of the loan.

call: the right of the lender to demand payment of the entire principal balance if the repayment terms of the mortgage loan are not being met.

lock-in: a clause that prevents the borrower from repaying the loan before a certain date.

Common Costs

points: an up-front fee charged by the lender to make the loan more profitable. One point equals 1 percent of the principal. Points are sometimes called the discount.

origination fee: like points, but usually a stated amount rather than a percentage of the principal.

application fee: amount charged to apply for the loan, usually nonrefundable. It can be any amount from $25 on up.

credit-report fee: amount charged for a credit report on the prospective borrower.

appraisal fee: amount charged for the bank appraisal of the property. Note that even though the borrower pays for the appraisal, it belongs to the lender.

Opportunities are as plentiful, but flung further afield. Creativity and knowledge pay dividends.

This chapter focuses on the concepts of investment real estate financing that are essential for effective borrowing. Remember, getting the right financing is a major part of getting a good deal.

How Much Can You Get?

How much can I get? That's the question everyone wants answered first. The nothing-down carnival barkers in this marketplace will tell you that you can get everything, the whole purchase price, maybe even more. Believe it or not, they're right—some of the time. There are government programs that will let you borrow the whole purchase price, and even beyond to include the cost of renovation. There are sellers who will take back a purchase-money mortgage with no down payment. There are "creative" deals you can work with bankers that feel a bit like card tricks but are, in fact, perfectly legal.

But let's anchor in reality. The majority of investment property is purchased with conventional financing through conventional sources. So let's start there.

> ## LEARNING THE LANGUAGE
>
> The term **purchase-money mortgage** refers to a mortgage lien given by the buyer to the seller in lieu of cash. You'll hear it said that the seller **takes back a mortgage.**

Banks Are in Business to Make Money

Where do banks get money to lend? From their depositors' savings, you answer. Well, that's partially correct. But given the American track record for saving, most banks would very quickly run out of money if they had to depend upon savings accounts or certificates of deposit (CDs) as their only source of funds. Banks can and do borrow money from the Federal Reserve at a low rate and lend out the money at a higher rate. That practice gives each bank a deep pocket, but it also brings about federal regulations and controls.

Federal Reserve regulations limit the amount of a bank's outstanding debt and set minimum requirements for cash to be kept on hand to cover future demands that might occur. The regulations effectively mean that if a bank were to hold all the mortgage loans it wrote until those loans were paid off, its borrowing rights would soon be cut off, and again it would run out of money to lend.

So if banks don't hold on to loans until they're paid off, what do they do with them? Most likely you've heard of Fannie Mae and Freddie Mac. If you haven't, you should know that these are not the names of pining lovers in a country-western ballad. They are the two most powerful corporations in the secondary-mortgage marketplace. That's where banks sell their loans.

Because they are not only powerful but also businesses run for profit, Fannie Mae and Freddie Mac want to buy only low-risk loans. Their definitions of "low risk" have come to set financing limitations, down-payment requirements, and qualification guidelines for most of the mortgage lending in the nation.

Even in the huge secondary mortgage marketplace, however, loan-to-value ratio requirements and qualification guidelines are changed from time to time, so check for these figures with your mortgage broker, your local lender, or on the Internet every time you are about to buy property. On the Internet, a recent search using non+owner+occupied+mortgage+loan on the Google search engine brought up 78,700 sites. Generally, these were mortgage brokers, some with offices in each state. For the most part, the Web sites included the qualification guidelines for programs with nothing down, 70 percent to 95 percent down, no documentation, and cash-outs. And they wanted

> ### LEARNING THE LANGUAGE
>
> **A portfolio loan** is a mortgage loan that the lender does *not* sell into the secondary market. Often these are loans anchored by good-risk properties where the buyer does not meet the prevailing secondary-mortgage-market qualification or down-payment guidelines. The lender usually charges a higher interest rate and higher fees for these loans. Sometimes portfolio holdings are shared-appreciation loans or participation financing (see page 173).

you to apply, right now, online. Surfing the net is a good method of gathering information, but don't be in too much of a hurry to apply instantly.

The Home-Investment Combination

Multifamily houses (two to four units) in which the owner occupies one of the units are a somewhat specialized mortgaging scene. Essentially, they are treated as home mortgages with the added advantage that rental income is calculated in when computing buyer qualification. Home/investment buyers are eligible for

---

DIGGING DEEPER

These are the major players in the **Secondary-Mortgage Market:**

Fannie Mae (formerly the Federal National Mortgage Association) is a government-sponsored corporation that sells mortgage-backed securities. For current guidelines for investment real estate mortgages and a wealth of other information contact it by phone or at its Web site.

> **Fannie Mae**
> **3900 Wisconsin Avenue, N.W.**
> **Washington, DC 20016-2892**
> **800-732-6643**
> **http://www.fanniemae.com**

Freddie Mac (formerly the Federal Home Loan Mortgage Corporation) is a stockholder-owned corporation that buys mortgages from lenders and issues mortgage-backed securities. For information on mortgage underwriting issues, check its Web site.

> **Freddie Mac**
> **8200 Jones Branch Drive**
> **McLean, VA 22102-3110**

> **800-424-5401**
> **http://www.freddiemac.com**

Ginnie Mae (Government National Mortgage Association) is the mortgage arm of the federal Department of Housing and Urban Development. Contact it at:

> **Ginnie Mae**
> **451 7th Street, S.W.**
> **Room B 133**
> **Washington, DC 20410-9000**
> **202-708-1535**
> **http://www.ginniemae.gov**

Neighborhood Housing Services of America (NHSA) works with local Neighborworks™ Organizations (NWOs) to provide a secondary market for nonprofit neighborhood revitalization loans. Contact it at:

> **Neighborhood Housing Services of**
> **America (NHSA)**
> **1970 Broadway, Suite 470**
> **Oakland, CA 94612**
> **510-832-5542**
> **http://www.nhsofamerica.org**

government-insured (FHA) and guaranteed (VA) mortgages, for low-down-payment, privately insured mortgages (up to 95 percent of appraised value), and for loans up to 100 percent (and sometimes even more) that are supported by Community Home Buyers Programs (CHBP, commonly called cherubs). Generally, the community revitalization programs have lower down-payment requirements (higher loan-to-value ratios) than conventional loans. Most of them also have less stringent and more flexible qualification requirements.

FHA Investor Programs

The Department of Housing and Urban Development (HUD), through the Federal Housing Administration (FHA), has several programs open to investors for both owner-occupied and nonowner-occupied properties. Some programs offer financing of 100 percent or more of the appraised value. The following is a list of programs for investors. For details and qualification guidelines, contact your local office of the FHA or snoop around on the Internet. (There's a box on page 166 to help you get started.)

- **203(k).** Rehab loans for existing properties from one to four units. The buyer can finance the entire cost of purchase, plus the cost of rehab.
- **221(d)(4).** Loans up to 90 percent of appraised value to build rental housing for moderate-income families.
- **223(e).** Insures loans for housing in declining neighborhoods where normal qualification and underwriting guidelines cannot be met.
- **223(f).** Insures loans for the purchase or refinancing of existing apartment buildings that are at least three years old.
- **231.** Insures loans to finance construction or rehabilitation of homes for the elderly or handicapped.

Seller Financing

Seller financing is much more common in investment real estate than in homebuying. Sometimes you can indeed finance 100 percent of the purchase price. But

DIGGING DEEPER

The **Federal Housing Administration** was established in 1934 to improve housing standards and conditions and to provide an adequate home financing system through insurance of mortgages. It is within the **U.S. Department of Housing and Urban Development** and today it insures both owner-occupied and investor mortgages (sometimes called NOOs—nonowner-occupied mortgages).

You can access information on all types of FHA mortgages at **http://www.hud.gov** by clicking on the FHA categories and searching out your areas of concern or inquiry.

The Internet is also crammed with private firms that handle government-backed mortgages. A good example of a Web site exclusively dedicated to FHA mortgage loans is **http://www.fhaloan.com** where various FHA loan offerings are explained and lists of lenders provided.

if you are considering this type of mortgaging, bear in mind that old saying that became the title of economist Milton Friedman's 1975 book: *There Is No Free Lunch.*

If you find a seller willing to hold the mortgage on the property, be aware that you may be paying a higher purchase price than you would pay with a cash deal financed with conventional financing. Also, the interest rate to be charged on the loan is sometimes higher than prevailing rates and the term of the loan is often shorter. (Both of these factors make for higher monthly payments.)

If you find a seller anxious to take back a mortgage, *ask why.* Is the mortgage market virtually shut down? Is there some reason why the property is not likely to appeal to conventional lenders? Has it been on the market a very long time, unsold at the current asking price? If the local market is moving well, does that mean that the price is too high? Is it indeed so far above market value as to be unsalable without the added incentive of nothing-down financing?

A property with the incentive of seller financing might get you into the investment real estate business without significant down-payment money, but the savvy investor will do some serious evaluation before signing that purchase contract. Consider:

- **Cash flow.** Will income from the property be sufficient to carry the loan payments, taxes, and expenses? Remember, negative cash flow can lead to foreclosure.

- **Market value.** Is the property worth the purchase price? When you bypass conventional lenders, you give up the safeguard of a bank appraisal. Pay for an appraisal of your own. Remember, circumstances change and you might want to sell this property sooner than you had planned.

- **Interest rate.** How much will the property really cost you if you add in the higher cost of borrowing?

- **Mortgage term.** Do you want to take on the risk of a short mortgage term that will almost certainly require refinancing? If you plan to sell before the mortgage comes due, what will you do if the market in your area turns cold?

Other Sources of Investor Financing

Borrowers who don't fit the guidelines established by the secondary-mortgage market are not without opportunities for financing. Sources of mortgage money that are not federally regulated have been increasing since the 1980s. Among these are credit unions, life insurance companies, pension and retirement plans, and private investors.

Loans from these sources may be written for higher amounts and at higher loan-to-value ratios. Buyer-qualification guidelines may be more lenient. Interest rates may be higher or lower than going market rates among federally regulated lenders.

STOP AND THINK!

Seller-held mortgages are often written for short terms, sometimes as little as five years, with the entire principal due at the end of the term, sometimes called a **balloon mortgage.** Some buyers plan to sell the property during that mortgage term. Most buyers intend to refinance.

Both groups must bear in mind that neither the real estate nor the lending marketplaces are predictable. Protect your property interests by refinancing with a longer-term loan as soon as qualification and financial advantage allow, but at least a full year before the mortgage comes due.

Many credit unions that once restricted their lending to home mortgages are entering the investment-financing marketplace and can be a direct source of money. If you belong to a credit union, inquire about its lending policies before you start to shop for your investment property. Credit unions can sometimes offer their members better financing than other competing sources.

Before the Internet brought us the possibility of obtaining instant information across the nation and around the clock, it was somewhat more difficult to make direct contact with pension funds, insurance companies, and private investment groups. Finding financing is a different game today.

DIGGING DEEPER

If you want to go beyond its effective use and really understand mortgage financing, you'll have to spend some time with specialized books. A good starting point is *Essentials of Real Estate Finance* by David Sirota, PhD (Dearborn Publishing).

If you key *investor mortgage loans* into a search engine on the Internet, you'll get thousands of responses. So many, in fact, that you may feel overwhelmed. For the individual investor buying a single building (as opposed to a shopping center or apartment complex), mortgage brokers and mortgage bankers are probably still the best path to information about sources of mortgage money that are not influenced by the secondary mortgage market. Especially so if you are not proficient at navigating the Net and don't have hours to spend weighing details and checking for credibility.

How Much Do You Need?

If you were developing a portfolio in the stock market, you would probably consider it a high-risk strategy to borrow cash in order to make your investments. Yet borrowing to invest is exactly what real estate mortgage financing is all about.

So why is it considered relatively safe to borrow to make money in the real estate marketplace and not in the stock market? These are the major reasons:

- **You have a tangible asset that is unique and wholly owned.**

- **You have direct control over management and policy decisions.**
- **Most real estate has a source of income in rents. (Raw land is the exception.)**
- **The real estate marketplace is not as volatile as the stock market and therefore at lower risk of sudden loss.**
- **Tax advantages and leveraging contribute to high rates of return.**

Those are pretty good safety factors, right? Well if borrowing is such a great idea, why not borrow as much as you can get?

Whoa! That idea can take you far out on thin ice. Yes, borrowing is the key to making money in real estate, but it can also be the downfall of any real estate investment. Remember: borrowing costs money. The secret of success is borrowing the right amount that will allow you to make the most money. That "right amount" depends upon the type of investment property, your plans and goals, and, essentially, your ability to make the scheduled payments.

Different Strokes for Different Choices

In Part II, we will discuss the best financing options for each of the seven starter investment vehicles. But being entrepreneurial and therefore always curious, let's just take a peek here.

Sometimes it's effective to borrow 100 percent of the purchase price or even more. Property in need of refurbishing is a good example. By borrowing the maximum amount available, the cash you have on hand can be used for repairs. Your plan must be to do the work quickly and sell quickly.

On the other hand, sometimes you can't borrow anything and must go for cash. Take raw land, for example. It's difficult to get mortgage financing on land that is not approved for development. Once subdivision approval has been granted by the local zoning board, however, you no longer have raw land, but salable building lots. (Approved lots have a much higher

> "To go beyond is as bad as to fall short."
>
> "Fish see the bait but not the hook; we see the profit but not the peril."
>
> Chinese proverbs

market value than raw land.) Many lenders offer mortgage loans for the purchase of building lots when home construction is planned within a short time (usually less than a year). Another loan, called a construction loan, is written after the lot has been purchased. It enables the buyer to draw money out to pay construction costs as they become due. When a building is complete, it must be sold, or the short-term construction loan must be refinanced with a long-term mortgage.

In rental-property investment, the amount you can or should borrow will often depend on whether your goal is monthly income from the property or appreciation and profit upon sale. If you want more positive cash flow, you borrow less. If you're betting on appreciation, future sales potential, and the benefits of declared losses on your federal tax return, you borrow more.

When buying vacation property, you may well choose to mortgage to the maximum available even though the rental income will fall short of covering costs. That may sound like a loser strategy, but some people see the loss as far less than they would pay to vacation elsewhere each year.

STOP AND THINK!

You can reduce the amount of your monthly mortgage payment by choosing a longer-term mortgage. This is important if positive cash flow is marginal.

Making the Scheduled Payments

No matter how you dance or juggle in the real estate investment marketplace, scheduled monthly payments will set the beat. It's a rhythm to which you must pay heed if you are to survive. Plan your borrowing, therefore, with careful consideration of cash flow from your investment. And maintain some reserve resources in case of vacancies or unexpected expenses.

Some investors even hold back some of their available down-payment money to establish an emergency reserve fund. This decision makes for a larger principal and higher monthly payments, but affords a security net. Other investors simply choose the longest possible mortgage term in order to obtain the lowest possible monthly debt payment and then put aside positive cash flow in the early years of ownership to establish a reserve fund. This strategy takes real self-discipline; it's always easier to spend cash in hand than to save it.

Weighing Your Options

In the best of all possible worlds, every investor would carefully consider his or her financing options before making an offer to buy any piece of real estate. To do so takes some number crunching and some paperwork and those activities require some stop-and-think time. That may sound pretty easy, but actually *doing* it demands strong self-discipline, especially when you're anxious to make that first offer and find out just how good a deal you can get. Bear in mind that in investment real estate, financing is a part of the deal, a big factor in success, and an element of risk.

Sources of Down-Payment Cash

Let's say that you're a first-time investor who is feeling a little gun-shy about those nothing-down deals. Where will you get the down-payment money?

Available cash is a real problem for many people because the sum you need always runs to tens of thousands of dollars. That's not the kind of money you can easily save in a short period of time. It's too much to count on winning at a casino, even if you're red hot. It's more than the typical annual bonus for us "regular" people. And very few of us win the lottery.

Of course, you might wait for your rich uncle to leave you a handsome inheritance. Actually, inheritance and windfall money is often invested in real estate. But if you don't find yourself suddenly flush, you can still get in. Look around among your current resources. And what do you see? Ah-ha, your home! It's the much touted, most valuable asset most Americans have and it's doing nothing for you except appreciating with the rest of the home marketplace.

Many investors who have considerable equity in their homes consider that equity a source of down-

> ## "Money is like manure. If you spread it around, it does a lot of good, but if you pile it up in one place, it stinks like hell."
>
> Clint W. Murchison, Texas financier

payment money for other real estate investing. There are two ways to tap this resource: so-called home-equity loans and refinancing.

Home-Equity Loans

Home-equity loans are really second mortgages. With the old-fashioned second mortgage, you can borrow a given amount to be repaid over an agreed-upon term. With the newer "revolving" or "flexible" equity line of credit, you can borrow and repay up to an established limit, and borrow again if you choose, paying interest on the outstanding balance only.

The interest rates on second mortgages and equity lines of credit are generally higher than interest rates on first mortgages. It's also important to remember that the home-equity loan is a lien on your property. If you should need to sell (for a business transfer, for example) you must repay the principal of both the first and second mortgages. That could leave you short of down-payment money for another home, unless you also sell your investment property.

If you are using a second mortgage on your home for the down-payment money to purchase investment real estate, be certain that you calculate the cost of that money when considering cash flow and potential profit. In most cases, the interest on a second mortgage on your home is deductible on your federal income-tax return, but that deduction does not entirely wipe out the cost of the loan.

Refinancing

Many investors who are using the equity in their homes to get a start in investment real estate prefer refinancing to taking out a second mortgage. The interest rate will certainly be lower than the going rate of home-equity loans and, if you are lucky and rates are low, you may even get a lower rate for the refinancing than you had on the original mortgage.

There is also an advantage in term. Few second mortgages are written for the 30-year term that is now common in first-mortgage financing. When you refinance, however, you start on a whole new 30-year term. Thus, by getting your down-payment money by refinancing, your new home-mortgage monthly payments will usually be lower than they would be if you were paying on both your established first mortgage and a new second mortgage.

Just as you would with a home-equity loan, however, consider the difference between your old mortgage payment and the proposed new home mortgage loan payment when evaluating your investment purchase. Also factor in closing costs on the refinancing. In some cases, you may be required to pay points and title insurance costs again.

Let's Get a Group Together

Group investing often works very well, with each investor contributing a portion of the required down payment and then sharing proportionately in the profits—and the expenses.

But there is potential danger here. You could easily lose friends or even start a family feud. To keep potential problems to a minimum, get an attorney to help you establish a partnership with written rules, or create a corporation.

When buying property with a group, be certain that the mortgages are *nonrecourse* loans. Without the nonrecourse provision, the personal property of every member of the group can be at risk in the event of default on the mortgage. This situation can be especially painful if default is caused by the withdrawal of financial support by one or more partners because of bankruptcy or personal problems.

Shared Appreciation and Participation Financing

Because the majority of real estate investments are profitable, there are a number of lenders who will lend money without adhering to the usual rules and guidelines of

---

LEARNING THE LANGUAGE

With a **nonrecourse** clause in a mortgage agreement, the lender waives the requirement for any personal liability on the part of the borrower or borrowers. In the event of default on the loan, the lender's remedies are limited to foreclosure of the mortgage and acquisition of the property. Each borrower's personal property and income cannot be touched.

good mortgage lending—that is *if* they get a share in the potential profits. In home financing, the practice is called a shared-appreciation mortgage (SAM). In commercial and investment projects, it's usually called participation financing. The financing arrangement can mean little or no down payment required and significantly reduced interest rates, but it will surely cut into your profits.

The SAM is usually used for single-family house and condominium purchases. The loan agreement allows the lender to secure an interest in the potential appreciation of the collateral property over a stated period of time. For example, a lender could reduce the down-payment requirement to 2 percent of the appraised value and the interest rate to a full point below the current prevailing rate in exchange for, let's say, a 20 percent share of the property's increased value over a four- to six-year period. Ownership of the property is recorded in the buyer's name only but the loan agreement spells out the lender's share in future increased value. Unless the property is sold during the term of the agreement (and there are usually strict rules about that), the buyer/borrower is generally required either to sell or to refinance the property at a stipulated time (during the last year of the term, for example) in order to pay off the lender's share. Refinancing, of course, requires that a professional appraisal be done.

The participation mortgage is really a partnership arrangement between mortgagor and mortgagee. In these deals, the lender usually accepts a higher loan-to-value ratio (meaning little or no down payment) and a lower interest rate, and in return takes a share of ownership in the property. The lender's ownership share may be as little as 5 percent, or as high as 50 percent and sometimes even more when workouts of failed projects are undertaken. (Workout is the financial jargon for debt refinancing after bankruptcy or failure to meet payment obligations.)

Should you consider this kind of financing? It works for some people. It's not always easy to find lenders, however, especially when times are lean or when you have no established track record in the real estate marketplace. But it does have an added feature: the borrower will get an extra (and well-experienced) opinion about the value of the property. The lender is very unlikely to enter into participation financing unless the odds of profitability are high.

DIGGING DEEPER

Several national and regional **mortgage-reporting services** are available to the general public. Try exploring these Web sites.

Bank Rate Monitor
http://www.bankrate.com

This site provides average national and state consumer bank rates and samples of lenders' rates in each state's metropolitan areas.

HSH Associates
237 West Parkway
Pompton Lakes, NJ 07444
800-873-2837
http://www.hsh.com

This company collects data from approximately 2,000 mortgage lenders in selected markets nationwide. You can purchase (online or by phone) individual weekly reports of lenders' offerings in your area.

Kiplinger Online
http://www.kiplinger.com

Kiplinger offers an extensive array of online mortgage shopping opportunities and "what if" financial calculators.

Quicken
http://www.quicken.com

This online service from Intuit, makers of Quicken money-management software, provides an online mortgage brokerage that features six large national lenders and includes online applications.

Picking Your Loan

Just as in making a real estate purchase, it's important to remember that every mortgage-financing deal is unique. It is tied to a particular piece of property (called the collateral), dependent upon the unique buyer's financial situation, and contracted to the agreed-upon payback terms. Add to this the thousands of potential lenders and you have an aspect of real estate investing that can sometimes feel overwhelming. Danger lies in seeing the purchase as more important than the financing and therefore accepting whatever financial arrangement is suggested to you.

No matter how distasteful it may seem, you must shop for financing. Ask the mortgage loan departments at local banks for their loan-to-value and qualification requirements. Tap mortgage-reporting and rate-quoting services and online mortgage brokers on the Internet. Compare offerings for seller financing with what is available in the mortgage marketplace. And use a mortgage broker to help you hunt for loans from sources not restricted by the secondary marketplace.

You can and should do a great deal of financial preparation even before you choose a property. Use the worksheet on page 177 to help you gather the necessary data. Then compare each factor lender by lender to find the loans that best suit your investment needs and goals. For added safety, when you are ready to buy, have your financing documents reviewed by a lawyer before you commit to anything. Attorney review is especially important if you are using unconventional financing agreements.

WORKSHEET FOR MORTGAGE SHOPPING

Lender _____

_____

Name of representative _____

Phone and Web site _____

_____

Loan type _____

_____

Loan-to-value ratio _____

Qualification requirements _____

_____

Interest rate _____

Points _____

_____

Other fees _____

_____

Notes _____

_____

_____

_____

KEEP IN MIND

- **Leverage can greatly increase profit** in the real estate marketplace.
- **Down-payment requirements vary,** depending upon the property and the lender.
- **There are some low-down-payment, low-interest-rate financing opportunities** available for home-investment properties (owner-occupied two- to four-unit houses) and for nonowner-occupied properties (sometimes called NOOs).
- **Beware seller financing.** Check it out before you agree.
- **Some investors choose to tap home equity** as a source for the down payment on investment property.
- **If you decide to purchase property with a group,** establish a legal partnership or corporation.

What About Taxes?

"Death and taxes and childbirth! There's never any convenient time for any of them."
Margaret Mitchell (1900–1949), *Gone With the Wind*

magine a builder's tract of upscale homes. Perhaps 20 houses are built and occupied, another 10 are in various stages of construction, and several of the remaining 30 vacant lots display "Sold" signs. Can you guess the topic of conversation most likely to come up at the first neighborhood cocktail party or backyard barbecue?

You guessed right! Real estate. Homeowners will almost certainly talk about the pace of sales, the builder's latest price increase and how much higher he's likely to go, the quality of construction, and local property taxes. Those who are a little worried that perhaps they paid too much might mention the fact that *new* houses are surely the best bet for staying ahead of inflation and rapidly rising property costs in the area.

But there are bound to be a few homeowners in this group who just won't talk about their particular deals. Often they're feeling the pinch of high monthly payments (mostly interest) that are the result of the low-down-payment deal the builder made with a nearby lender. Many of these homeowners hang on knowing that the interest is deductible on federal income tax returns. That deduction is likely to result in a hefty tax refund come April. Uncle Sam again comes to the aid of the property owner.

You might even find a homeowner or two in the group who is thinking that he or she has really bought more house than was needed, wanted, or could be afforded. Thoughts of selling in a couple of years and moving down in price are cushioned by the tax break that was created in the Taxpayer Relief Act of 1997. That law allows married couples filing jointly to take up to $500,000 profit on the sale of their homes tax-free (single taxpayers are allowed $250,000), without the obligation to buy an equal or higher-priced home. (You can do this once every two years if you have lived in the home, but only for your primary residence.)

If you're a homeowner, chances are you've already had an introduction to the give-and-take relationship that exists between owners of real estate and the IRS. Perhaps you're even thinking that tax benefits are really one of the plus points of real estate investment, not something to be worried about. Well, be warned: You haven't even seen the top of the mountain yet!

Taxation laws regarding investment real estate are different from and far more complex than those regarding home ownership. Investment-property tax laws can sometimes even make negative cash flow look appealing.

LEARNING THE LANGUAGE

Tax shelter is an all-inclusive term referring to any method used by investors to avoid or reduce tax liability legally. Investment real estate is considered a tax shelter because of allowable deductions for interest paid on mortgages, maintenance costs, depreciation, and, under certain circumstances, the ability to defer payment of capital gains taxes.

If you don't already have one, now is the time to get yourself a good tax lawyer or a CPA who specializes in tax issues because these tax laws are not only complex but also full of opportunities for tax shelter. It is *not* a good idea to attempt to do your own tax returns when investment property is a factor. If you do, you might just find yourself mired down in a stormy April. With good professional advice, however, April need not be the cruelest month.

Tax laws can work for or against real estate investors. A decision made at any time during the year may turn out to be costly or cost-saving at tax time. That's why it's important to use the services of a tax professional both before the deal is done and frequently during the course of ownership. Investment real estate purchases, financing, improvements, and sales made with the tax laws in mind can save you many thousands of dollars, not to mention some severe stress headaches.

Tax professionals can also keep you up-to-date on changes in the tax laws and how they might affect you and the property you hold. Without professional training, it's often difficult to make the connections between new legislation and your particular situation. It is very important to remember that tax laws can and do change and that printed information about them can be out-of-date by the time you actually read it. So read tax material carefully to understand the *concepts* of real estate taxation. Then check with your tax advisor for the current figures and status before you act.

According to the IRS . . .

The two most common kinds of income a taxpayer can have are ordinary income and capital gains. Both are part of your real estate investment plan. Ordinary income includes wages, bonuses and commissions, rents, royalties, and bank interest. It is taxed on a sliding scale at various rates according to the amount of the annual income, up to a maximum rate of 35 percent. Capital gains are generated when you sell possessions for a profit, including stocks and real estate.

Capital gains fall into two classifications:
1. Long term (ownership for 12 months or more)
2. Short term (ownership for less than 12 months)

Short-term gain is taxed at the same rate as ordinary income. Long-term gain is taxed at a maximum of 15 percent. (Taxpayers in the 10 percent to 15 percent income tax brackets with incomes less than $58,100 on joint returns or $29,050 on single returns have capital gains taxed at 5 percent as of May 6, 2003. As of 2008, the proposed rate for these taxpayers is 0 percent.)

Rent (or more correctly, the positive cash flow from your rental building) is taxed as ordinary income. Your profit from the sale of your property is taxed at the capital gains rate if you owned it for more than a year. In either case, both lowering the amount of tax liability and delaying the need to make tax payments (sometimes for many years) are possibilities. In fact, getting as many tax benefits as possible is the goal of every smart investor. And it's all perfectly legal.

Most small-property real estate investors have "day jobs" that generate the major part of their income outside the real estate marketplace and in professions unrelated to real estate. Sometimes exactly how much time they spend in the real estate investment marketplace makes a difference on their federal tax returns. The IRS taxes part-time investors differently from those who buy and sell real estate as a profession.

According to the Internal Revenue Service, real estate professionals are persons who perform at least half of their services in businesses related to real estate and spend at least 750 hours a year working at it. (That's 20-plus weeks of full-time work or 14½ hours a week for 52 weeks a year.) These "professionals" are considered "active" investors and are allowed to claim all the real estate loss deductions they have coming in the year that they incur them.

LEARNING THE LANGUAGE

Tax evasion is the failure to pay taxes that are due or the falsifying of information on a return to reduce the amount of tax due. It can also include failure to file a return or provide complete information on a return. It is illegal and punishable by fines and imprisonment.

Tax avoidance is reducing the amount of tax due by the timing of income and expenditures within the limitations set by current tax law. It is legal.

STOP AND THINK!

To claim many of the tax benefits associated with investment real estate, you must show that you are "actively involved" in its management. The IRS has interpreted actively involved to mean that you set the rent, approve tenants, and decide on capital improvements. This does not mean that you cannot hire management help; you

simply must remain in control. For more details, read IRS Publication 527, *Residential Rental Property (Including Vacation Homes)*.

IRS publications are available online at **http://www.irs.gov** or by calling **800-829-3676.**

Everyone else is considered a "passive" investor and has limitations on the deductibility of current expenses. But don't panic. There are allowances for good behavior, and the deal really isn't bad at all. Even if you are classified as a passive investor, all you have to do is prove that you are "actively involved" in the management of your property and you will qualify for substantial deductions.

For details defining passive investor, read IRS Publication 925, *Passive Activity and At-Risk Rules*. Meanwhile, here's a quick take on what you get if you're a passive investor who is actively involved.

- **You can deduct against your rental income** all property losses, including damage, theft, and depreciation (more about depreciation in the next section), and expenses such as maintenance, management fees, property taxes, debt service, and insurance.

- **If you come up with a negative number** (a loss for the year), you can deduct up to $25,000 ($12,500 if married and filing separately) in rental-property losses against your other income, such as salary, bonuses, or capital gains.

- **If your adjusted gross income is more than $100,000** ($50,000 if married and filing separately) you will be denied 50 cents of the loss allowance for every dollar you make over $100,000. (The entire $25,000 loss allowance disappears at an adjusted gross income of $150,000.)

- **Loses that are disallowed in one year,** however, can be saved and applied to reducing rental or other "passive" income that you might make in future years.

- **If you do not get a chance to use disallowed losses** during the time that you own the property, the IRS says in Publication 925:

  "Any passive activity losses (but not credits) that have not been allowed (including current year losses) generally are allowed in full in the tax year you dispose of your entire interest in the passive (or former passive) activity."

In readable English that means: *When you sell the property, you can deduct the total losses that have been disallowed on it to this time.* But there are some restrictions (if you

---

STOP AND THINK!

Avoid the IRS's **"dealer"** designation. People who buy and sell multiple properties in a year can be considered dealers by the IRS. The dealer does not get capital gains tax benefits because all profits on property are considered ordinary income. The dealer cannot depreciate property (even if held for the long term) and all rents are counted as ordinary income. Most investors who turn over many properties a year do so in names other than their own, such as separate corporations or limited liability companies.

---

give the property away or if you will it to someone, for example), so be sure to consult with your tax advisor before applying this loss.

Protecting Your Investment Income

We discussed how to calculate your cash flow in Chapter 6. To review briefly, you can deduct from rental income all of your expenses in running the building including repair and maintenance costs, management fees, debt service, property taxes and special assessments, insurance, and even a mileage allowance for all those times you must go there to collect overdue rent, settle a dispute, or unclog a sink. What we haven't yet discussed is the tax benefit that allows you to put more of that cash into your pocket. It's called depreciation.

Down, Down in Value . . . No Matter What!

Depreciation is the principal way of sheltering positive cash flow from taxation. With it, you have the right to claim as a deduction a certain portion of the value of a property just because you own it, with no relationship to whether or not it is wearing out or losing value. In the past, depreciation could be accelerated in the early years, but according to today's tax laws, only straight-line depreciation can be used. Properties purchased before tax-law changes in 1993, 1986, and 1981 continue to be depreciated according to the more taxpayer-friendly laws prevailing at the time they were put in service.

As of this writing, if you purchase residential rental real estate (single-family houses, multifamily houses, condominiums, or apartment buildings), the IRS has established 27.5 years as the economic life (recovery period) of the property and requires that you depreciate it over that time. You must use straight-line depreciation, which means that for each full year of ownership, you can deduct a depreciation loss of 1/27.5 of the price you paid. (That's about 3.64 percent.) The depreciation loss for the first year is partial, prorated according to the proportion of ownership time in that year.

If you invest in nonresidential investment property (office buildings, warehouses, or stores, for example) your recovery period will be 39 years. In each year after the first year, you can deduct a depreciation loss of 1/39 of the price you paid for the building. (That's about 2.5 percent.)

If you invest in mixed-use property (part commercial and part rental residential), you will have to

> **"There are occasions when it is undoubtedly better to incur loss than to make gain."**
>
> Titus Maccius Plautus (c. 254–184 BC), Roman playwright

LEARNING THE LANGUAGE

When the word **depreciation** is used in doing federal tax returns, it means a loss in value that is created by an accounting procedure used for the purpose of tax deduction. Tax depreciation has no relationship to whether the property has gained or lost value in the marketplace.

Straight line-depreciation reduces the value of the property by set equal amounts each year over its established economic life. In other words, the same amount is deducted each year as a depreciated loss whether you're in year two of ownership or year 22.

The period of time during which depreciation is allowed is called the **recovery period.**

establish the proportion of each in the building and calculate two depreciation schedules accordingly. If you purchase a building that is partly your home and partly residential or commercial property, you will also have to prorate depreciation on the investment portion of the building, according to the proper schedules. (The portion of the building that is your home cannot be depreciated, but remember that you are exempt from paying capital gains taxes on up to $500,000 profit from that portion for a married couple filing jointly, $250,000 for a single person.)

Before you begin running off figures to see how much depreciation you can take, you must always take into account the fact that land is not depreciable. Your calculations, therefore, must be done on the value of the buildings only. The easiest way to determine the value of the buildings is to refer to your local tax assessment, which will show valuations for land and buildings separately. If the figures do not add up to your purchase price, calculate the percentage that has been allotted to the land and to the buildings and apply it to your purchase price.

You can also consult the breakdown done by the insurance company for the property. Land is not only not depreciable but also not insurable, so an insurance company separates out the value of the land when it appraises property. If you are still not comfortable with the figures, consult the bank appraisal that was done with your mortgage application. The appraisal technically belongs to the lender, but you can request a copy.

STOP AND THINK!

Every time ownership changes, the property is said to be **"put in service"** and the depreciation schedule starts all over again. It makes no difference if a house is 10 years old or 100 years old when you buy it, according to the IRS, it has an economic life of 27.5 years after the date title passes from one owner to another.

And remember, land is not depreciable!

Keeping the Records Straight

Every real estate investor wants to get his or her maximum allowable break on taxes. To do that, you must keep records and those records must be clear, accurate, and documented. You'll need them to prepare your tax return every year. And you'll need them if you ever face a tax audit.

Apart from satisfying government requirements, you'll also need these records to evaluate the performance of the property before you decide to improve it or put it on the market. You'll need the records to refinance if you want to get some of your profits out of the property while still holding ownership (more about that in just a bit). And you'll need good records to help convince someone else to buy the property when you are ready to sell.

In fact, if you are worried about any aspect of your real estate investment plan, you can begin the work of addressing that fear by keeping and reviewing records relating to it. Good records will allow you and your tax advisor to run figures using every available method of calculation. Working with records at hand, you can

---

HOW DEPRECIATION LOWERS YOUR FEDERAL INCOME-TAX LIABILITY

Let's assume that you are in the third year of ownership of a two-unit house. You paid $250,000 for the property. The value of the land is $50,000. Your basis for tax depreciation purposes, therefore, is $200,000. You are allowed to depreciate 1/27.5 of the basis. $200,000 divided by 27.5 equals $7,272.7272, so your annual depreciation deduction is $7,272.73.

Annual rental income	**$12,000.00**
Deductible expenses	− 10,500.00
Positive cash flow	$ 1,500.00
Depreciation	− 7,272.73
Taxable income (loss)	**($ 5,772.73)**

The tax loss (up to $25,000) can be applied against ordinary income to reduce tax liability for those who are actively involved in the management of their real estate investment (see limitations noted in the text).

better anticipate and avoid problems. *And* you can go after the most favorable tax treatment.

Now, the idea of all that recordkeeping sounds very high-minded, but there remains one essential question: *What should you keep records of?* Let's go through the basics. Later you can add any other topics that you think are important to your particular property or investment situation.

- **The purchase contract and closing statement.** It is essential that you document the price that you paid for the property because it establishes the basis upon which depreciation will be calculated and from which your capital gains will be figured for tax purposes.

- **Documentation for all expenditures on capital improvements.** If capital improvements are made to the property before putting it into service and collecting rents, their cost can be added to the purchase price and used to raise the basis. If capital improvements are made after the property has been in service for some time, they can still be depreciated but must be done so separately from the purchase price basis depreciation. Your tax advisor will introduce you to the Modified Accelerated Cost Recovery System (MACRS, pronounced mac-ers) that has been in use since 1986. Your records of capital improvements and their depreciation will be needed to establish your *adjusted* basis. (Read "Learning the Language" on page 189.)

- **Documentation for all operating expenses.** Operating expenses include management fees, maintenance and repair costs, utilities, advertising costs, property taxes, interest paid on mortgage debt, insurance, real estate commissions, travel expenses to and from the property, and legal and accounting fees. These are deductible from rental income and will reduce your tax burden.

- **Documentation for all rental income.** Records should be kept not only for rent received but also for security deposits and their disposition and for vacancy periods.

LEARNING THE LANGUAGE

Basis is the value of the property to be used for determining depreciation and tax liability. When a property is purchased, the basis is the cost (price), whether it is fully paid for or not. When a property is inherited or gifted, special rules determine the establishment of the basis, usually based upon a fair market value appraisal.

A **capital improvement** is an improvement made to extend the useful life of a property or add to its value. A new roof is a capital improvement; painting the interior of an apartment is a maintenance item. The installation of new windows is a capital improvement; repairing a broken window is not. Capital improvements can be depre-

ciated according to MACRS; maintenance costs cannot.

The **adjusted basis** is the figure used for computing capital gains on investment property. In most cases, it is determined by taking the original basis (the purchase price) and deducting the total amount of depreciation that has been claimed on the building during the entire period of ownership. Then take capital expenditures and deduct the total amount of the depreciation that has been claimed against them. Add the balances together to get your adjusted basis. The requirement to subtract the total amount of depreciation claimed will lower your basis and thereby increase the "profit" figure upon which you will be taxed.

Capital Gains When You Sell

Profit from the sale of investment real estate is considered a capital gain and taxed as such. As mentioned above, the maximum tax rate for long-term capital gains is 15 percent (lower if your marginal rate for ordinary income is lower and if the gain does not put your total taxable income into a higher tax bracket).

After enjoying the tax benefits of depreciation and operating-cost deductions through all of the years of ownership, investment property owners must pay the piper when they sell. The question every investor ultimately faces is: *How do I pay the least possible tax that is allowed by law?* The answer rests in recordkeeping and in knowledge of the current tax laws.

STOP AND THINK!

Consider **holding time** carefully before you sell a quick-turnaround property. Short-term capital gains are taxed at the same rate as your ordinary income. Selling a property after 11 months of ownership could cause you to lose a significant tax reduction. If possible, you will want to hold a property for at least 12 months to reap the long-term capital gains tax break.

Your first step is to determine your adjusted basis. That is your purchase price minus the depreciation that you have claimed over your years of ownership, plus the cost of major improvements, minus the depreciation you have claimed on those improvements.

Next, determine the adjusted selling price. Take the current selling price of the property and subtract from it the real estate commission, closing costs, and all other expenses that are associated with the sale, such as inspections or tests and the repairs required to close contract.

Finally, subtract your adjusted basis from the adjusted selling price and you have your taxable *profit,* which is the capital gain upon which you will pay taxes. If the adjusted selling price is less than your adjusted basis, you have a loss.

It would be nice to say that the most you will have to pay the IRS is 15 percent of the figure you come up with in your capital gains calculation. But, alas, life on the real estate investment road is not quite that simple. In the ever-changing tax-law area, one of the latest additions has added a new wrinkle of complication. Here it is: Any profit attributable to depreciation after May 6, 1997, is taxed at 25 percent rather than the capital gains rate of 15 percent. In other words, you pay the traditional capital gains tax only on the amount the property has appreciated in value over the years you held it. You must pay a rate of 25 percent on the difference between original purchase price (basis) and the total depreciated value assigned to the property when you sell it.

Because of increased taxation on depreciation, those investors who are selling property that has appreciated only slightly often find themselves with a whopping tax bill, big enough in some cases to wipe out any cash profit. What do they do? Many of them find a way to avoid paying taxes. Read on.

How to Put Off Paying Taxes

If you watch late-night television, you may have seen some "infomercials" where the "host" and the "guests" discuss tax-free exchanges of real estate

COMPUTING YOUR CAPITAL GAIN

Using the same two-unit house example from the box on page 187, let's assume you sell after six years of ownership. All of the figures in this box are approximations because depreciation deductions are prorated to the actual month in which title passes, and tax liability is actually dependent on many variables. If you follow these numbers, however, you'll understand the concept of capital gains taxation on your real estate investment. Be sure to get help on the actual tax return from your professional tax advisor.

Purchase price	$ 250,000
Capital improvements done in year six	+ 25,000
Claimed depreciation	− 43,636
Adjusted basis	$231,364
Selling price	$ 350,000
Real estate commission	− 21,000
Closing costs	− 900
Adjusted selling price	$ 328,100
Adjusted selling price	$328,100
Adjusted basis	−231,364
Taxable capital gain	$ 96,736
Taxable capital gains rate: $53,100 at	
15 percent =	$ 7,965
Claimed depreciation rate: $43,636 at	
25 percent =	+ 10,909
Total tax liability*	$ 18,874

* Payment of taxes can be postponed with a like-kind exchange. See "Learning the Language" on page 192.

investment properties. Don't pin your hopes on these sales-pitch dreams. Aside from the sale of one's primary residence, there are no tax-free profits in real estate. The come-pay-for-my-seminar guys on TV are talking about tax-*deferred* exchanges. Under the deferred-tax exchange laws, you can continue to defer tax payment until you sell an investment property and do not buy another.

That sounds pretty tempting, right? Beware! Exchanging to defer tax payment on investment property capital gains is a complex process. If you break one of its rules, you will become ineligible for the exchange and you will be required to pay your tax. There's no leeway or courteous exception made in this arena.

The 1031 exchanges (named for the section of the Internal Revenue Code that describes them) are done through a neutral third party called a facilitator, exchanger, or qualified intermediary. To qualify, the exchanger cannot be a relative, a business partner, an employee, your real estate agent, or your attorney. When doing an exchange, the money obtained from the sale of your property is held in escrow by the exchanger. If you actually hold the money, even for one day, the exchange is disqualified and you will owe taxes.

LEARNING THE LANGUAGE

The **1031 exchanges,** sometimes called **Starker exchanges,** allow for the postponement of capital gains tax payment when another property of like-kind is purchased within a specified time period.

When dealing in investment real estate, the IRS has defined like-kind as any property held for business, trade, or investment purposes. The liberal definition means that you can use a 1031 exchange to defer taxes when you sell an apartment building and buy raw land, or vice versa.

A tax credit is a direct (dollar credit for dollar spent) reduction in tax liability. In contrast, a **tax deduction** reduces tax liability only by the percentage of the taxpayer's bracket. A tax credit is deducted after the tax liability is computed. For example, an investor whose tax liability computed to $15,000 would pay only $10,000 if he took advantage of a $5,000 tax credit.

Once you sign an agreement with an exchanger stating your intention to exchange, you have 45 days after the close of the sale on your old property to identify a new property for purchase. You must close on the purchase of your new property within 180 days of the date of closing on your old property—no exceptions.

To avoid paying taxes, you must acquire property that is of equal or greater value and equal or greater in debt (mortgage) than the property you sell. If you withdraw equity from an exchange, you will pay tax on the amount you withdraw. You are not allowed to exchange property in the United States for property in another country.

Because of the complexity of the exchange process, it is essential that you choose a well-qualified exchanger. Most commercial real estate brokers, real estate attorneys, and tax advisors will be able to recommend exchangers working in your area.

> ## STOP AND THINK!
>
> You are not taxed when you take equity out of an investment property before you sell it. For example, suppose your first property has appreciated in market value by 50 percent. You want to buy another property using a part of the increased equity as a down payment. You know, however, that equity will be decreased by selling costs and taxes if you sell.
>
> Rather than sell, many investors refinance the original property. Even though the amount you take out of the property by refinancing is more than you put in, you are not taxed on the withdrawal of funds. Bear in mind, however, that you will pay taxes on the entire profit when you sell the original property. Hopefully by then the equity you withdrew will also have grown into a significant positive return far greater than the taxes due on it.

A Few More Ways to Save on Taxes

On specific types of property, the federal government offers some additional tax incentives. Generally, the rules are both detailed and complex, so if any of the following investments appeal to you, be sure to confer with your tax advisor before proceeding.

Historic Structures

The Tax Reform Act of 1986 provides a 20 percent tax credit for rehabilitation of historic buildings. To qualify as a historic building, the building must meet the following two criteria:

1. **The building must be a certified historic structure.** That means it must be an investment property (depreciable) that fits at least one of three categories. It must be: (1) listed in the National Register of Historic Places; (2) located in a historic district designated under state or local statute as containing standards satisfactory to the Secretary of the Interior; or (3) located in a Registered Historic District and certified by the Secretary of the Interior as being of particular historic significance to the district.

2. **The rehabilitation itself must be certified** by the Secretary of the Interior as being consistent with the historic character of the property or district.

Older Commercial Buildings

The federal tax law allows a 10 percent tax credit for rehabilitation of nonresidential structures built before 1936. These buildings are not required to have any historic significance.

Low-Income Residential Buildings

If you buy low-income housing that is at least ten years old, you may qualify for a 4 percent annual tax credit for up to ten years. If you build new low-income housing or if you significantly rehabilitate an older building for low-income housing, you may be able to qualify for a 9 percent annual write-off that can continue in effect over a ten-year period.

KEEP IN MIND

- **Because tax laws** for investment property are more complex than those for home purchase and sale, it is essential to use a professional tax advisor both before buying or selling and during the period of ownership.
- **Tax avoidance is legal;** tax evasion is not.
- **To be regarded by the IRS** as "actively involved" in your real estate investment, you must set the rent, approve tenants, and decide upon capital improvements.
- **By claiming depreciation,** you establish a paper loss that can be deducted from rental income and allows you to keep more of your positive cash flow or to create a beneficial paper tax loss.
- **Current law allows** only straight-line depreciation for real estate.
- **Every time ownership changes,** the depreciation schedule starts all over again.
- **Careful recordkeeping** is essential to establish the basis for depreciation, account for all capital improvements, document operating expenses, and document all rental income.
- **Capital gains tax** is paid on the adjusted basis. The tax rate is a maximum of 15 percent on the appreciation of the property above the nondepreciated basis, and 25 percent on the depreciated amount.
- **The 1031 tax exchanges** defer tax liability; they do not eliminate it.
- **There are some federal programs** that offer tax credit on rehabilitated property.

Single-Family Fixer-Uppers

"Own your own cave and be secure."
Fred Flintstone

Single-family houses are among the most popular and the least popular investment vehicles available today.

"How can that be?" you ask. "It's either one or the other."

Not at all. The appeal of single-family houses depends very much on the investment goals of the buyer. They are the most popular among two groups of buyers: (1) short-term investors who want to take their profit quickly and move on and (2) first-time investors who want to use sweat equity as a means of getting started on their real estate investment plan. Single-family houses are rarely chosen by investors who want long-term positive cash flow from their property.

Why Buy Single-Family Houses?

Most single-family houses bought by investors are properties in need of repair. Their degree of distress ranges from fixer-uppers that really need only cleaning and cosmetic improvements to total rehabs that require structural repair as well as refurbishing. The four most common reasons for choosing this investment vehicle are:

1. **Below market-value purchase price**
2. **Short holding time**
3. **Quick and significant profits on a relatively small capital investment**
4. **No tenants**

Below Market-Value Purchase Price

For the investor, the attractiveness of single-family fixer-uppers lies in the fact that they are generally unattractive to the homebuying public. Most homebuyers want clean and pretty, even when they say aloud that condition and cleanliness don't matter. In most cases, emotion weighs in on their buying decision and they just can't see themselves living in "such a mess."

So the number of potential buyers for a single-family house in need of repair is limited. That limited demand creates a buyer's market. A buyer's market means a weak negotiating hand for the seller. As a result, most single-family houses in need of repair sell at prices well below market value for a similar house in good condition. In other words, fixer-uppers are usually bargain properties. How to be certain you're actually getting a bargain will come into the spotlight in just a bit.

LEARNING THE LANGUAGE

Holding time or **holding period** is ownership time. When used by the IRS, the term refers to the length of ownership time used to determine if an investment qualifies for long-term capital gains tax treatment.

Short Holding Time

Holding time for the fixer-upper is the time from the purchase closing date to the sale closing date. It includes the time necessary to complete the repairs, market the property, and await the closing paperwork.

The length of holding time depends on:

- **The amount and complexity of the repair work that must be done**
- **The number of owner/investors doing the work**
- **The time they have available to give to the project**
- **The number of professional contractors that must be scheduled and their availability**
- **The on-the-market selling time, which depends upon the desirability of the property after repairs have been completed and upon the pace of the local real estate marketplace**

Quick and Significant Profits

Your capital investment in a single-family fixer-upper is the total of the down payment, the repair costs, the costs for obtaining and carrying the mortgage loan, property taxes for the period of ownership, insurance, and closing costs (including title insurance). By using leverage, the successful investment choice brings a return that can be double the capital investment or more within a relatively short period of time.

Depending on the length of holding time, the profit will be taxed as ordinary income or a capital gain. You must hold the property for 12 months or more to qualify for the long-term capital gains tax rate. If you sell before the year is out, the short-term rate, which is the same as your rate for ordinary income, will be used.

No Tenants

Ask any professional real estate investor and he or she will almost certainly tell you that the worst headaches in the business come from tenants. Rental real estate investment is management intensive, and that management must deal not only with recordkeeping and maintenance but also with the people who are living in your investment property.

For those who do not want to work with long-term leases and tenant problems, the fixer-upper is frequently the investment vehicle of choice. It limits management problems to planning, doing the repairs, and marketing the property.

Getting in through the Back Door

In many areas where state and municipal homesteading programs are in effect, the beginning investor can buy a fixer-upper with little or no down payment just by moving in and calling the place home. After living there for two years or more while the repairs are being done, the investor can sell the property for a profit without paying federal income taxes on the gain (assuming the profit is no more than $500,000 for those filing jointly or $250,000 for those filing single returns).

> ## "Remember that time is money."
>
> Benjamin Franklin
> (1706–1790), American statesman

STOP AND THINK!

Remember: To qualify for the **homeowner tax exemption,** you must live in the property for at least two years and it must be your primary residence.

The cash you take away from the closing table in the sale of a fixer-upper called "home" can be used, of course, as a down payment on another home, but that use is not required by the current tax laws. You can use part of the profit as a home down payment and part as down payment on another investment property. Or you can buy two investment properties.

Your Profile for Success

Are you the type for fixer-uppers? Let's look at how the criteria we talked about in Chapter 3 apply to this investment vehicle. Each characteristic will be rated high demand, moderate demand, or low demand.

- **Assertiveness** (high demand). If you want to get in on good deals and get quality repairs done quickly, you must be willing to speak up and to act. There are few rewards in this arena for the passive personality. You must be willing to make things happen.
- **Attention to detail** (high demand). Appearances can be deceiving. What looks good on the surface can be bad, and vice versa. Especially when estimating the cost of a fixer-upper, you must look beyond the obvious and take careful notice of the small and inconspicuous. The *quality* (and often the effectiveness) of repair and refurbishing work is also dependent upon attention to detail, whether you are doing the work yourself or supervising the work of contractors.
- **Awareness** (high demand). Your knowledge of the pace of the marketplace, the desirability of the location and the housing style, and the local demographics can translate into significant differences in investment choice, selling time on the market, and profit. Sometimes awareness means gathering and evaluating words heard and over-

---

SINGLE-FAMILY FIXER-UPPERS: A PROFILE FOR SUCCESS

Assertiveness:	XXXXXXXXX
Attention to detail:	XXXXXXXXX
Awareness:	XXXXXXXXX
Creativity:	XXXXXXXXX
Initiative:	XXXXXX
Perseverance:	XXXXXXXXX
Rational judgment:	XXXXXXXXX
Self-confidence:	XXXXXXXXX
Strategic planning:	XXXXXXXXX
Tact:	XXX

heard on the golf course, on public transportation, at zoning board meetings, or while coaching Little League baseball. Sometimes you must read beyond the facts reported in the local newspaper to grasp trends or likely happenings.

- **Creativity** (high demand). The ability to see beyond the surface is essential in this investment vehicle. But that's still not enough. Creativity not only enables an investor to envision new concepts but also to solve problems.
- **Initiative** (moderate demand). In most cases, the demands upon your initiative in the single-family fixer-upper will be generated by the structure and condition of the building. You will have to make a plan for doing the repairs and follow it. You will not be required to go out seeking new battlegrounds. If you are contemplating an addition or a change in the use of the property, however, you will have to initiate the paperwork for changes that require zoning-board approval.
- **Perseverance** (high demand). Once you begin a fixer-upper project, you must stay the course and finish it. Partially finished projects almost never bring a good market price.
- **Rational judgment** (high demand). The financial success of a fixer-upper is almost always dependent on careful analysis of the costs involved in repair and the projected time needed for those repairs. Even before you take on cost estimates, however, it is essential that you use good judgment in selecting a property.
- **Self-confidence** (high demand). If you don't believe that you can succeed, you probably won't. Lack of self-confidence can also cost you big bucks if you have to pay contractors to do tasks or complete projects that you could have done yourself.
- **Strategic planning** (high demand). Planning is to success in the fixer-upper as training is to success in track and field events—it's awfully hard to win without it.
- **Tact** (low demand). Except for dealings with your repair contractors, this vehicle puts high demands on mental and physical skills rather than social skills.

> ### STOP AND THINK!
>
> In the eyes of prospective buyers, **some repairs and renovations count for more** and therefore bring a better return than others do. Basically, buyers are more concerned with results that they can see rather than with results that do not change the appearance of a piece of property. If you buy a fixer-upper that needs to have lead paint removed to satisfy state laws, for example, it may not be easy to get the cost of doing so reflected in your selling price. On the other hand, an exterior paint job can return ten times its cost in added value.

Time, Work, and Money

OK! You think you have what it takes in character traits to take on the fixer-upper. Now test out the time, work, and money demands of this investment vehicle.

Holding Time and Taxes

The single-family fixer-upper's holding period can be as little as two or three months or longer than a year. Although repair work and the resale marketing time are the primary factors in length of ownership, federal income tax laws sometimes become yet another factor. In certain situations, investors intentionally delay closing on the sale of their properties to meet the 12-month holding time that allows them to qualify for long-term capital gains tax treatment. For example, a contract for the sale of the property can be written with occupancy granted in advance of the closing date. There is usually a payment arranged for the period of occupancy before closing.

To lower the carrying costs while marking time for tax purposes, fixer-upper properties are sometimes rented for short terms before or even after the fix-up work is completed. Some after-fix-up rentals are really part of a sales-incentive deal. When the prospective buyer is short on down payment money, some sellers use a lease with option to buy to facilitate the sale. In the rent/buy arrangement, it is agreed that some or all of the rent will be applied toward the purchase price if the tenant exercises the option and closes the deal.

Why give away this rental money? Well, to start with, a seller can often command a higher purchase price and higher rent in a lease-with-option deal because the rent is being credited against the purchase price. The seller also benefits because the promised credit toward purchase price increases the likelihood that the option will be exercised. In other words, it encourages the prospective buyer to close on the purchase rather than walk away. If the option is not exercised, all those rental credits toward purchase are lost as ordinary rent.

Holding time without rental or lease/purchase agreements can be expensive. It all depends upon your financing agreements. Sometimes financing agreements arrange for interest to be paid at the end of each year and the principal in a lump sum upon sale of the property (called a *straight-term mortgage*). This eliminates (or more accurately, *postpones*) the largest single monthly carrying cost. Most fixer-upper investors also do not make monthly property tax payments, waiting instead until the closing of the sale to do so. Finally, short-term loans can sometimes speed up the work on a fixer-upper by providing funds for materials and labor.

> ## LEARNING THE LANGUAGE
>
> In the real estate marketplace, an **option** is the right to lease or purchase a piece of property at a named price on or before a named date and at agreed-upon terms. In most cases, a **consideration** (sometimes a flat fee, sometimes a percentage of the agreed-upon purchase price) is paid for the option. Sometimes the option fee is applied to the purchase price when the option is exercised, and sometimes not.
>
> **A lease with the option to buy** is a rental agreement that includes the option to buy the property on or before a given date at agreed-upon price and terms. Sometimes all or part of the rent can be applied toward the purchase price.

Working Time

While holding time in the single-family fixer-upper is usually short by real estate standards, the working time can seem grueling and never-ending. If you do all or most of the work yourself, you will need skills, supplies, and available working hours—not to mention endurance and a good, working shower on-site. If you use

"We continue to overlook the fact that work has become a leisure activity."

Mark Abrams, *The Observer*, June 3, 1962

professional contractors for all or part of the work, you will be required to find qualified people, schedule their work, and either supervise or evaluate their performance. Not to mention find the money to pay them.

Both houses in need of a cosmetic face-lift and houses in need of refurbishing are likely candidates for the beginning investor's strategy of living in the house while doing the repairs. Total rehabs that require major repairs, however, can rarely be occupied while the necessary work is in progress; and even if you can find a way to live in part of the house while working on the remainder, the process is generally long and costly, and often stressful. Because of the risks involved in living in close proximity with unfinished construction and repair work, the live-in rehab option is usually not suitable for families with young children.

Putting Money In

Working cash is a major concern in the fixer-upper investment because the property usually generates no income during holding time. It is important, therefore, to allow for repair and carrying costs in your borrowing plan. Remember these three points:

1. **Repairs may take longer than you anticipated.**
2. **Repairs may cost more than you estimated.**
3. **Once repairs are completed, the property may take longer to sell than you planned.**

Don't cut your allowance of available cash too closely. It is preferable to borrow more than you think you will need and pay interest on that extra cash rather than to find yourself short and possibly facing mechanics' liens and foreclosure proceedings. That kind of financial pressure leads to negotiating compromises when an offer to buy is made. Such compromises inevitably lead to reduced profits.

Consider the market value of the improvements you choose to make. The "Stop and Think" box on page 205 will give you some examples of cost versus return. Also factor in time. Improvements that require a great deal of time are usually costly.

STOP AND THINK!

Consider the cost and return relation-ship of these improvements.

- New windows
- New roof

Low Cost with High Return
- Exterior and interior painting
- Yard cleaned and landscaped
- New kitchen flooring
- Hardwood floors sanded and refinished
- New lighting fixtures

High Cost with High Return
- Kitchen remodeling, including cabinets and appliances
- Bathroom remodeling, including tile and fixtures
- Addition of a bathroom
- Addition of a garage

High Cost with Little or No Return
- Bracing, buttressing, or rebuilding foundation
- Waterproofing foundation or regrading to eliminate water seepage
- Decontaminating soil around once-buried oil tank
- Radon remediation, lead-paint removal, or elimination of other health hazards
- Termite-damage repair and/or termites eradicated
- New well, pumping equipment, filtration system, and storage tank
- New septic tank, dry well, or leech lines
- Chimney repairs

Checkpoints for a Good Investment

Before you buy a single-family fixer-upper, read Chapter 6 again. Because this investment vehicle usually brings in no sustaining income during the ownership period, its potential for profitable sale is more time-sensitive than rental property and therefore more dependent upon your accurate evaluation of market conditions and property values in the local area.

Investors who call their fixer-uppers "home" feel less time pressure to sell quickly. The requirement for careful market analysis still applies, however. Fixing up the wrong house in the wrong neighborhood can get you stuck where you are currently living. Being unable to sell for a profit can curtail or greatly delay your investment plans.

Location

The value of a given location is a composite of many factors, but probably the most important for the single-family house investor is the character of the surrounding houses. When a fixer-upper is your investment vehicle of choice, search for:

- **Areas close to higher-priced neighborhoods or new construction**
- **Areas experiencing turnaround where scattered houses have already been refurbished or renovated**
- **Areas that are stable and well kept and in which the investment property is among the smallest and/or the only run-down house**
- **A small house in a neighborhood comprised primarily of larger and higher-priced houses**

When commuting is a part of the character of a town, a house located in an area with easy access to public transportation and interstate highways is usually desirable, but avoid houses that abut or overlook these facilities. And of course, houses in municipalities with good reputations for security and highly regarded school systems get bonus points.

Market Appeal

When you buy an investment fixer-upper, you should know the housing features that appeal to the greatest number of potential buyers and try to select property with as many of them as possible. Look for:

- **At least one bathroom or lavatory on each floor**
- **An eat-in kitchen with as much sunlight as possible**

LEARNING THE LANGUAGE

In real estate, the words **gradient** and **grade** refer to the degree of the slope of the land. When you hear **"above grade"** or **"below grade"** in talk about houses, however, the terms usually refer to the relationship of a property to the grade of the road surface on which it fronts.

- **A front-entrance foyer—most buyers object to front doors that open directly into the living room**
- **A gathering room (family room, den) on the main floor of the house (basement "rec" rooms do not add value to a house)**
- **At least a one-car garage (two or more is preferable)**

Whenever possible, avoid properties with additions that cause awkward floor plans or the need to walk through one room to get into another. Also avoid houses that have poor window placement resulting in dark interior spaces, and houses with minimal closet space. Generally, houses that are built below grade level, houses on steep or oddly shaped lots, and houses that have an architectural style that is not in harmony with the neighboring properties are less desirable to the homebuying public and therefore more difficult to sell.

Price, Cost of Repairs, and Profit Potential

Just about everyone thinks he or she knows how to get a good deal in real estate, even if they've never bought an investment property before. Often overheard at the country club are statements such as: "If a property is run-down, you should get 25 percent off the price."

It is *not* a good idea to use asking price as a factor in your property evaluation. Asking prices are almost never selling prices, and they do not necessarily have a relationship to market value. Remember: Asking prices are set by sellers, sometimes by sellers with big dreams. For example, if a property is priced 20 percent above its fair market value and you get 15 percent off the asking price, you've paid too much!

> **DIGGING DEEPER**
>
> If the single-family fixer-upper is your investment vehicle of choice, you might want to consult some more specialized books. Here are some books on the topic:
>
> - *Flipping Properties: Generate Instant Cash Profits in Real Estate* by William Bronchick and Robert Dahlstrom (Dearborn Trade Publishing)
> - *Buy It, Fix It, Sell It: Profit!* by Kevin C. Myers (Dearborn Trade Publishing)
> - *Buying Low, Fixing Smart, Adding Value, and Selling (or Renting) High* by Jay P. DeCima (McGraw-Hill)
> - *Fix It and Flip It: How to Make Money Rehabbing Real Estate for Profit* by Kate Hamilton (McGraw-Hill)

STOP AND THINK!

Often the first offer sets the parameters of the negotiations. And the buyer makes the first offer. When you are the buyer, never pick a number out of the air and never use a fixed percentage of the asking price as your guideline.

In fact, even getting a significant percentage off the fair market value does not guarantee a good deal in the fixer-upper marketplace. Before you start negotiating, calculate two factors:

1. **The market value of the property if it were in good condition**
2. **The cost of repairs that will bring it to marketable condition**

Subtract the cost of repairs from the fair market value. Now you have a starting point—but don't start anything yet. No matter how far your starting-point figure is below the asking price, it does not yet represent a "good deal."

A good deal allows the investor to make a profit. The next step to arriving at your good-deal figure is to factor in (subtract) the cost of carrying the financing, the costs of two closings (buying and selling), insurance during the holding period, and property taxes. Then you must estimate the real estate commission on your probable selling price and subtract that. And still the number you get is not your good-deal price.

Read again the bulleted items in the box titled *Stop and Think* on page 205. It gives you a quick overview of cost and return for a sampling of improvements. If everything takes longer and costs more than you anticipated, your good-deal purchase price might look a lot like a porterhouse steak, well marbled with fat!

You should buy a fixer-upper property anticipating a juicy profit. And then if everything doesn't work out perfectly (and it never does), you'll still come away well rewarded for your efforts.

So how do you arrive at this juicy-deal optimum purchase price? After you've deducted every anticipated cost from an accurate evaluation of the fair market value of the property if it were in good condition, you'll have your breakeven figure. Now look at the amount of capital you have at risk: How much return can you expect for your investment of time and money? Do you want to double your investment? Do you want a 30 percent return? Set a realistic goal.

Now reduce your breakeven figure by your anticipated profit. The result is your target price for purchase. Then begin your negotiating at a lower figure. How much lower depends on the pace of the marketplace, the desirability of the property, and all the information you can gather about the seller's motivation and financial position.

Safeguards in the Contract

In the fixer-upper marketplace, more than with any other investment vehicle, your contract must include contingencies for professional inspections. Read again the inspection-contingency wording rec-

---

LET'S MAKE UP A DREAM DEAL

Seller's asking price	$200,000
Market value with repairs completed	$240,000
Estimated cost of repairs	− 20,000
Starting point for property valuation	$220,000
Miscellaneous and carrying costs	− 7,500
Anticipated real estate commission upon sale	− 14,400
Break-even price	$198,100
Your cash investment	$ 10,000

To triple your investment: Deduct $30,000 from $198,000 = your target price of $168,000
To double your investment: Deduct $20,000 from $198,000 = your target price of $178,000
To make a 50 percent return: Deduct $15,000 from $198,000 = your target price of $183,000

---

ommended in Chapter 8. Be certain that you can withdraw from the contract for any dissatisfaction. Also be certain that you can arrange for more than one inspection because the primary inspection may raise questions that require you to get opinions and estimates from specialized contractors.

Do not allow the seller the option of making repairs and holding you to the contract. You may not like the repairs as the seller chooses to do them. The condition of the property must be to *your* satisfaction before the contract can be binding and before you close title. For a fixer-upper that may mean pretty poor condition, but a condition in which you are *aware* of the problems and choose to work with them. If the seller will not agree to an inspection contingency in the contract, you can arrange to have an inspection done *before* you make an offer and sign a contract to purchase. If the seller won't agree to an inspection, watch out.

In addition to the chance to have the structure and working systems inspected by professionals, the inspection-contingency clause buys you time to:

- Consider your purchase as an investment
- Get competing bids on some of the work that must be contracted out
- Consult with an attorney or financial advisor
- Look at other properties for the sake of comparison
- Price out carefully the cost of materials for the work you plan to do yourself

When setting a cutoff date for the inspection contingency in the contract, allow yourself plenty of time—as much time as you can get the seller to sit still for. Two to three weeks is the most commonly allowed amount of time. Ideally, however, your inspection contingency should run as long as your mortgage contingency, or in some cases even longer.

Speaking of the mortgage contingency, be very specific in the contract. Specify exactly how much mortgage financing you will need and the maximum interest rate you are willing to pay. Remember: You need to have extra money to do the repairs, but you want the

---

DIGGING DEEPER

It's always a good idea to know what your inspector is inspecting. You might want to do some background reading even before you have your first fixer-upper purchase inspected. Here are some suggestions:

- **The Home Inspection Troubleshooter** by Robert Irwin (Dearborn Trade Publishing)
- **Complete Book of Home Inspection** by Norman Becker (McGraw-Hill)
- **Inspecting a House: A Guide for Buyers, Owners, and Renovators** by Carson Dunlop & Associates Ltd. (Dearborn Trade Publishing)
- **Real Estate Home Inspection: Mastering the Profession** by Russell W. Burgess (Dearborn Publishing)

---

lowest possible interest rate. If there is no limit on the interest rate written in the contract, you could be forced to borrow at a high rate. Interest to be paid will reduce your profit.

Maintenance responsibility between the date of the purchase contract and the closing of title is another important point in the fixer-upper purchase contract. Be certain that your contract includes a clause stating that the seller is responsible for delivering the property in the same condition as on the day you signed the purchase contract. Read Chapter 8 again—and take pictures!

Some Financing Tips

One of the best places to find good fixer-upper investment properties is on the REO lists of your local lenders. Often properties that go into foreclosure proceedings are run-down because the owners were unable to afford or not interested in doing repair and maintenance work. Once the lender takes possession, these properties are usually sold on an as-is basis. Even when the lender has arranged to have some of the necessary repairs done by contrac-

Among lenders, **REO** stands for **real estate owned.** The term is used in the real estate marketplace to refer to properties that have been acquired by financial institutions through foreclosure or by deed in lieu of foreclosure. Another term for these properties is **nonperforming assets.**

Deed in lieu of foreclosure is the process by which a mortgagor (borrower) avoids looming foreclosure and the financial stigma associated with it by deeding the property back to the mortgagee (lender).

tors, REOs require careful inspection. The repairs might be cosmetic only.

The good news, however, is that lenders do not want to hold REOs and therefore can often be persuaded to carry the financing for an interested investor, sometimes at terms better than those generally available in the mortgage marketplace. And don't be intimidated by the idea of negotiating with a bank. Banks will often offer attractive deals on properties they have been holding for a period of time.

For those people who want to get started in investment real estate by choosing a home/investment fixer-upper, there are bond-backed community-redevelopment projects in many states. These projects offer lower-than-market interest rates with little or no down payment. Some programs even allow fixer-upper investors to borrow without the requirement of owner-occupancy. Fannie Mae, HUD, and some of the larger nationwide lenders are

DIGGING DEEPER

For information about HUD's 203(k) program to support community revitalization, you can visit its Web site where you'll be able to search online for lenders who participate in the program.

http://www.hud.gov/progdesc/203k—df.cfm

If you would like to browse through printed pamphlets describing other government-supported offerings, or if you would just like to talk with a real person, you can visit you local HUD office. It is listed in the blue pages of your phone book. Most mortgage brokers will also help you to access government-supported programs.

also offering mortgage-loan programs for community revitalization.

As we saw in Chapter 9, the federal government's 203(k) program will allow investors to borrow the cost of purchase *and* the cost of repairs with little or nothing down. This idea of financing both purchase price and fix-up costs has spread to the private sector. For information on program offerings in the private sector, contact your mortgage broker.

You've probably seen advertisements in your local newspapers for HUD-owned properties that are offered for sale or are being auctioned off. The Department of Housing and Urban Development acquires properties through foreclosures on FHA-insured loans. Like other foreclosures, most of these properties are in need of some degree of repair. The Department of Veterans Affairs (VA) also handles some foreclosed properties. Both the FHA and the VA sometimes offer financing on these properties when mortgage loans are not available through conventional sources.

KEEP IN MIND

- **Most of the single-family houses** purchased by investors are fixer-uppers.
- **Bargain prices,** short holding time, quick and significant profits, and no tenants are the reasons for choosing this investment vehicle.
- **You should not use a percentage** of the *asking* price as a guideline for making your first offer.
- **A deal is a good deal** only when it allows the investor to make a profit.
- **Reduce your breakeven estimate** by your anticipated profit. That's your target purchase price.
- **Inspection contingencies** are essential in the fixer-upper purchase contract.
- **You won't be rewarded financially** for fixing environmental or structural problems.
- **You can look for good deal packages** (with financing sometimes included) among the REOs of local lenders.

Multifamily Houses

"It is always wise to look ahead, but difficult to look farther than you can see."
Sir Winston Churchill (1874–1965), British statesman

What exactly is a multifamily house? One dictionary defines it as a building occupied by more than one family. But that definition does not work in the real estate marketplace. We're not talking about a boardinghouse or a big, run-down old mansion in which many immigrant families (without green cards) are illegally housed for high rents.

Multifamily houses are freestanding buildings that have from two to six separate living units, each having its own bedroom, kitchen, and bathroom facilities. Most were built in and around cities, both large and small, during the first half of the 20th century. Some have a single unit on each floor (sometimes called a "flat"), others have two units to a floor, and others, more recently built, often have multifloor units side by side under the same roof. We often call them "town houses."

Why Buy Multifamily Houses?

The four most common reasons that investors choose multifamily houses as their investment vehicle of choice are:

1. **As an entry into the real estate marketplace**
2. **As a chance to use sweat equity to build wealth**
3. **For positive cash flow**
4. **As the first block in a wealth-building pyramid**

"No bird soars too high, if he soars with his own wings."

William Blake (1757–1827), British poet and mystic

The Way In

If you don't yet own any real estate, if you have minimal cash savings, if you have an entry-level salary at the start of your career, and/or if you want to combine your first homebuying experience with your first investment property, you will enter the real estate marketplace much like a child coming into a high-tech theme park. Some of the "rides" look too big and some too scary. Where should you go first?

A multifamily house may well be your first step to financial security, maybe even wealth. It is an investment property that can provide shelter (home) for the investor while also being supported by rental income. As mentioned in Chapter 9, there are a number of federal, state, and community financing programs that allow for the purchase of an owner-occupied multifamily house with little or no down payment. Qualification guidelines for these mortgages are less stringent than in any other investment vehicle, and the rent from the unit or units that you do not occupy is considered as part of the qualifying income.

Sweet Sweat Equity

The maintenance demands of the multifamily house are not much different from those of the single-family house, and both owners and owner-occupants often find that they can save considerable money and build sweat equity by doing much of the maintenance work and renovation themselves. For those investors seeking long-term capital gains, especially owner-occupants, the work can be done over time as cash becomes available and units become vacant and ready for renovation. For those investors seeking a turnover situation more like that of the single-family fixer-upper, cash received from rented units in a multifamily investment can ease the financial drain of carrying the property while renovations to other units, the exterior, or the grounds are in progress.

More Cash Coming In—Less Going Out

If you are comfortable with the requirements of rental-property management, a well-chosen multifamily house can be a long-term positive cash-flow investment. Because most multifamily investment properties are managed by their owners, operating costs are reduced.

Vacancy of a unit, however, can cut into your cash flow. In an owner-occupied two-unit house, all income ceases when the rental unit is vacant. In an owner-occupied four-unit house with one unit vacant, the income is reduced by one third. If at the outset you are dependent upon rents to meet the operating costs (mortgage, taxes, maintenance, insurance, etc.), be very careful to choose a property in an area where demand is high and the vacancy rate low—even if you must pay a little more for the property. The added income security is worth the stretch. And besides, properties in high-demand areas generally appreciate better than properties in marginal areas.

A Building to Build Upon

A multifamily house is commonly the first purchase made by a beginner in a real estate investment plan. The capital required for purchase is relatively small and the potential resale market is quite large, including all the beginners who will be coming after you. Although multifamily houses usually sell less quickly than single-family houses, property turnover is faster than in mixed-use buildings, commercial property, or small apartment buildings.

For nonowner occupants, a 1031 tax-deferred exchange (see Chapter 10) can move your entire profit from the sale into another, larger multifamily property. In another strategy, as an owner-occupant, you can sell after two years and take the portion of the profit equivalent to your living space tax-free. With careful financing and a good track record of on-time mortgage payments, you can expand your investment into two multifamily buildings. Then you can continue the pattern at two- to five-year intervals to constantly increase your net worth.

On the other hand, if you want to continue holding your first owner-occupied multifamily property because it's "home" and/or because it's a source of present and future positive cash flow, there is an alternative to resale. Once you've increased equity by refurbishing, renovation, and appreciation, you can refinance the property while you're still an occupant, thus getting owner-occupant rates and qualification guidelines. Then you'll have cash for a down payment on another property. Once the refinancing on your original property is in place and some time has elapsed, you can move to the new place, or you can look for a single-family home using money you've saved as your down payment.

Be careful, however, to watch the numbers closely. When you refinance based upon appreciation and the improvements that you have made, you will have higher mortgage loan payments. Be certain that increased rents will cover these debt service payments. You may also have higher municipal taxes if your improvements have been taken into account in a tax reassessment.

STOP AND THINK!

Investment in multifamily houses is **management intensive.** This is a hands-on purchase that calls for grass to be mowed and sinks unplugged. Especially at the outset, the owner-occupants usually do the managing. At that time the cost of a professional management firm is usually too large for the operating budget. When a nonowner-occupant owns several multifamily houses, however, management companies are often hired.

Your Profile for Success

Do you have what it takes to make money in multifamily houses? Here's a review of the criteria we talked about in Chapter 3. Each characteristic will be rated high demand, moderate demand, or low demand.

- **Assertiveness** (moderate demand). You won't need to elbow your way into this investment vehicle; the properties are there for the taking. You will, however, need some assertiveness and strength of character to deal effectively with tenants.
- **Attention to detail** (high demand). As in the single-family fixer-upper, the cost of refurbishing or renovating must be carefully calculated. Add to this the requirement for cost-effective maintenance work

---

MULTIFAMILY HOUSES: A PROFILE FOR SUCCESS

Assertiveness:	XXXXXX
Attention to detail:	XXXXXXXXX
Awareness:	XXXXXXXXX
Creativity:	XXX
Initiative:	XXXXXX
Perseverance:	XXXXXX
Rational judgment:	XXXXXXXXX
Self-confidence:	XXXXXXXXX
Strategic planning:	XXXXXX
Tact:	XXXXXXXXX

---

and the need to keep careful rental records. And don't forget the details in the lease and in tax records.

- **Awareness** (high demand). Because most multifamily houses are located within city limits, awareness of the desirability of a neighborhood and both current and proposed programs or trends toward revitalization or deterioration can significantly affect profitability.

- **Creativity** (low demand). In the multifamily housing section of the marketplace, pragmatism usually overcomes creativity. Adjectives such as *useful, durable,* and *comfortable* are more important (and more commonly used) than *beautiful* or *awesome.* You'll do well to paint walls beige rather than fuchsia.

- **Initiative** (moderate demand). Because rental income helps with carrying costs, project start time is not always crucial. Many owners respond to problems rather than initiating changes. For those seeking optimum return, however, it's important to make a plan and then work toward its goal.

- **Perseverance** (moderate demand). Just as in a single-family fixer-upper, when you begin a renovation, you must complete it. Partially completed projects *decrease* market appeal. But time pressure is not as intense as in the fixer-upper because you have some rental income and/or a place to live while renovations are in process. In the property-management aspect of this investment vehicle, your perseverance may well be tested when tenants are late in rent payments or when they must be evicted.

- **Rational judgment** (high demand). Everything said about the fixer-upper applies. You'll need careful evaluation of property value and probable appreciation; careful analysis of costs to refurbish or renovate; and careful evaluation of time demands and allotments. In addition, you have the human factor. You must be able to select tenants, deal with their complaints without emotional response, and enforce the provisions and restrictions of the lease.
- **Self-confidence** (high demand). As a landlord, you must make rules and decisions and stand behind them. There is no space for a weak and wavering personality in this investment vehicle.
- **Strategic planning** (moderate demand). It's important to have a plan for your multifamily house investment, but it's equally important to be flexible

DIGGING DEEPER

Key "landlord" into the Barnes and Noble Web site and you'll come up with almost 700 titles. To help you develop a workable and comfortable management style, here is a selection of some of the best and most recently published:

- *Every Landlord's Legal Guide* (7th edition) by Marcia Stewart and attorneys Janet Portman and Ralph Warner (Nolo Press)
- *Every Landlord's Tax Deduction Guide* by Stephen Fishman (Nolo Press)
- *Landlording: A Handy Manual for Scrupulous Landlords and Landladies Who Do It Themselves* (9th edition) by Leigh Robinson (Express)

- *The Landlord's Kit: A Complete Set of Ready-to-Use Forms, Letters, and Notices to Increase Profits, Take Control, and Eliminate the Hassles of Property Management* by Jeffrey Taylor (Dearborn Trade Publishing)
- *The Landlord's Troubleshooter: A Survival Guide for New Landlords* (3rd edition) by Robert Irwin (Dearborn Trade Publishing)
- *The Successful Landlord: How to Make Money Without Making Yourself Nuts* by Ken M. Roth (AMACOM)
- *What Every Landlord Needs to Know: Time and Money-Saving Solutions to Your Most Annoying Problems* by Richard H. Jorgenson (McGraw-Hill)

enough to change that plan in response to changes in the community or in the needs of your tenants.

- **Tact** (high demand). Sometimes finding the "politically correct" or more pleasant way to say something can make a tremendous difference in the response the words elicit. Tact does not mean softness, however. This trait must be combined with self-confidence and perseverance for maximum effectiveness.

Time, Work, and Money

Holding time for a multifamily investment property may be long or short depending on your goals and the pace of the local marketplace. Working time, however, is ongoing and may sometimes seem endless.

The most frequent problem for investors in this vehicle is tenant complaints. The toilet always seems to overflow at 2:00 AM. Lightbulbs in hallways seem to grow feet and walk away soon after they are installed. The second-floor tenant doesn't like the tricycles and basketballs in the yard; the first-floor tenant doesn't like the late-night music playing upstairs.

Even when there are no complaints, frequent visits to the property are necessary to maintain a sense of owner presence. You can make your visits at regular and predictable intervals (the first of each month, for example) or at unpredictable times and dates—or both. The predictable intervals give tenants a secure point of contact at which to voice concerns or make requests. The unpredictable visits increase awareness of the tenant/landlord relationship and therefore can result in more cleanliness and less property damage.

In addition to maintenance and peace-keeping activities, the owner-investor of a multifamily house must spend some time each month in recordkeeping. Rent receipts, expenditures, and operating costs including maintenance, accountant's fees, property insurance, and liability insurance, must be recorded and documented.

And sometimes all of this work doesn't seem to bring in much money. An owner-occupied multifamily house

---

LEARNING THE LANGUAGE

The implied warranty of habitability refers to the landlord's responsibility to provide livable premises when a unit is rented and to maintain that condition throughout the rental period. Every state requires that rental property meets basic structural, health, and safety standards, but the specific requirements vary from one state to another.

In rental real estate, **a nuisance** is anything that is dangerous to human life or detrimental to human health. Insufficient lighting, heat, and ventilation are some examples.

Nuisances in rental property are prohibited by local housing codes. If they are not corrected, landlords are subject to fines and penalties.

According to municipal law, **attractive nuisances** are conditions that might attract inquisitive children or other people. Some examples are abandoned vehicles, appliances, wells, scaffolding, or excavation. Attractive nuisances on rental property are prohibited by local ordinances. If someone is hurt by an attractive nuisance, the landlord may be liable.

---

often has a negative cash flow for several years. Remember, however, that the minus numbers are usually related to your share of the mortgage payment. Fully rented investments should show positive cash flow within a short time of purchase unless the financing is intentionally structured to show losses for tax purposes.

Speaking of taxes, remember that only the rented portion of an owner-occupied multifamily property is depreciable. Maintenance expenses must also be apportioned according to the proportions of owner/tenant occupancy. And finally, upon sale of an owner-occupied multifamily property, only the proportion of the profits equal to the proportion of owner occupancy is exempt from taxation, according to the Taxpayer Relief Act of 1997, section 312.

Checkpoints for a Good Investment

Everything you read in Chapter 6 applies to multifamily investment purchases. You need to pay special attention to:

■ **Location**

■ **Size and condition**

■ **Price**

In the Neighborhood

Everyone wants a neighborhood that is clean and safe. If your investment property is in a desirable neighborhood, the units will bring higher rents and the resale value will be higher. Your real estate agent can help you get neighborhood demographic profiles and information on vacancy rates and going rents in the area.

It's a generally accepted maxim in the investment marketplace that neighborhoods with a high ratio of owner-occupants are better maintained and hold their value better than neighborhoods that are heavily rented. You can check for owner occupancy by going to the local tax-records office and noting the owners of record for each property in an area of several blocks. Then compare those names with the occupants listed at each property in a current street directory, which is generally available in real estate broker's offices.

DIGGING DEEPER

Many real estate firms subscribe to a professional Internet service called eNeighborhoods, Inc. The company calls itself "the nation's premier compiler of home and neighborhood information." To help the real estate professional, eNeighborhoods provides detailed information about any neighborhood in the country, including facts about schools, home values, crime rates, cost of living, and other demographics. The company charges a subscriber fee for use of its site, but if you are working with an agent who is already a subscriber, you can ask him or her to help you access the site.

If you want information on schools (grades K through 12), you can get it free at http://www.greatschools.net, which reports on both public and private schools throughout the nation. The service is available to everyone.

Accessibility to public transportation and shopping is another plus factor in a multifamily investment property. Be aware, however, that property values are higher when these conveniences are close by but not contiguous to or visible from the rental space. Also remember that both tenants and buyers prefer a strictly residential neighborhood to mixed-use zoning.

Because a vacancy can cut rental income by a large percentage (50 percent in the case of a duplex), it's very important that you consider the economic base of the community before you buy. The risk factor goes up for multifamily houses in communities where there is only one major employer. If that employment source falters, layoffs or a plant closing can mean nonpayment of rent, a high vacancy rate, and virtual nonliquidity of your investment.

STOP AND THINK!

Be aware of the distance factor when you buy multifamily investment properties. Because multifamily houses require owner management, you will want to choose investment property as close to your own residence as practically feasible. The IRS does, however, allow a deduction for mileage to and from the rented property for inspection, rent collection, and maintenance.

Is Bigger Better?

Value and return on your investment in a multifamily house can be influenced by two physical characteristics of the property:

1. The total square footage of available living space

2. How that space is divided up

Let's imagine the same two-story house divided inside in two different ways. In one example, you have two three-bedroom units, each with a living room, kitchen, and bath. In the other, you have four one-bedroom units each with a small sitting room, a kitchen alcove, and a bath. The one-bedroom units each bring in $500 a month. The three-bedroom units each bring in $750. Do the math!

In addition to being more lucrative, the four-unit house is also a safer investment because a single vacancy reduces rental income by 25 percent, not by 50 percent as in the three-bedroom example. You can afford to have a unit vacant for refurbishing and still collect the same amount of rent that you would get from the two-unit house.

The size of the units also determines the type of tenants you will have. The three-bedroom units are likely to attract families or groups of young adults sharing space. The one-bedroom units attract singles and sometimes couples.

STOP AND THINK!

Because a landlord can be liable for environmental hazards, your professional inspection service should check for and report on them. The most common hazards are asbestos, lead paint, and radon. Be aware that if these hazards are present, you as landlord will be required to notify tenants and to comply with your state's regulations for remediation or control.

How Good Is "Good Condition"?

The professional-inspection contingency in your purchase contract is extremely important in a multifamily investment property. Few buyers have a large contingency fund in the first years after purchase. During that time, a single major breakdown (a furnace or a roof replacement, for example) can put the investment into negative cash flow for many months.

In some cases, you will be negotiating an especially low price because the property is in need of repair. When estimating your profit potential, bear in mind that you, as new owner, may not have full control over what will be done in the way of refurbishing. Many local and state ordinances now require that rental residences be inspected by a municipal buildings inspector whenever a property changes ownership.

Residential or commercial usage that was allowed under the principle of grandfathering may become illegal upon change of ownership until compliance with local building and health codes is undertaken. Bringing a building up to code usually means significant up-front expenditures. It's a good idea, therefore, to get a copy of the local codes and discuss them with your professional inspector.

It is becoming increasingly common for investors to make code compliance a contingency of the purchase contract, with the seller responsible for the cost of making whatever changes or improvements are necessary. In some cases, however, the agreed-upon purchase price can be lowered still further to compensate for the projected costs of bringing the property up to code.

Punch the Price

The price on multifamily houses is always negotiable. Everything in Chapter 7 applies to this investment vehicle, especially when you are negotiating with independent investors, much like yourself, rather than lenders

---

DIGGING DEEPER

ASBESTOS. Strict regulations for asbestos were established by the U.S. Occupational Safety and Health Administration (OSHA) in 1995. Landlords are required to comply. For information on rules, inspections, and control, contact:

> **OSHA**
> **Department of Labor**
> **200 Constitution Avenue**
> **Washington, DC 20210**
> **800-321-6742**
> **http://www.osha.gov/SLTC/asbestos/**

OSHA offers a program called *Asbestos Advisor* that will help you to locate and deal with the problem. You can download it (free for Windows) at http://www.osha .gov/dts/osta/oshasoft/asbestos/index.html.

LEAD. Landlords of all buildings built before 1978 are required to give tenants the booklet, *Protect Your Family from Lead in Your Home,* which is authored by the Environmental Protection Agency (EPA). Copies are available from regional offices of the EPA or by calling the **National Lead Information Center at 800-424-5323.**

To download a copy of the booklet *Lead-Paint Disclosure Rule* or to seek more

information on the subject, you can visit HUD's Web site at http://www.hud.gov/ offices/lead/disclosurerule/.

For specific questions about how regulations apply to you, call the **Lead Paint Compliance Assistance Center at 866-483-1012.**

RADON. There are currently no laws that require a landlord to detect and report the presence of radon. However, the EPA estimates that unacceptable levels occur in over 25 percent of American homes. A precedent for landlord liability for radon poisoning has been set in New York State [*Kaplan v. Coulston,* 381 NYS 2d 634 (1976)].

For information about the detection and removal of radon, visit the EPA's Web site at http://www.epa.gov/iaq/radon/, where you can read online the EPA's publication, *A Citizen's Guide to Radon.*

For answers to other questions about radon, call the **National Radon Information Line at 800-767-7236.**

holding REOs, state or local agencies, or corporations. That is not to say, however, that government-held or corporate-held property is not negotiable. Sometimes these big guys can afford to take a loss just to get rid of an annoyance. That loss could be your gain.

While taking into consideration that the amount of necessary repairs and the prospective income from the property are important factors in your negotiating strategy, the most important consideration in this investment vehicle should be the local marketplace. Ask yourself and your real estate professionals: *What are other multifamily houses selling for? How fast is the turnover time? How much below asking price is the average selling price?*

After you have done all your calculations, imagine that you might want to sell this property in three months. Do this even if you think you are buying a long-term, positive-cash-flow investment. What do you think the property will sell for? This is actually the price you are now willing to pay and constitutes a fair market figure. Now ask yourself how much less you would have to pay today to make a sale in three months profitable. (Subtract real estate commission, closing costs, financing costs, and carrying costs.) Your answer is your target price. You may not get the seller to go that low, but if you do, you'll have an excellent safety net.

"Caveat emptor!" (Let the buyer beware!)

Traditional ancient Latin saying still alive in the real estate marketplace

Safeguards in the Contract

In every real estate transaction, the written contract can (and should) be the document that will ensure your safe passage through the precarious demilitarized zone between a fully executed agreement and the transfer of title. It's that important. So read Chapter 8 before every real estate purchase you make, ever. Meanwhile here are some points that are particularly pertinent to multifamily houses.

Rental Income and Operating Expenses
In addition to the usual buyer-protection clauses, the purchase contract for a multifamily house should be contingent upon the buyer's right to inspect and approve the seller's records and documentation for income

"We all know how the size of sums of money appears to vary in a remarkable way according as they are being paid in or paid out."

Sir Julian Huxley
(1887–1975), British biologist

and operating expenses and all current leases. But multifamily-house sellers hardly ever issue the detailed type of financial statements used by condominiums and apartment complexes. So you may have to snoop around and put puzzle pieces together. Often, the best place to get accurate income and expense information is the seller's federal income-tax return. Ask for copies of Schedule E, Supplemental Income and Loss, for the past three years.

Because sellers are prone to exaggerate income and "forget" some of the expenses when talking with prospective buyers, tax returns are the best source of this information. It's a truly rare American who would ever report to Uncle Sam more income than was received or fewer expenses than were paid out. Tax returns are also a good place to note when major repairs or appliance replacements were done, if in fact they occurred.

Leases and Security Deposits

Some leases survive a change of ownership and some do not. The purchase contract for a multifamily house should specify the lease terms currently in effect. If you, as buyer, want to occupy one of the units, make the contract contingent on the vacancy and availability of that unit at closing. The current landlord will then be responsible for negotiating and arranging the departure of the current tenants. (This usually costs the seller some money to be paid to the tenant as an incentive.)

With all the details involved in the transfer of multifamily properties, tenants' security deposits are sometimes overlooked by the buyers when a purchase contract is drawn. That memory lapse could cost you money. Be certain that the amount (including interest, if applicable) and location of all security deposits are recorded in the contract and that the contract clearly states that the monies are to be turned over to the escrow account of the new owner at closing.

Is the Place Legal?

Some especially large, single-family houses (think early 20th century city dwellings) have been converted to multifamily rental properties. Usually, the conversions work and all is well. Except for the fact that some conversions have not been recorded in municipal tax, buildings, and zoning offices. You do not want to buy a structure that has undergone an unrecorded change-of-use.

Worst case: You could buy such a property for rental income from, say, four units and then be required by the zoning board to convert it back to single-family occupancy. To prevent such an occurrence, your purchase contract should state that the property is in compliance with local zoning laws or that the owner has obtained the appropriate variances and/or nonconforming-use permits. (Check at the town hall anyway. Or have your real estate agent or attorney check. Get a copy of the documentation.)

> **LEARNING THE LANGUAGE**
>
> **A nonconforming use permit** allows for usage of the property that does not conform to the zoning in the neighborhood—for example, a multifamily-house conversion in an area zoned for single-family residences.

In the purchase contract, the seller should also warrant that:

- **There are no pending citations for violation of building and safety laws.**
- **There are no pending special tax assessments.**
- **The building is legally located within the property lines and that there are no encroachments on adjacent property.**
- **There are no unrecorded liens on the property.**

Some Financing Tips

There are a few financing opportunities and cautions that apply especially to multifamily houses, whether owner occupied or not. Check the following to see if any of them might apply to your deal.

Assumables

Some multifamily houses are advertised with "assumable" FHA mortgages. All FHA loans that were originated before December 1, 1986, are assumable by a new borrower without qualifying through the FHA. The liability in case of default on these loans remains with the original borrower. For loans originated after December 1, 1986, the new buyer must meet FHA qualification guidelines to assume the loan.

It doesn't happen much anymore but when investors sell a property with an old-style FHA assumable mortgage, they can give the buyer a purchase-money loan for all or part of the difference between the FHA mortgage balance and the selling price. This is called a seller carryback. It is written as a second mortgage loan.

Wraparounds

Mortgage loans that contain a due-on-sale clause (the provision that the entire balance is to be paid when ownership changes hands) cannot be assumed. In the 1980s, some sellers were trying to avoid the due-on-sale clause by offering "wraparounds." The wraparound mortgage is an arrangement whereby the original mortgage (usually with an interest rate lower than the one prevailing at the time of the wraparound sale) was kept in place by writing a new mortgage for the remaining principal plus the additional money needed to meet the purchase price, with the seller as mortgage holder. (This is the mortgage that would be "wrapped-around" the original mortgage.)

In times when interest rates are high and climbing, some buyers get a break on interest with a wraparound mortgage by calculating the mortgage payment using two different interest rates: the old rate for the balance that has been assumed and the new rate on the difference between the purchase price and the balance. In other wraparounds, the seller charges the buyer one rate (the current higher rate) and pockets the difference between that payment and what is due on the old mortgage.

In most wraparound deals, the seller would continue to make the payments on the old mortgage, hoping that the original lender would not find out that the property had changed ownership. There were many court cases across the country as a result of this practice, and most found in favor of the original lenders. As a general rule, wraparound arrangements should be avoided.

Rehab Loans

FHA 203(k) programs, which provide money for rehab within the mortgage loan, are available to both owner-occupants and investors in multifamily houses. Repairs that can be factored into the loan can include replacing or repairing windows, roof, gutters, siding, floors and floor coverings, stairs, plumbing, and heating, cooling, and electrical systems. Loan money is also provided for improvements outside the house, such as landscaping, patios, or driveway repair.

The FHA's 203(k) loans make it possible for a buyer to do repairs before occupying or renting a fixer-upper multifamily house. While the repairs are under way, the borrower does not have to make mortgage payments. However, property taxes and insurance premiums must be paid during this period when there is no rental income.

Bond-Backed Mortgages

Multifamily houses are the most common candidates for bond-backed mortgages. These loan programs are sponsored by state and commu-

---

DIGGING DEEPER

For information regarding the approximately 180 public agencies that provide mortgaging assistance to buyers, contact:

National Council of State Housing Agencies
444 North Capitol Street, N.W., Suite 438
Washington, DC 20001
202-624-7710
http://www.ncsha.org

Or search online or in the blue pages of your phone book for your state's housing agency.

---

nity revitalization groups. They make financing available at lower interest rates and lower down-payment requirements to candidates who might not qualify under conventional financing guidelines.

The problem is that most people don't know where to find these mortgages. Mortgage brokers can help. So can your state housing agency (look in the blue pages of the phone book) and the National Council of State Housing Agencies (see the box on page 231).

How Much Can You Afford?

When money is readily available, there's always the temptation to get as much as you can. Remember, however, that you must pay back what you borrow. And if you don't or can't pay it back on time, you can lose the down payment you made as well as your ownership interest in the property.

Even when loan terms are very appealing, calculate carefully to be sure that you can make the payments. You should have reserves at the outset that will cover you for several months' payments and for an unexpected expenditure on repairs. If necessary, borrow a little more to give yourself this security fund.

KEEP IN MIND

- **Multifamily houses** are among the least costly and least risky entry vehicles into the real estate investment marketplace.
- **This is a management-intensive vehicle** requiring both time and do-it-yourself skills.
- **Positive cash flow** and equity can both be increased when owners do maintenance and repair work themselves.
- **Rental-property ownership** carries with it legally enforceable responsibilities to provide tenants with safe and healthy living space.

- **Location and unit size** are important factors in determining market value and cash flow.
- **Landlords must be aware of asbestos, lead, and radon hazards.**
- **Inspection of the seller's federal income-tax returns** is the best way to check on rental income and operating expenses.
- **Be careful not to take on more mortgage debt** than you can carry.

Condos and Co-ops

"Property has its duties as well as its rights."
Thomas Drummond (1797–1840), Scottish engineer and statesman

T he legal concept behind condominium ownership goes back to apartment buildings in the Roman Empire. But the idea didn't catch on in modern America until after 1961, when legislation was enacted at the federal level that defined and permitted condominium ownership throughout the country. Once condos got going, however, the concept took hold like wildflowers in the woods. Today every state has its own condominium legislation and "everyone, everywhere" knows about condos.

Or do they? Shared-space ownership is more complex than any other fee-simple estate (see the box on page 234). Few buyers fully understand what they're getting into when they buy a condominium unit. Some even equate condos with co-ops, when co-ops aren't really a form of real estate ownership at all. Are you confused? Let's review the basics.

What's a Condo?

W hen you own a condominium apartment, you own space—the airspace enclosed by the walls, floors, and ceilings described in your deed—and you own an undivided interest in the common areas. An undivided interest is one that cannot be severed or separated from the whole. For example, you own an undivided interest in the swimming pool, which means that you own an undivided interest in every drop of water in the pool. Your undivided interest, however, does not allow you to take a bucket of water out of the pool and call it your own. Likewise, you own an undivided interest in the exterior walls of the buildings but not even one brick is yours alone.

Despite the fact that your share in the land and buildings is an undivided interest, you can sell the *space* designated as yours within the condominium because you hold that *fee simple*. Ownership of that space, however, requires that you contribute a designated share (your monthly maintenance fee) to the maintenance and operation of the common areas. Because of your fee simple ownership, you can get a mortgage loan on condominium space in exactly the same way that you would get a mortgage loan for a single-family house.

Condos come in a large variety of sizes and shapes. There are condominium communities that are high-rise, mid-rise, and low-rise, and there are condominium patio homes and town houses. There are even condominiums comprised of detached single-family houses, where the common areas are limited to land, roads, and

---

LEARNING THE LANGUAGE

Fee simple refers to ownership of real estate that allows for unrestricted power to dispose of the property by sale, gift, or inheritance. In modern-day America, fee simple is pretty much synonymous with the concept of property ownership. In everyday usage, **shared-space ownership** is pretty much a synonym for condominium ownership.

Common elements or common areas in a condominium are the land and those portions of the building or buildings and amenities that are owned by the condominium association and used by all the unit owners (for example, roof, exterior walls, stairwells, hallways, foundation, plumbing, windows, swimming pool, tennis courts, and parking areas). All unit owners share in the common expenses of maintaining and operating the common areas.

amenities. In addition to residential condominiums, investment opportunities are available in commercial and office condos. There are condos in every state, in cities, suburbs, and even in rural and vacation areas.

What's a Co-Op?

People talk about "buying a co-op," but in fact no one actually owns the co-op apartment he or she occupies. You buy *into* a co-op. And when you do, you own shares of stock in the corporation that owns the building.

Like stockholders everywhere, you have voting rights in electing the management (called a board of directors) of your corporation. Unlike most stock holdings, however, your co-op ownership share carries with it a financial responsibility to keep the building (corporation) solvent. Your maintenance fee is your apartment's share of the building's mortgage payments, municipal taxes, and operating expenses.

LEARNING THE LANGUAGE

A **proprietary lease,** sometimes called an **occupancy agreement,** assigns a co-op shareholder the right to occupy a specific unit.

But if you don't own any real estate, how can you call an apartment your own? When you buy into a co-op you get a proprietary lease on your unit. Each unit has a given number of shares in the corporation assigned to it, and that number determines your voting strength at shareholder meetings. The number of shares designated to a unit cannot be changed without the unanimous approval of the stockholders.

Technically speaking, co-ops cannot be mortgaged because they are not fee-simple real estate holdings. In practice, however, the loans made for co-op purchases feel, look, smell, and taste very much like mortgages. Even the IRS looks upon co-op ownership as home ownership.

When you finance your co-op purchase, the lender will hold your stock certificate, your proprietary lease, and a promissory note, rather than holding a deed. If you fail to make your payments, you will be evicted and lose your ownership interest. That eviction can happen without foreclosure proceedings. There are no co-op sales on the proverbial *courthouse steps*.

You'll find co-ops primarily in and around larger cities, especially Chicago, Miami, New York, and Washington, D.C. Some co-ops date as far back as the late 19th century, others were established in the 1920s, and still others in the 1940s. Condominium conversion has now far outpaced the creation of co-ops, but the process is still going on. The most recent co-ops are usually converted rental-apartment buildings. (More about opportunities in conversions in just a bit.) There are also some vacation-resort communities structured for co-op ownership and investment.

Why Buy Condos or Co-ops?

In the 21st century, condos and co-ops appeal to many buyers, both homebuyers and investors. They appeal to people who are just starting out in life, to people who have experienced a change in their lives such as divorce or widowhood, to people about to retire or in retirement, and to city dwellers of all ages and temperments. Let's look at a few reasons why.

No Responsibilities

Condos and co-ops are sometimes called the lazy-investor's vehicle. People fantasize about gathering monthly rent checks while the owners' association or board of directors does all the work of supervising building maintenance and management. Such a dreamy vision, if not perfectly true, is true enough to make lack of management responsibility the primary attraction of shared-space investment.

Low Prices

Condos are generally priced somewhat below the going market price for the similar living space in single-family and multifamily houses. Furthermore, one-bedroom units, hard to find among houses for sale, are commonly available in shared-space communities. The low prices

---

STOP AND THINK!

The survival of a co-op apartment building depends on the sustained contributions of its shareholders. This fact increases risk. If several shareholders default on payments, the remaining shareholders must make up the difference, which usually means significant increases in monthly maintenance fees. The co-op board of directors, therefore, has the right to reject prospective purchasers for almost any reason. Usually, the board places great emphasis on financial qualification and stability.

---

and small-unit size allow investors to hold several investment properties concurrently.

Generally, holding a larger number of small rental units brings a greater return in rent per dollar invested than holding a small number of large rental units does. Holding many small units also affords the maximum flexibility for liquidating individual investment units at opportune times. For small investors, condos and co-ops may also be one of the few residential investment vehicles available in our major cities.

Long-Distance Investment Opportunities

Condos and co-ops are good candidates for long-distance ownership. Because management by an owners' association increases the likelihood of good maintenance and protection of property value, many investors choose to buy condos or co-ops in areas where potential appreciation is greater than it is where they are currently living. Some investors choose holdings in areas where they would like to retire. Tax allowances are made for trips to attend annual owners' association meetings, to inspect the property, or to do repairs and refurbishing

---

LEARNING THE LANGUAGE

Rent control is a law placing a maximum price, or a "rent ceiling," on what landlords may charge tenants. It began as a temporary price control during World War II but is still in effect in more than 100 cities, including New York City, Washington, D.C., and Los Angeles. Be sure you know if local rent controls are in effect in your area. Thirty-one states have adopted laws and constitutional amendments forbidding rent control. The issue is controvercial where it is not prohibited. If rent control is in effect, it will have bearing on investment returns.

---

between tenants. Most condominium bylaws allow for long-term leases (from three months to a year or more). Many co-op boards, however, restrict rentals or require board approval of the tenants.

Appreciation in Blocks

In cities where rent control is in effect, some investors have made handsome returns on their investments by purchasing several occupied apartments in buildings that are undergoing conversion to co-op or condominium ownership. In this situation, several occupied apartments are bundled for sale at one heavily discounted price, called a block.

Because the rent-controlled leases on the newly converted units generally survive the conversion, there is often some negative cash flow in the early years of this investment holding. Once the apartments are vacated, however, each unit often sells for more than the original price of the entire block.

New construction offers a different kind of opportunity to purchase blocks of condos on the basis of paper plans. It's a high-risk investment.

Some builders offer heavily discounted preconstruction prices. Investors sign up to buy several apartments, writing the right to assign the contract into the agreement. (Assignment is defined and explained in Chapter 17.) As construction of the building nears completion, these speculators hope to sell their rights to purchase the units they have under contract. They are betting that the builder will have significantly raised the asking price on units as the building or community nears completion. (This usually does happen.)

There are two inherent risks in signing a contract to purchase to-be-built units. Consider these possibilities:

1. **The builder goes bankrupt without completion of the project.** Depending on what was done with your earnest money, you could come out even or you could lose. If the contractual earnest money was turned over to the builder, it is usually lost. If it was held in escrow by a neutral third party such as a lawyer or a real estate broker, it is usually returned to the investor.

The problem is that most builders make turning the earnest money over to them a stipulation in the contract for the discounted multiunit price.

2. **The builder completes the project but the market turns sour and there are no buyers to be found for the units under contract.** The investor must purchase the units or lose the deposit monies. If the investor can get financing, the units can be rented. The cash flow might be negative for several years, however.

Your Profile for Success

So far, does it sound as though condos and co-ops are appealing investment vehicles? If so, are you the type? Here's a review of the criteria we talked about in Chapter 3. Each characteristic will be rated high demand, moderate demand, or low demand.

■ **Assertiveness** (high or low demand). In the first decade of the 21st century, condos are hot in hot areas. In other areas where the marketplace is slow or overbuilt, shared-space community appreciation is not keeping pace with other forms of residential investment. In real estate's hot areas you must be very assertive to find a good buy, sometimes even can-

---

CONDOS AND CO-OPS: A PROFILE FOR SUCCESS

Assertiveness (slow market):	XXX
Assertiveness (hot market):	XXXXXXXXX
Attention to detail:	XXXXXXXXX
Awareness:	XXXXXXXXX
Creativity:	XXX
Initiative:	XXXXXX
Perseverance:	XXX
Rational judgment:	XXXXXXXXX
Self-confidence:	XXX
Strategic planning:	XXXXXX
Tact:	XXXXXXXXX

vassing large communities with flyers on car wind-shields. In areas where the pace of the market is slow, agents will take you to condo after condo, all looking alike, all waiting to be bought. You won't have to fight your way into this marketplace.

■ **Attention to detail** (high demand). Choosing a good condo or co-op investment requires careful attention to annual financial statements. Is the community being well managed? Is there a reserve fund? Have maintenance fees remained relatively stable?

You should also read the fine print in a condo-minium's declaration, bylaws, and house rules or in a co-op's corporate charter, corporate bylaws, and proprietary leases. These details are often tiresome, but it's better to examine them yourself than to lis-ten to a quick recitation by an agent or seller.

A detailed structural and working-systems in-spection is required, not only of the unit being pur-chased but also of the entire common areas of the building and of the grounds. Are buildings and grounds well maintained and in good repair? Re-member that unexpected maintenance and repair

---

LEARNING THE LANGUAGE

In the overall real estate marketplace, a **special assessment** is a lien against property by a government office to pay the cost of public improvements that directly benefit the property being assessed. (Some examples of special assess-ment improvements are sidewalks, city water, sewers, or streetlights.)

A special assessment in a condominium community is a one-time fee levied on all the units to pay for repairs or improve-ments. Sometimes payment is allowed in installments over a year or two, but the assessment is separate from and in ad-dition to the maintenance fee. (Some examples of condo-minium special assessments are elevator replacement or repair, swimming pool repair, or repaving of parking areas.)

problems can mean special assessments or significantly increased monthly maintenance fees, both of which will threaten your investment with negative cash flow.

- **Awareness** (high demand). You must thoroughly understand the demographics of the community where your investment apartment is located. Has the apartment vacancy rate been stable for the past five years? Are the major employers in the area reliable? Is there a large university that creates relatively constant demand for rental space? You must also be aware of building and development plans in the area. Competition from new apartment construction can mean empty condo or co-op units in your investment community.

- **Creativity** (low demand). Shared-space rental units do best in plain vanilla.

- **Initiative** (moderate demand). Change of tenants will require cleaning and perhaps refurbishing, advertising the unit, and selection of new tenants. You probably won't be asked to start up anything else.

- **Perseverance** (low demand). You won't need very much stick-to-itiveness unless you are required to evict a tenant. Or unless you try to change the by-laws or house rules.

- **Rational judgment** (high demand). Palm trees by the pool or waterfalls in the lobby must not influence your purchase decision. You must crunch the numbers without emotion.

- **Self-confidence** (low demand). There is security in numbers in condo or co-op investment. The owners' association works as a group to maintain the value of the investment.

- **Strategic planning** (moderate demand). It's important not to let your shared-space investment stagnate. Evaluate its performance each year, and ask yourself if this is the best investment vehicle for your current and future needs.

- **Tact** (high demand). Your ability to deal tactfully with other owners, officers of the board of directors, and tenants is an important factor in success for shared-space investment vehicles.

Time, Work, and Money

In its simplest form, the time and work required for managing shared-space investments is limited to choosing tenants, collecting rent, paying the maintenance fee, and keeping records. Knowing that efficient and effective management protects property value, however, many investor-owners serve as officers of owners' associations or co-op boards of directors.

Work on the board can be very time-consuming and usually there is no pay. Often you will be working with politically hot topics and opposing cliques among the owners. Just as in a rental building, you'll have to deal with owners who don't make their payments, budget restrictions, and cash-flow problems. And that's not to mention owners and/or tenants who break the house rules or bylaws.

Among the most difficult and time-consuming challenges a board member may face in shared-space housing is a proposal for change or improvements. The infighting could rival that of the U.S. Congress. Some rule changes require unanimous consent; many others require nothing more than a simple majority. You may well find yourself lobbying for improvements resisted by other condo owners or co-op shareholders on the basis of cost or some other factor. Like Gandhi, if you feel strongly about your position, you may have to hold out against derision and active opposition, smiling patiently while you stand firm. This is not always easy when you are living in the community and sharing amenities with those who oppose your views. It can be even more difficult for the nonresident owner.

Checkpoints for a Good Investment

Generally, all the factors that make for a good investment in single-family or multifamily houses are also important in shared-space housing. But because of the larger number of persons sharing facil-

---

DIGGING DEEPER

These organizations are good sources of information, training, and other support for condo and co-op owners and board members. They also offer online bookstores that sell their publications.

Community Associations Institute (CAI)
225 Reinekers Lane, Suite 300
Alexandria, VA 22314
703-548-8600
http://www.caionline.org
This group works to improve community living and management. It sponsors national seminars and publishes a variety of materials. You can read excerpts of publications in the online reading room.

National Association of Housing Co-operatives
 (NAHC)
1707 H Street, N.W., Suite 201
Washington, DC 20006
202-737-0797
http://www.coophousing.org
This group provides technical assistance and training to housing cooperative boards and keeps members informed of changes in laws and regulations.

The Urban Land Institute (ULI)
1025 Thomas Jefferson Street, N.W., Suite 500W
Washington, DC 20007
202-624-7000
http://www.uli.org
This organization provides information about the planning, design, and development of real estate projects that include the creation of community associations.

> **"First they laugh at you, then they fight you, then you win."**
>
> Mahatma Gandhi (1869–1948), Hindu spiritual leader

---

ities and because of the competition of similar apartments on the resale market, some things are more important than others. Let's look at some points specific to condos and co-ops.

Location of the Building

Is the town desirable (relatively low taxes, good schools, low crime rate, economic growth, good recreation facilities)? Are neighboring areas safe and attractive or improving? Are shopping and transportation convenient?

Gather information on the demographic profile of the town and its surrounding areas. You can even expand demographic profiles to look at whole regions of the nation. For example, the state of Florida is growing rapidly whereas some states are actually losing population. Remember: demand for housing is a factor of demographics.

Vacancy Rate

Have your real estate agent help you ascertain the rental unit vacancy rate in the community. Is it low and stable? What is the vacancy rate in the condominium community or apartment co-op? (The lower the better.) Talk with board officers to find out what proportion of units are owner-occupied. (The higher the better.)

Desirability is a factor in vacancy rate. If the condo community has been in existence through some economic ups and downs, check back through records to see how it fared through the bad times. Apartment buildings that are particularly appealing stay pretty near capacity even when other buildings have higher vacancy rates.

Location of the Unit

Many units in a given community or building are generally similar in floor plan and amenities. The location of a unit within the complex, therefore, can significantly affect value.

Corner units, units with a view, units with privacy, and units located high in the building usually bring a better return both for rental and upon sale. Avoid units that are near the elevators, the pool, or the maintenance facilities, and, in garden-type complexes, units that are near the gate or main-access roads.

Maintenance History

Be certain that the condominium community or co-op building has been well maintained. Determine what repair, replacement, or refurbishing has been done in the past five years. How was it paid for? What repairs or replacements are scheduled in the near future?

Check back through records to determine if monthly maintenance fees have been relatively stable. How much have they gone up during the past five years? If there has been a significant increase, try to find out what caused it. Does the community have a contingency fund for emergency repairs? How much?

Special Features

The right amenities in shared-space housing can mean higher rents and better resale. Look for these plus factors: more-than-adequate parking, public areas (meeting rooms, exercise rooms, gardens with seating), recreational facilities (swimming pool, hot tub, tennis courts, golf courses, walking trails), good security systems, on-site day care, views, surrounding green acres.

Price

As the baby boomer population bubble moves toward retirement age, condos and co-ops, with their no-maintenance features, are becoming more and more popular. In destination retirement areas such as Arizona, Florida, and North Carolina, prices are climbing and good investment deals are getting harder to find. Don't jump at a unit just because it's the only one available. Check the price against other units in the building and against the prices of units in nearby communities.

When looking for investment property, it's rarely a good idea to choose the most expensive unit. On the other hand, the least expensive, if it has some detrimental quality, may not be a good investment, either.

To find bargains in shared-space housing near vacation areas, look for anxious sellers, often second-home owners who have fallen on hard times. Check with officers of the community to determine if there are delin-

> **"The buyer needs a hundred eyes, the seller not one."**
>
> George Herbert (1593–1633), British clergyman and poet

quencies in maintenance fee payments. Apartments being disposed of in estates are another good opportunity for finding lower-than-market-value prices.

In areas that are overbuilt or in economic downturn, shared-space investments can be found at the proverbial *dime a dozen*. Well, not exactly. But they are sometimes so plentiful that it's hard to tell one from another. Yes, you can get a deal, but your main question should be: *Can the unit be rented profitably?*

Safeguards in the Contract

For the purchase of a condominium unit or co-op apartment, you will use essentially the same contract form and terms that you would use in the purchase of a multifamily house. So begin with a review of Chapter 8 and then go on to pay due attention to the following documents that pertain to condos and co-ops only.

Make your contract contingent on your unconditional approval of everything in these documents. Have your real estate agent or closing agent get them to you as soon as possible after the purchase contract is signed. Most states require that they be delivered within a few days.

LEARNING THE LANGUAGE

A **plat plan** (sometimes called a **plat map**) is a drawing showing how a parcel of land is divided into lots or ownership units.

In real estate, **a covenant** is a written agreement or assurance set forth in the deed.

CC&Rs (covenants, conditions, and restrictions) is a term used in some areas to refer to the limitations placed on property in the deed. The CC&Rs remain with the property through all changes of ownership. Sometimes they are simply called **deed restrictions.**

Pertinent Paperwork for Condos

The following are the documents that will influence the purchase of a condominium unit.

THE DECLARATION. Sometimes called the **Master Deed,** the Declaration creates the condominium and is its principal document. It must include a plat that shows the exact location of all the structures on the land owned by the condominium and architectural drawings and/or legal descriptions that show the exact location of each unit within those structures.

The Declaration also establishes the percentage of undivided interest in the common areas that is assigned to each unit. Check this number carefully regarding the unit you intend to buy because the percentage assigned reflects and affects the value of your unit. Usually it cannot be changed without unanimous approval of all of the owners.

Also check for any covenants, conditions, and restrictions (called CC&Rs) that might affect your ownership plans. Your attorney or closing agent can point these out. Be aware that these deed restrictions remain with the property through all changes of ownership.

THE BYLAWS. These keep the condominium running by setting forth and controlling its self-government. They are so important that everyone who buys or rents a unit must agree to abide by them. This agreement is usually secured by a covenant written into the Declaration. The covenant usually states that the mere acquisition, rental, or act of occupancy of any residential unit in the condominium has the effect of signifying that the bylaws of that condominium are accepted and will be complied with.

In addition to the government of the condo, the bylaws also affect life within the community. They enable the board to establish a budget and collect funds. They determine who may use the common areas and when. They rule on pets (and sometimes children) and sometimes the ability to rent the individual units. Be certain that there is nothing in the bylaws that will limit your plans for the use of your unit. Getting bylaws changed is difficult (some say virtually impossible).

THE INDIVIDUAL UNIT DEED. This document enables the owner to convey title (in other words, sell the property). In most cases, it repeats much of the information in the Master Deed and it states where that deed is on file (usually in the county land-records office).

Pertinent Paperwork for Co-ops

The following are the documents that will influence the purchase of a unit in a residential co-operative.

THE CORPORATE CHARTER. Sometimes called the **Certificate of Incorporation,** this document establishes the corporation that owns the building, just as the Declaration establishes the condominium. It must include the name of the corporation, its location, and the state law under which it is incorporated. It must also state the purpose of the corporation as the acquisition of land and building(s) to provide residences for its shareholders.

THE CORPORATE BYLAWS. These establish and describe the working systems of the corporation. Most co-op bylaws reserve the right of the board of directors (or in some cases the majority of stockholders) to approve or reject the sale of stock—and therefore the sale of an apartment—to a potential purchaser. This control measure has been tested in the courts and decisions have been handed down repeatedly that support the rights of a co-operative corporation to refuse a sale for any reason or no reason, except that a refusal cannot be based on race, color, creed, or national origin. In other words, the board of directors is not required to justify a decision. They can refuse to sell a unit because the prospective buyer wore yellow tennis shoes.

THE STOCK CERTIFICATE. This document states exactly how many shares a shareholder has purchased in the co-op corporation. This number establishes his or her voting power and determines his or her share

---

STOP AND THINK!

In order for co-op shareholders to qualify for homeowner tax breaks, the primary use of a co-op building must be for private residences. The tax law allows for up to 20 percent of the building space to be used for commercial rental. If commercial rental goes above that figure, all of the unit holders' homeowner tax benefits will be wiped out. Be aware, however, that this law does not prevent subletting. You can get more information regarding residential rentals from IRS Publication 527, *Residential Rental Property,* available online at http://www.irs.gov/publications/p527/ar02 .html, or you can call to request a copy at 800-829-3676.

---

of the corporation's maintenance expenses. Stock certificates are usually held by the lender when an apartment purchase is financed.

THE PROPRIETARY LEASE. The lease determines which unit you will occupy. It also spells out the respective responsibilities of both the landlord (the co-op corporation) and the tenant (the shareholder).

Some Financing Tips

When interest rates are low, assumable mortgages have little, if any, appeal. But just in case things change, it's good to remember that assumable FHA loans are available for condos. If you are buying for a short term (an apartment that needs cosmetic attention, for example), you can save some of the cost of mortgage application and origination by assuming the original loan for the term of your ownership. Of course, you will have to pay the seller the difference between the remaining principal and the sale price.

Some condos are available on foreclosures and sometimes these units sell well below market price. If the bank appraisal is truly based on market value and not your purchase price, it's possible that the standard loan-to-value ratio will require less money down than you were expecting to pay.

As was mentioned, loans on co-ops are not mortgages, although they are indeed structured like mortgages and the interest is usually deductible on federal income tax returns. Generally, interest rates are a bit higher than home-mortgage rates (to make up for the added risk, so say the lenders) but the financial marketplace is competitive, and you should shop for the best rates and terms.

KEEP IN MIND

- **Condos and co-ops** are two different types of investments. Condo owners hold real estate; co-op owners hold a share in the corporation that owns a building.
- **In shared-space investment real estate,** you do not have control over maintenance and management decisions.
- **Condos and co-ops** require minimal time, work, and money.
- **Because of owners' association** and board-of-directors management control, apartments are good candidates for long-distance investing.
- **Check these important aspects** of your shared-space housing investment: the location of the building in the community; the vacancy rate in the community and in the building; the location of the unit within the building or complex; the maintenance history of the unit; available amenities in the building or condo community; and the price of the unit relative to others in the complex.
- **You should receive and examine these condo documents:** the Declaration (Master Deed), the bylaws, and the individual unit deed.
- **You should receive and examine these co-op documents:** the Corporate Charter, the corporate bylaws, the stock certificate for your unit, and a proprietary lease.

Vacation-Area Properties

"I must confess that I am interested in leisure in the same way that a poor man is interested in money."
Prince Philip, Duke of Edinburgh

A generation ago the words *vacation home* brought to mind images of a cabin by a lake or a cottage by the sea. For many people, those images still come up, but today the field of possibilities is much greater. Shared-space housing has entered the marketplace in a big way.

If you imagine a high-rise on the beach when someone says vacation home, carefully read Chapter 13 again. In addition to condos of virtually every type imaginable, built on virtually every type of terrain, the marketplace includes investment co-ops and planned communities of single-family houses sharing a lakefront, a clubhouse, a golf course, several tennis courts, and maybe even a stable and a few bridle paths.

Some vacation-area investors avoid all the new construction and seek out charming and traditional architecture, such as rambling Victorians or gabled Early Americans in the small towns around destination cities or near major recreational attractions. With this investment property, they create a gathering place for family and friends with separate units that can also be profitably rented. Or they might convert the houses into rental units, timeshare offerings, or perhaps a bed-and-breakfast inn. Some simply renovate the property for resale.

And of course, there's land. New construction techniques can ease and facilitate the work of putting up a weekend hideaway that will someday bring a good return on resale. On a larger scale, speculators often successfully invest in land around the proposed locations of theme parks, golf-course communities, or other recreational developments. (Be sure to read Chapter 17.)

So what are we looking at in this chapter? Virtually every kind of real estate (which means you'll have to read at least one other chapter in Part II to get the full picture of your investment's pros and cons). What makes this investment vehicle special enough for a separate chapter? The where and why of ownership.

A successful investment in vacation-area real estate is destination sensitive. (How far is it from the primary residence of the owner? How desirable is it to prospective tenants?) Probably more than any other real estate investment, a vacation-home investment is also influenced by the personal needs of the investor. (Will this property provide pleasure as well as profit? Can it work as a future retirement location?)

> ### STOP AND THINK!
>
> Vacation property responds more sensitively than any other type of real estate to changes in the economic health of the nation or the region in which it is located. Be sure you can carry the property through "bad times" when rental income is minimal and resale unlikely.

Why Buy Vacation-Area Property?

Before you enter this area of the real estate marketplace, take a clean sheet of paper and print five letters on it: T-H-I-N-K. While vacation-area investment property can be a source of both pleasure and profit, it can also be a pesky pet or an ogre that eats money. In addition to knowing the principles of real estate and the local marketplace in the area where you plan to buy, the secret to this pleasure-and-profit path is knowing what you want, why you want it, and how much money you are willing to commit to satisfying those wants.

The three most common reasons for buying vacation-area property are:

1. **Purely for pleasure.** The buyer is looking for a leisure hideaway, a place to get away from it all, to have fun,

to enjoy family activities, to entertain. The investment aspect of the purchase is long-term resale value.

2. **For cost-free pleasure.** The buyer is looking for all of the above but would like enough income from rent to pay the mortgage, taxes, and operating expenses.

3. **Purely for profit.** Speculation is not uncommon in vacation areas. Fixer-uppers and opportunistic purchases for quick turnover come onto the market from time to time everywhere. In areas where there is a long "season" or where "in season" rentals are in very high demand, investors buy and hold properties for the positive cash flow of high weekly rentals.

Your Profile for Success

Do vacation-area properties call out to you? Is ownership the pot of gold at the end of a rainbow you've been chasing for a long time? Do you have what it takes to deal successfully in this area of the marketplace? As with the other investment vehicles, let's review the criteria we talked about in Chapter 3 and see how they apply to investing in vacation-area properties. Each characteristic will be rated high demand, moderate demand, or low demand.

VACATION-AREA PROPERTIES: A PROFILE FOR SUCCESS

Assertiveness:	XXXXXX
Attention to detail:	XXXXXXXXX
Awareness:	XXXXXXXXX
Creativity:	XXXXXXXXX
Initiative:	XXX
Perseverance:	XXX
Rational judgment:	XXXXXXXXX
Self-confidence:	XXXXXX
Strategic planning:	XXXXXX
Tact:	XXXXXX

- **Assertiveness** (moderate demand). If you're an escape-place (purely for pleasure) buyer, assertiveness is probably a character trait you'd like to leave behind, temporarily at least. For vacation-area landlords and speculators, assertiveness comes into play when marketing the property and dealing with tenants. Sometimes assertiveness helps in getting an opportunistic purchase (such as waterfront property after a hurricane, or a condo in Scottsdale that is part of an estate with the heirs thousands of miles away).

- **Attention to detail** (high demand). It's the details (often unnoticed) that make a vacation place appealing and comfortable. For example, most vacation places are rented furnished, so appropriate furnishings contribute to desirability and thus to the amount of rent your investment will bring in. Because of vacation-home tax laws (see the box on page 256), the details of recordkeeping can be troublesome if you're not a detail-oriented person. And attention to the details of preparing the property for the off-season closing can save megabucks.

- **Awareness** (high demand). It's important to be aware of the local factors that make a particular vacation-area property desirable and to respond to changes in these factors. (For example, a doughnut shop and a Internet café/video-game parlor have opened on the next block. Do they add to local color or indicate the coming of honky-tonk?)

- **Creativity** (high demand). Charm, especially charm that captures the unique sense of a locale, is an important factor in renting for top dollar. Creativity can contribute to building, remodeling, and decorating with local charm. Creativity can also influence the choice of the most desirable condominium complex, the one that prospective vacationing tenants will find enticing from printed brochures or Web site ads and choose above all others. Also the one they are willing to pay a little extra for.

- **Initiative** (low demand). Vacation property by its nature doesn't demand a lot of get-up-and-go. The exception, of course, is the fixer-upper bought on spec.

- **Perseverance** (low demand). Under most circumstances, you won't have to knock on doors or keep pressing when the person in charge says, "Not interested." The exception is the vacation-property owner who needs a zoning change for an addition or change of use.
- **Rational judgment** (high demand). This character trait is in higher demand than all the others because buying under the influence of emotional response is a real danger in vacation areas.
- **Self-confidence** (moderate demand). You may not need lead-the-parade assurance in this investment vehicle, but you do need to trust your own responses to and evaluations of what is happening in the local area. Consider if changes or trends might affect your investment positively or negatively.
- **Strategic planning** (moderate demand). Most vacation properties are held for the long term, but planning does come into play in deciding how much time to rent, what rental periods will bring the best return, and what improvements will be most appealing to prospective tenants.
- **Tact** (moderate demand). Vacationers are somewhat more demanding and somewhat more destructive than ordinary tenants. You'll have to combine tact with assertiveness in dealing with them. You'll also need your fair share of tact in dealing with condo owners' associations and management companies.

Time, Work, and Money

Time, work, and money—aren't those the very concerns you're trying to get away from when you invest in vacation property? Well, they follow you around, especially if you want a little return on this investment while you're also enjoying it.

Time and Work
Vacation property can consume as much or as little working time as you wish to allow. It can be an outlet for hammer-and-nails creativity or simply an investment

> **"A man builds a fine house; and now he has a master, and a task for life; he is to furnish, watch, show it, and keep it in repair the rest of his days."**
>
> Ralph Waldo Emerson (1803–1882), American essayist

DIGGING DEEPER

The IRS has several publications and topic discussions on tax and rental factors for vacation homes. *Tax Topics—Topic 415 Renting Residential and Vacation Property* is available for reading on the IRS Web site at http://www.irs.gov/taxtopics/tc415.html, or, if you prefer, you can get a listing of all government tax-related publications by visiting http://www.irs.gov/formspubs/index.html.

If you would rather use the phone, call 800-829-3676 and ask for Publication 527, *Residential Rental Property,* which includes the rules for vacation-area property.

that demands an hour or two a few months out of each year to keep records up to date. It all depends upon the type of vacation property you choose. Just be certain that you pick the type that suits your schedule and your personality.

Holding time in most vacation property is long. In fact, one of the most common reasons for choosing a particular location is its potential as a retirement destination. Some vacation homes are not sold, but are passed on from generation to generation. Certainly, a factor in calculating the return on this investment vehicle is happiness.

Money

Money to be spent is another matter. If you have an endless supply, you can choose vacation-area property without a thought to paying for it and its upkeep. But that's not the situation for most of us. The typical vacation-property investor must consider the following factors.

COST. This includes not only the price but also the financing and the resulting monthly payments. How will these payments affect your monthly living budget? How will they affect your other investment plans?

MAINTENANCE. What will it cost to keep the property "in good shape"? Coastal properties are affected by the corrosion caused by salt-laden moist air and they are subject to the threat of damage from windstorms. Lakeside properties often have septic-system problems. Cabins in the woods are susceptible to termites and the invasion of rodents or bats. When buying vacation property, consider all the usual maintenance items, plus any factors particular to its location.

If the vacation building is used only for a portion of the year, also include the cost of securing it for the off-season and then reopening it again. Even condos that have been closed for the off-season may require periodic insect and pest fumigation, shuttered windows, phone and cable disconnects and reconnects, and occasional inspections.

Interior appointments such as floors and floor coverings, appliances, furniture, and window treatments are another source of cash outgo not always covered by cash income. To repeat: *Vacationers are tough tenants.*

TAXES AND FEES: In addition to property taxes on every type of vacation property, don't forget to factor in maintenance fees in a condo community and asso-

---

STOP AND THINK!

Is This a Vacation Home or a Rental Property?

Vacation Home

You, the owner, your spouse, or your blood relatives *must* use the property at least (1) 15 days each year or (2) more than 10 percent of the number of days that it is rented at fair market value, *whichever is greater.* (For example, if the percentage is used, you must use the property 26 or more days when the property is rented for 250 days in a year.)

Advantages

- Mortgage interest and property taxes are deductible on federal income tax returns.
- Maximum personal use.
- If the property is rented for no more than 14 days, no deduction for expenses can be claimed, but the income from the 14 days need not be reported on federal income tax returns.

Disadvantages

- Property cannot show a tax loss.

Rental Property

You, the owner, your spouse, or your blood relatives can use the property *no more than* (1) 14 days each year or (2) 10 percent of the total number of days that it is rented at fair market value, *whichever is greater.* (For example, if you use the percentage, you can use the property for 25 or fewer days when the property is rented for 250 days in a year.)

Advantages

- Mortgage interest, property taxes, and expenses allocated to the rental period can be deducted against the rental income and can exceed that income, creating a tax loss.
- The property can be depreciated for tax purposes.

Disadvantages

- Limited personal use.

ciation fees in a planned vacation community. Also consider membership and use fees for recreation facilities such as golf, tennis, swimming, skiing, riding, etc.

And then there are the federal income taxes related to vacation-property investment. Here you choose whether you use the property as a "second home" or a rental property. There are separate rules for each. There's a summary in the box on the previous page, but consult an accountant before filing your federal income tax return.

Checkpoints for a Good Investment

In addition to all those timeless principles of good real estate investment that we've been talking about so far, you'll need to review the specific checkpoints for the type of property (single-family, multifamily, condo, etc.) that you choose. There is one factor, however, that overrules all others in your vacation-property choice: location, both its physical factors and its socioeconomic factors. Let's focus on that.

Location: Physical Factors
Knowledge of the geographic area is essential. Never buy a vacation property based on in-season visits only. You will own this property 12 months a year, every year (unless, of course, your vacation-property choice is at a timeshare resort). The better you know the area, the more appropriately you can deal with maintenance issues and rental opportunities. Beyond climate and terrain, you should consider the following as plus points in the town, neighborhood, lot, and condominium complex.

The Town
- **On or near a body of water.** Look for opportunities for swimming, boating, and fishing.
- **Historic character.** Much of the tourist activity in Maryland and Virginia, for example, is motivated by historical events and locations.

- **Natural beauty and attraction.** Proximity to a national park is a plus, for example.
- **Ample support and recreational facilities.** Look for restaurants, shopping, children's activities, sports, nightlife, medical facilities, police, and fire protection.
- **Easy access by road or air travel.** You don't want to be next to the airport or highway, but you want to be able to get there without much fuss and without too long a distance to travel.
- **Relatively low property taxes.** Low taxes don't increase the appeal to tenants but they do contribute to positive cash flow.
- **Friendly people.** If locals are antagonistic toward tourists, everyone feels uncomfortable.

The Neighborhood

- **Well-maintained properties.** Like most real estate, vacation home values are affected by the care and attention given to neighboring properties.
- **Some homogeneity in housing value.** Many cottage communities are a hodgepodge of architectural styles. For maximum investment protection, the housing units surrounding your property should be relatively close in price and rental value.
- **Clean and well-maintained public areas.** Clean streets, walkways, beaches, parking lots, etc., that are in good condition indicate a municipality that takes maintenance seriously.
- **A sense of safety.** Can you walk about safely at night? Can children play in the neighborhood? Some vacation areas have little or no police protection. Some say they don't need it. Make your own evaluation.

Your Lot

- **Waterfront or water access.** Oceans and lakes are America's favorite vacation spots.
- **Close to the central attraction of the area.** For example, if you own a ski chalet, you want to be on the ski slope or as close as possible.
- **Views.** It's truly amazing what people will pay for a good view.

- **Abutting forest, park, open marsh, or other land dedicated to open space.** Visitors who live in cities often want to take their vacations far from the sounds of traffic.
- **Level.** Even in hilly terrain, the more level the individual lot, the better.
- **Good parking area or garage area.** We are a nation of drivers. People want to park their cars (even their rental cars) close to where they are staying.
- **Play area.** Many vacation homes are rented to families. A swimming pool, a yard for volleyball or croquet, a basketball hoop, or even a sandbox can make a difference in rental desirability.
- **Good drainage.** Avoid the lowest lot in a development or any property that will collect water during a heavy rainstorm or during spring runoff from melting snow.
- **Privacy.** A hedgerow or a stand of trees between houses adds to value. If houses are built very close together, the positioning of windows and outdoor-use areas such as patios becomes important.

The Condominium Unit

- **High in a high-rise.** Tenants claim it's quieter near the top of the building. Some probably get a sense of power, or maybe just awe, from being high above the buzz of life on the ground.
- **View.** Vacationers like to look out upon something, something that is different from what they are accustomed to every day, even if it's city lights.
- **Noise-free.** Try to choose a unit that is away from elevators, trash chutes, laundry rooms, and most common-use recreation areas.
- **Corner units.** Corner units usually have more windows, more light.
- **Close to parking.** Parking for condominium units often depends on the style or type of the community. In "garden style" communities, parking should be close to the unit. In high-rise communities, people prefer covered parking. Most tenants prefer an assigned space for each unit rather than whoever-comes-first parking.

LEARNING THE LANGUAGE

Timesharing is the purchase of an undivided condominium interest in a vacation-area resort for a fixed or variable time interval each year, usually a week. Some owners take **fee-simple title** to a particular unit for a particular week (which means that theoretically there can be 52 owners of that unit). Other "owners" buy a **right-to-use leasehold** for, say, 20 years, with their choice of which week they will use to be applied for and assigned each year.

Many large developers arrange for the owners' ability to trade "weeks owned" for weeks in the developers' other projects across the nation. There are also timeshare trading groups that make trade arrangements around the world for a fee. Timeshare trading Web sites are now becoming popular. These sites allow you to sell, rent, or trade timeshares without the use of a timeshare membership group. Key "timeshare rental" into a search engine. You'll get tens of thousands of responses.

Location: Socioeconomic Factors

Knowledge of the demographics and economics of your vacation-area investment can mean the difference between just a pleasant place to spend leisure time and a valuable asset that will weather the normal swings of economic change. Before making a purchase, survey rental rates in the community and the area as a whole. Generally, higher rent areas fare better during economic turndowns.

Consider the geographic draw of the area. Do vacationers come primarily from nearby cities? The Pocono Mountains in Pennsylvania are a good example. The draw is from New York City, Philadelphia, Newark, and other New Jersey, New York, and Pennsylvania cities. In contrast, think about Orlando or Maui where the draw is international. The wider the draw, the more likely an area is to withstand fluctuations in economic conditions.

STOP AND THINK!

Timeshare ownership is rarely a good real estate investment. Because the marketing for new resorts is so intense and the pricing so inflated and because the resale market is so weak, most unit owners find that they must sell their weeks for far less than their original price, sometimes for as little as 20 cents on the dollar. Purchase of a timeshare, however, may indeed be an investment in happiness. It can provide you with many opportunities for dream vacations if you are not good at searching them out on your own.

The size and type of the rental unit and the local attraction that brings vacationers to the area also affect the type of tenants you are likely to get and the appeal for resale. Generally, both large, single-family houses and remote cabins attract families and groups. One-bedroom condominium units appeal to singles and couples, while two-bedroom units attract both small families and retired couples traveling together.

Structure and Condition

All of the usual recommendations for inspecting structure and working condition apply to vacation properties, but there are also some focal points that are more important or more likely to be troublesome when dealing in this marketplace. Here's a list to start your thinking.

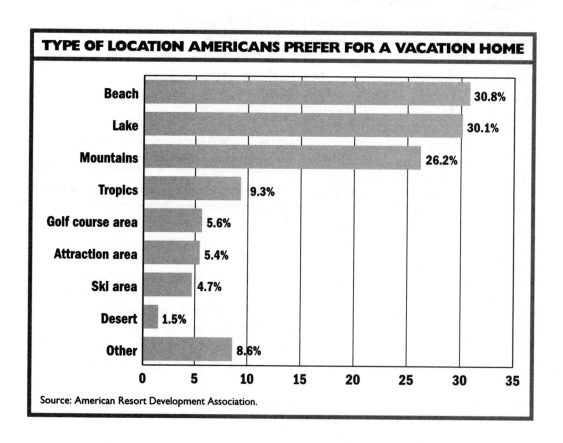

TYPE OF LOCATION AMERICANS PREFER FOR A VACATION HOME

Location	Percentage
Beach	30.8%
Lake	30.1%
Mountains	26.2%
Tropics	9.3%
Golf course area	5.6%
Attraction area	5.4%
Ski area	4.7%
Desert	1.5%
Other	8.6%

Source: American Resort Development Association.

THE FOUNDATION. Is the land stable? Shifting or unstable land can cause cracking and buckling of the foundation. Stability is an important consideration for vacation houses that are built cliffside to enhance the view.

If the house is oceanside and on pillars, are the pillars high enough and strong enough to withstand potential storm damage? Are there enough of them? How much beach erosion has taken place in the past five years? Will there be firm land left by the time you are ready to sell the property?

Is the property located near the top or bottom of a hill? Near the bottom tends to collect water in the basement. Water seepage can even damage a foundation if the land is fairly level. A great deal depends upon the grading of the lot. If the house is closed during the rainy season, poor grading and drainage can allow water to accumulate in the basement. Standing water can cause serious damage and invite molds.

WATER. If the vacation-area property relies on water from a private well, you must check for potability. If water is supplied by a community system, check to see if it is turned off during the off-season. If it is, determine the exact dates. Be aware that the property will be virtually unusable when the community water is off. Find out if there is the possibility of having a well dug for you on the property. Could a well mean the possibility of year-round usage?

LIQUID-WASTE DISPOSAL. Does the vacation area have a sewer system? Will you be paying a sewer-use tax or special fee or is that fee included in the maintenance fee?

If there is no municipal waste disposal system, determine what type of private system is being used.

LEARNING THE LANGUAGE

Potable water is water suitable for drinking. Lab tests on water taken from a private well will show what substances are present in the water and in what quantities. Both states and municipalities set standards for safe drinking water that must be met. Most lenders will not finance a property without proof of potable water.

Septic tank, leech lines, dry well—there are a number of options. Try to get a map showing the plan and location of the waste disposal system. (For newer buildings, the plan may be on file with the building permit in the municipal records office of your town.)

While still negotiating the price and terms, ask for information on the last cleaning of the septic tank. Who did it? Try to get proof.

HEAT AND AIR-CONDITIONING. What type of heating system is used? How old is it? Is it adequate for winter weather? Will the air-conditioning keep the unit cool on the hottest days of summer?

Be particularly careful if you are buying a property that has an addition built on. Often the heating system changes in the new area. Sometimes there is no heat in the added area, relying on heat from the original system. Get a home inspector to check this out. Trying to remedy an error in design can turn out to be more expensive than doing the job the right way in the first place.

ELECTRICITY, PLUMBING, AND APPLIANCES. Will the current systems serve the probable number of occupants during peak season? Does the system have circuit breakers or fuses? Are there enough outlet boxes to discourage tenants from running and overloading extension cords?

Is the capacity of the hot water heater adequate? How old is it? (After ten years, you might find a leak on any given day.)

Is cable TV available in the area? Many tenants want it.

PESTS. When buildings stand unoccupied by humans, wild "guests" sometimes set up house. Have you checked the property for evidence of mice, squirrels, raccoons, bats, termites, carpenter ants, roaches, palmetto bugs, or whatever the local most-likely bother seems to be? What protective measures are currently installed in the building? Is there a pest control service in the area?

How much does protection cost on a monthly or yearly basis?

SECURITY. Because vacation properties often stand empty during the off-season, many owners choose to install security systems. In more remote areas, it's common to hire a local person to check on the property periodically.

Shared-Space Resort Management

If you buy a unit or block of units in a condo or co-op resort for the purpose of profitable rental, consider carefully the rental policies and success rate of the management company. Here are some questions to help you.

■ **Are marketing and advertising used to attract renters?** What are the target markets? Where is advertising placed? Does the management keep records showing the amount of response to various types of advertising?

■ **What is the percentage of occupancy during high season?** Low season? The rest of the year?

■ **How does the management company choose which unit is to be rented?** (This is important because there are many owners in a condominium resort, each with his or her own unit or units in the rental pool.) Ask to see the rental records for the past three years for the unit you plan to buy.

■ **What is the annual rental agent's fee for the unit you are considering?** What services does it include? Is rental income distributed unit by unit as each one is rented? If so, is there an additional "commission" for rental of individual units? Or is rental income distributed through a pool? What portion of the pool does your intended unit get?

Safeguards in the Contract

As with every other investment real estate vehicle, you'll need a tight, buyer-protective purchase contract to guard your interests. In addition to the points discussed in Chapter 8, here are a few things to watch out for specifically in vacation properties.

> **"Give me the luxuries of life and I will willingly do without the necessities."**
>
> Frank Lloyd Wright (1867–1959), American architect

Condo or Co-op Restrictions

Condo and co-op community boards can restrict the number of rentals allowed per each unit each year, the number of occupants allowed per unit, the number of parking spaces per unit, and what type of vehicle can be parked on the premises. (Usually no trailers.) They can also decide whether or not to allow pets (and what kind). Some 55-plus (seniors) communities do not allow children. In some communities, tenants must apply to use the recreational facilities and sometimes there is a fee. Clarify all of these points before you buy; it could well make a difference in your potential tenant pool.

To be certain you get accurate answers to your questions, make the contract contingent on your acceptance of rental and use restrictions in the bylaws or house rules, and get these in writing. You want the potential to rent the unit as often as your plan for the investment indicates. That may be one tenant for five years or a different tenant every week during high season with a vacant unit during low season. Many upscale condominium communities located in seasonal vacation areas require that three months be the minimum rental period to each tenant. This ensures some stability in the community, but it often makes rental less profitable for the owner.

Your main concern in researching the character and the rules and regulations of a condominium community is harmony. You'll want to choose one where you feel comfortable and where your plans for use or rental will not trigger objections or resistance from the other members of the condominium owners' association.

Monies Due

While unpaid back taxes usually result in a recorded tax lien, unpaid association dues or assessments may not be recorded in public records. Be sure that the seller warrants in the contract that there are no unpaid association dues or assessments at the time of sale. Then check with the board of directors. You want all outstanding debts paid off before you take title.

Building Permits and Setback Lines

Vacation properties are notorious for having decks and porches, patios, outdoor shower stalls, parking areas, storage sheds, and basketball hoops added or erected without the owner ever checking the

> ### LEARNING THE LANGUAGE
>
> **Setback lines** are part of the local zoning ordinances. Setback lines establish the closest distance from each property boundary line where improvements may be constructed.

zoning regulations or obtaining a building permit. The new outdoor shower stall and dressing room built and installed by the seller may look like a major property plus, but if a corner of it extends over the setback line and that condition is discovered after you have taken title, you could be liable for all the expenses of getting a zoning variance or for moving the shower stall. The same goes for outbuildings (a storage shed, for example) or additions (perhaps a deck) that were built without a permit and don't meet code.

Making a trip to the local buildings department and checking that everything currently standing meets the current code or is "grandfathered" can be a bothersome chore. Sometimes a real estate agent will help. In any case, it's work that should be done to avoid surprises (sometimes very expensive surprises) later in the ownership time.

Be sure that your contract is *contingent* upon a survey in which everything is as it was represented to be. Then have the survey done. Your survey can be compared with the previous survey, if the seller has a copy, or with town tax records. You can note if any changes to land use or structure were made.

In the contract, the seller should warrant that no structural changes or additions have been made during his or her ownership. Or if changes have been made, a list of those should be included in the contract with a warrant that these conform to local codes and zoning laws. Building permits are kept on file in the town records office and are open to inspection. Again, be sure to check that all necessary permits and permissions were obtained for the property.

DIGGING DEEPER

You can get more information on what makes a desirable resort and a good vacation-property investment from the American Resort Development Association (ARDA). It operates a library, maintains a database, and conducts seminars and conferences.

American Resort Development Association (ARDA)
1201 15th Street N.W., Suite 400
Washington, DC 20005
202-371-6700
http://www.arda.org

Promised Rentals

Because vacation rentals are typically for short periods of time (from a few days to a month or two), a common imagined nightmare is two tenants showing up for the same week, each with deposit receipt in hand. The nightmare intensifies for the new owner who was not told about promised rentals of the previous owner.

Your purchase contract should state that there are no pending rentals. Or if there are pending rentals, the rental agreements and the deposit monies should be turned over to the new owner. If you do not wish to accept a pending rental, the seller will have to arrange with the prospective tenants for a return of their deposit money. Get written verification that this was done.

Some Financing Tips

Vacation property is financed by much the same means as other real estate. Sometimes larger down payments are required for oceanside property or property in remote areas. And sometimes buyers will refinance their primary homes in order to get the down payment required for a vacation-area property.

It can be difficult to obtain a mortgage loan from conventional sources for seasonal cabins or camps because most financial institutions regard them as a high lending risk, similar to undeveloped land. Sometimes you can, however, get seller financing, and sometimes a good mortgage broker can put you in touch with private loan sources. Interest rates tend to be higher than the going rates for owner-occupied houses or other investment properties. Many investors refinance some other piece of property to pay cash for the vacation home.

Condo purchases in established buildings or resorts are usually attractive to local lenders. Sometimes in new resort construction, the developer makes arrangements for financing with a local lender. And occasionally, these prearranged loans are actually at a rate slightly below market.

KEEP IN MIND

- **Vacation-area investment opportunities** range from the primitive cabin in the woods to the most luxuriously appointed condominium penthouse.
- **Rational evaluation of cost and investment potential** is essential in this vehicle where the buyer's emotions and personal needs often play a role in purchase motivation.
- **Correlate the time, working skills, and money you have available** with the time, working skills, and money demanded by the vacation property you are considering.
- **Be aware of the vacation-home tax laws.** Your property qualifies for different treatment as a "second home" or as a rental property. Depending upon which you choose, your time for personal use will be affected.
- **Both the physical and socioeconomic aspects of location** are important to success in vacation-area investment.
- **Condo units in established resorts can be rented** by a management company on a unit-by-unit basis or as a part of a rental pool.
- **Before buying, be certain that your rental plans can be accommodated** within the bylaws and house rules of a condo or co-op community.
- **You may need the help of a mortgage broker** to finance your vacation-area property.

Mixed-Use Buildings

"You can't steal second base if you don't take your foot off first."
Mike Todd (1900–1958), American film producer

We commonly think of commercial real estate as a gathering of shops. Size and scope runs the gamut from local strip malls with half a dozen stores to regional indoor malls with footprints bigger than the village green used to be. These are multimillion-dollar properties. But you, the individual investor, can still own commercial real estate.

"How can I possibly get into that scene?" you ask.

Well, you just have to think out of the box as we talked about way back in Chapter 1. Commercial space does *not* have to house a national franchise. It doesn't even have to house a retail business. You can get into this area of the marketplace if you will think smaller and hedge your bets with some residential space.

A mixed-use building is one way to get into commercial real estate investment without the big-bucks clout of a corporation, public limited partnership, or real estate investment trust. (Public limited partnerships and REITs are discussed in Chapter 17.) A good place to start is a building of two to four stories that houses both commercial and residential tenants.

Such buildings exist in virtually every town and city in the U.S. and they are often within the price range and management demands of the independent investor. Typically, they are older buildings that were built for other uses. They might once have been the mansions of the richest families in town, small factories, grade schools, or the town hall.

Today, commercial tenants are most commonly housed on the street level, with the residential units on the upper floors. Some typical examples of street-level usage are:

- **A food establishment,** such as a restaurant or coffee shop
- **A specialty shop,** such as an independent bookseller, a yarn store, an educational toy store, or an antique shop
- **A mail-order fulfillment center**
- **Professional offices,** such as a pediatrician, a psychologist, a hairdresser, or a Realtor
- **Day-care facilities** for children, disabled individuals, or the elderly

LEARNING THE LANGUAGE

A **sale-leaseback** allows a building-and-business owner to sell the real estate and lease back the commercial space from the new owner, usually for a long-term lease. Although the leaseback technically follows the sale, both are negotiated at the same time and are part of the same transaction. This financial arrangement is a means of raising cash when the business and building owner has significant equity. It provides the buyer with an already-in-place, long-term tenant who usually anchors the value and cash flow of the building.

Some mixed-use investment properties appear on the marketplace with both the business and the residential tenants firmly established with leases in place. For experienced investors who are doing a 1031 exchange for tax purposes (see Chapter 10), there is sometimes an opportunity to work a sale-leaseback with the current owner of the building and business. Sometimes, however, real opportunity for the investor lies in finding an appropriate building and converting it into mixed-use space.

Buying a mixed-use building as an investment vehicle is not for the faint of heart. Think about the following factors.

- **Each building is unique and uniquely situated.** Questions regarding the appropriate use of space are applicable on two different levels (commercial use and residential use). Parking is almost always an issue. The location of stairways and access doors is another.
- **Most available buildings are older and not a part of the current trend toward homogeneous units in a row.** This out-of-fashion status raises questions regarding

desirability and functionality for both the commercial and residential uses. For example, an owner might have difficulty finding a tenant for the second floor unit in a converted Victorian-style mansion when the first floor and basement levels are occupied by a funeral parlor.

■ **Commercial and residential tenants have different goals and needs.** This diversity again raises questions of functionality and appropriateness. For example, think electricity, heat, phone, and hot water when there's a beauty shop on the first floor and two residential units on the second.

For most independent investors, the first venture into this area of the marketplace can be an intimidating experience. Generally, price tags are higher than for the other entry-level vehicles we've been discussing. But then again so are rent receipts.

Can you juggle these balls of different sizes? It feels risky and certainly calls upon some investor courage, not to mention vision and perseverance. Demanding as it is, however, it can be just as rewarding for the investor who is willing to do the necessary research.

Why Buy Mixed-Use Buildings?

There are three basic reasons why investors should consider taking on the challenges that come with ownership of mixed-use buildings:

1. **For income**
2. **To create value**
3. **To house a business**

Income

Income from commercial tenants is usually greater per square foot than it is from residential tenants. In addition, many commercial leases stipulate that the tenant is responsible for paying utility bills and general maintenance costs and sometimes even taxes and insurance. (See "Learning the Language" on page 71 in Chapter 5.)

Commercial tenants also stay longer than most residential tenants. Leases have renewal options that are often executed with rent raises spelled out ahead of time. Sounds pretty good, right? So why not have all commercial tenants? Basically, because most above-street-level space in mixed-use buildings is not suitable for business. Also on the downside, vacant commercial space is much more difficult to rent than residential space. Getting the right tenant may take many months, sometimes more than a year.

Residential tenants in apartments above the commercial space provide a safety net for the investor. Rents from the residential space help to carry the mortgage and pay expenses in those periods of vacant space between commercial tenants.

Creating Value

In addition to bringing in more rent, the mixed-use building generally sells for a higher price than the all-residential building of the same size in nearby or similar locations. Some investors add to their wealth by converting obsolete and often vacant real estate to mixed-use function. The additional value created is usually considerably higher than the return from a fixer-upper or even a multifamily conversion. Bear in mind, however, that conversion costs are also higher and that the economic health of the neighborhood will remain a factor in occupancy.

Some investors sell the converted building for a quick return. *Quick* being a relative term here because the conversion process takes time as does the marketing and selling process. Most conversions to mixed-use buildings qualify for capital gains tax treatment (ownership for 12 months or more). Other investors (the majority) hold the mixed-use building for a period of time, taking in the rental income and benefiting from depreciation allowances.

STOP AND THINK!

Depreciation is a bit tricky in a mixed-use building. You must allocate your depreciation schedule to usage. The residential portion of the building is depreciated over 27.5 years, the nonresidential portion over 39 years. This is an area where an accountant can be helpful.

To House a Business

Many self-employed professionals and businesspeople buy a small mixed-use building to house their own office or retail space. Just like a first homebuyer who chooses to buy a multifamily house because the rents help carry the mortgage, the mixed-use building owner aims to have the residential units pay a portion of the mortgage payment and the building's operating expenses. This arrangement often gives the fledgling business the opportunity to get established and begin to show positive cash flow.

Your Profile for Success

Mixed-use buildings create a complex pattern of ownership and management demands that goes beyond the scope of the traits used for the success profiles in this book. But the following evaluations will give you a sense of what ownership and management can mean in your life. Each trait is rated high demand, moderate demand, or low demand.

- **Assertiveness** (high demand). It's the risk-taking aspect of assertiveness that predominates in mixed-use building investments. Inhabitable residential space can almost always be rented if the price is low

A PROFILE FOR SUCCESS	
Assertiveness:	XXXXXXXXX
Attention to detail:	XXXXXX
Awareness:	XXXXXXXXX
Creativity:	XXXXXX
Initiative:	XXXXXXXXX
Perseverance:	XXXXXXXXX
Rational judgment:	XXXXXXXXX
Self-confidence:	XXXXXX
Strategic planning:	XXXXXXXXX
Strategic planning:	XXXXXX
Tact:	XXXXXXXXX

enough. The demand for commercial space, however, is greatly affected by the local economy (a factor beyond the owner's control). It may not rent easily and quickly at any price. Risk in this investment vehicle runs neck and neck with reward. It takes an assertive person to go out into the marketplace to find the right mixed-use property and take it on.

- **Attention to detail** (moderate demand). Because mixed-use buildings serve two functions (commercial and residential), the details involved in purchase and management are almost doubled. So why the "moderate" rating? This is an area where delegation is essential. (See self-confidence below.) Pay for good professional help. Instruct them to pay attention to the details. Then check up on their work regularly.
- **Awareness** (high demand). The most essential trait for success in mixed-use property investment is sensitivity to the needs and trends in the community.
- **Creativity** (moderate demand). In the case of a conversion, you must be creative enough to see the potential for an alternative use. But in managing the mixed-use building, pragmatism, efficiency, economy, and responsiveness to the preferences, needs, and requirements of the community are more important characteristics.
- **Initiative** (high demand). No one is going to come knocking on your door saying, "I have a great mixed-use building for you." You've got to go out into the marketplace and find one, or you've got to be able to see potential in an all-residential or all-commercial building and initiate the procedures for converting it to a mixed-use building. Among the challenges might be a zoning variance or nonconforming use permit, building permits for remodeling and code compliance, and architectural design.
- **Perseverance** (high demand). If you start a conversion, you've got to see it through. Unfinished projects usually sell below market value, if they sell at all. You must also be able and willing to persevere when problems arise regarding maintenance, supervision of a custodian, rent collection, and eviction.

- **Rational judgment** (high demand). You *must* pay attention to the numbers. Facts must rule over dreams of wealth and power. Ask yourself: Is mixed-use feasible? Is there enough demand for rental housing in the area to keep the residential units occupied? Is the location desirable as a site for a business? Will this building be profitable?
- **Self-confidence** (moderate demand). Whether you're managing an existing mixed-use building or converting a property into one, you will need professional help. Likely to be among your "consultants" will be an accountant, an attorney, a professional engineer, an architect, an electrician, a heating and air-conditioning contractor, and a plumber. Overconfidence in an arena that demands the skills of people trained in many different disciplines can be a fatal flaw.
- **Strategic planning** (high or moderate demand). In a conversion for quick resale, strategic planning is absolutely essential to success. For long-term holding and positive cash flow, the demands on your planning abilities diminish somewhat.
- **Tact** (high demand). The usual politically correct mandates for landlords prevail here, but the areas of focus are slightly different for residential tenants, commercial tenants, and contractors. Demands on this character trait are highest during zoning and planning-board appeals for a conversion or when working with the local buildings inspector.

LEARNING THE LANGUAGE

An **entrepreneur** is a person who takes on the risk of loss along with the opportunity for profit in a business venture. In real estate, an entrepreneur gathers land, buildings, labor, and capital and puts them together to realize a vision.

Time, Work, and Money

Time, work, and money requirements all depend upon your choice of investment mode. The mixed-use building investment can be a quiet source of positive cash flow or a stormy moonlight career. The age-old cliché rings true here: *Don't bite off more than you can chew.*

Converting Existing Property to a Mixed-Use Building

Do you really want to be an entrepreneur? Are you looking for a glorious, turreted Victorian house, a vacant municipal building (a former police station, for example), or something overlooked by others that makes your heart pump more quickly with thoughts of created value? Buying it with the intent of conversion will be a major commitment to a business venture. Think about these demands on your time, skills, and money:

- **Finding a suitable building**
- **A feasibility study**
- **Professional inspections** (note the plural; it's almost always more than one inspection)
- **Negotiating the price**
- **Applying for zoning changes** or nonconforming use permits
- **Working with architects** for redesign
- **Repairs, construction work,** heating and plumbing, and building code requirements
- **Finding tenants** (both commercial and residential) and negotiating leases
- **Remodeling** to meet the specific needs of a business tenant
- **Marketing the property** for (very) profitable resale

The In-Service Mixed-Use Building

Generally, the purchase of a building with commercial and residential tenants already in place makes few unusual demands for time and work. In addition to the typical problems and commitments of managing residential rental property, however, you will also be confronted with the need to remodel each time a commercial tenant leaves. (If you're lucky, this may never happen during your term of ownership.)

The demands on your money supply depend on your choice of

STOP AND THINK!

Location and access rank higher in importance than price when retail space is a part of your mixed-use investment. Do not buy simply because a building carries a bargain price tag. In the wrong location, you may never be able to rent the commercial space in your investment.

investment. Usually after the first year or two of ownership, when the up-front down payment, purchase, and rehab costs have been spent, you should be showing positive cash flow. One relatively small additional expenditure that you may want to consider is increased liability insurance because you are the landlord for both residential and commercial real estate.

Checkpoints for a Good Investment

Because the commercial space in a mixed-use building not only distinguishes it from a multi-family house investment but also accounts for the greater part of its market value and income potential, let's focus on the factors that determine a good commercial-space investment. Also read Chapter 12 for a view of residential-ownership factors before you hop aboard this investment vehicle.

There are five factors to be considered when investing in commercial real estate:

1. **Location**
2. **Physical characteristics**
3. **Legal constraints**
4. **Local market analysis**
5. **Your investment analysis**

It's All About Location

In all real estate investment, the importance of location has a double focus. Think of a theatrical spotlight. It can focus tightly on the central character or broadly on the whole stage. In the same way, location must be considered with a focus on the property in question and on the town or area in which it exists.

In mixed-use building investment, the challenge is greater than in other investment vehicles. You must consider the site of the property, the quality of the land, and the character of the neighborhood and of

> **LEARNING THE LANGUAGE**
>
> When referring to the location of commercial property, **access** means more than roads and driveways. It also includes the surrounding environmental and municipal characteristics (bridges over streams, stairways that climb a steep bank, complex highway-exit systems, and one-way streets, for example). These factors, external to the building, influence both the ease and the safety involved in getting to and from a given piece of property

"It's a recession when your neighbor loses his job; it's a depression when you lose your own."

Harry S Truman (1884–1972), American statesman

the town each separately in terms of appropriateness for residential use and for commercial use.

LOOKING AT THE FOCUSED SPOTLIGHT. Access and neighborhood are the most important aspects of the site location. To be desirable, a commercial location must be easy to get to and inviting for customers, clients, employees, suppliers, and the other businesses that interface with it.

Although the construction, maintenance, and appearance of the other buildings in the neighborhood are important, the *appropriateness* of the neighborhood to the prospective business is the more important determinant of success in creating value. For example, the owner of a chain of stores that sell French country-home décor would not find a mixed-use building in the commercial district of a midsize city appealing for a new branch store, unless that city had a historic tie to French-American history and the mixed-use building was next door to a house where Lafayette once slept.

LOOKING AT THE BROAD VIEW. Both the rent return and the resale value of a mixed-use building will be strongly influenced by the direction and rate of economic growth (or decline) in the surrounding area. It is important, therefore, to be familiar with the master plan, including current or proposed construction and proposed road building.

You, as an investor, should also study predictions for economic growth or decline and forecasts of change in the demographics of the area. Get whatever professional help you may need to review the items listed in the box on page 281. You might search at the chamber of commerce, the local Realtor board, municipal offices, and even the local library. The Internet can also be helpful. Check "Digging Deeper" on page 223 in Chapter 12.

LEARNING THE LANGUAGE

Master plan is a zoning board term for a comprehensive map for the development of the entire municipality. Ideally, the plan will allow for orderly growth that is both economically and ecologically sound. Most cities and towns, even small towns, in the United States have a master plan.

All That You Can See and Touch

The physical characteristics of the property that determine value are the land and the buildings. The lot must be large enough to hold the building and provide ample parking for the typical number of daily customers plus the residential tenants (or municipal parking must be nearby). There must be enough sidewalk or road frontage so that prospective customers will notice the business. And topography and drainage must not inhibit use.

When evaluating a building, look at construction quality, functionality, and support systems. What kinds

---

A CHECKLIST TO EVALUATE COMMUNITY ECONOMIC HEALTH

When you are evaluating the current economic health of a community and its prospects for the future, check the following:

The Master Plan and Land-Use Maps for the Area
- ❑ Recent changes
- ❑ Pending zoning appeals
- ❑ Environmental issues

Current Population and Employment Statistics
- ❑ Total population
- ❑ Population broken down by age groups
- ❑ Employment by industry
- ❑ Ratio of total employment to total population
- ❑ Unemployment ratio
- ❑ Income levels of the employed population
- ❑ Income levels per household

Community growth trends
- ❑ New industry types
- ❑ New industry locations

- ❑ New industry wage scales
- ❑ Population growth
    - ❑ past ten years
    - ❑ projection for next ten years
- ❑ Retail sales
    - ❑ past ten years
    - ❑ projection for next ten years
- ❑ New school construction
- ❑ Property taxes
    - ❑ current
    - ❑ ten years ago
    - ❑ projected

Character of the Community
- ❑ History and historic locations, if any
- ❑ Climate
- ❑ Topography
- ❑ Ethnic makeup
- ❑ Crime rate
- ❑ Educational institutions
- ❑ Cultural attractions and opportunities
- ❑ Recreational opportunities
- ❑ Transportation

LEARNING THE LANGUAGE

Eminent domain is the right of the government to acquire property for the public good. Fair and just compensation must be paid to the owner.

In real estate law, **police power** means the power of the state to overrule the individual in questions of safety, health, and the general welfare of society. It is the basis for building codes and zoning laws.

of commercial establishments would work in such a building? Is there a possibility for expansion? Do residential tenants have means for private access? Are there fire escapes? Can electrical, heating, and plumbing systems be reconfigured to separate commercial and residential use?

The Letter of the Law

Under the mandate of the state's police power and, sometimes, eminent domain, real estate is highly controlled and regulated. Investors in mixed-use building conversions must be aware of building codes, health standards, the current zoning restrictions, and the likelihood of obtaining necessary variances.

Municipal ordinances can also regulate the business operations that are permitted at a given site. For example, the law may not allow an establishment that sells or serves alcoholic beverages within a certain distance of a school. You must do the necessary research on allowable land use before making an offer on a prospective property. Spend some time in the municipal offices. Ask questions until you are directed to the answers.

A Matter of Trade

An investor in mixed-use buildings should remember that the demand for commercial rental space will reflect the demand for the business activities that might use that space. Think about the types of businesses that might function well in the property you're evaluating. What is the current demand for their goods and services? How will predicted changes in demographics affect that demand? How many businesses in the field compete in the local area? How much appropriate real estate is available to these businesses?

Because supply and demand determine value, it's important to look at other mixed-use buildings similar to your prospective purchase. What are rental rates for the commercial space? The residential space? Do rates vary significantly from one area of town to another? What is the vacancy rate for commercial space in town? For residential space?

The Residential Part of the Deal

Whether your mixed-use investment is a two-story house with one commercial unit and two residential units or a four-story apartment building with three commercial units and six residential units, rent from the housing space will be an important contributor to positive cash flow. Evaluate this part of the investment just as you would a multifamily house (see Chapter 12). Be aware, however, that in mixed-use buildings you may have to deal more frequently with municipal authorities and you may be held more closely to compliance with local housing laws in addition to federal and state fair-housing statutes.

Some municipalities have periodic inspections of rental units and health-department inspections of

---

STOP AND THINK!

The federal **Fair Housing Act** and **Fair Housing Amendments Act**, which are administered by the Department of Housing and Urban Development (HUD), prohibit discrimination in housing for any of these reasons:
- **Race**
- **Color**
- **Religion**
- **National origin**
- **Familial status**—includes families with children under 18 and pregnant women
- **Physical or mental disability**
- **Sex**

For more information, visit the Web site of HUD's Office of Fair Housing and Equal Opportunity at http://www.hud.gov/offices/fheo/index.cfm or contact your local HUD office (check the blue pages of your phone book).

---

some commercial establishments. In some areas, a buildings inspection will be required whenever residential rental property changes ownership. (If that is the case in your area, be sure to make your contract contingent on the building being up to code.)

Rent control is still in effect in some metropolitan areas, particularly in the northeast and California. (See "Learning the Language" on page 237 in Chapter 13.) If you are considering buying property in these areas, be aware that rent-control limitations may strongly affect the potential income from the residential portion of the building.

About Carrying Costs and Cash Flow

Last but certainly not least among your checkpoints for a mixed-use building investment is your analysis of the investment itself, its demands and opportunities, its current market value, its cash flow, and its projected appreciation. You will need to go to Chapter 6 and work the numbers.

Bear in mind that you should allow for extra fix-up money in your calculations because most commercial tenants expect renovations to suit their needs. And you should establish a larger contingency and emergency fund than you would in multifamily house investments because a vacancy in the commercial space may be lengthy.

Safeguards in the Contract

Everything said about purchase contracts for multifamily houses applies to mixed-use buildings. In addition, include in your contract contingencies that the zoning changes or nonconforming use permissions you anticipate will be granted and/or that the structural changes you anticipate doing will be approved. These contingencies could postpone the closing date by many months and may well be a point of negotiation. Pay special attention to zoning regulations that might affect the businesses you see as prospective tenants.

Carefully review the local building codes if you plan to remodel or put on an addition. A building permit may be required even for an interior restructuring of space. Those changes can move a building out of its "grandfathered" designation and then you will be required to bring everything up to current code.

Your contract should also state the name in which you will take title. This could be an individual, group, partnership, or corporation. To protect yourself against increased personal liability as the landlord of a building that houses a business open to the public, consider forming a limited liability company (LLC) to buy the property. The LLC is looked upon as a partnership for tax purposes by the federal government (even if there is only one partner) and recognized as a separate legal entity in the majority of states. This separation means that the LLC, not you or your bank account, is liable for any awards or settlements won by injured tenants or customers.

> ## DIGGING DEEPER
>
> You should consult with an attorney if you are considering the creation of a limited liability company. These books can also help you with background information:
> - *How to Profit by Forming Your Own Limited Liability Company* by Scott E. Friedman (Dearborn Trade Publishing)
> - *Nolo's Quick LLC: All You Need to Know About Limited Liability Companies* by Anthony Mancuso (Nolo Press)
> - *Starting a Limited Liability Company* by Martin M. Shenkman, Samuel Weiner, and Ivan Taback (John Wiley & Sons, Inc.)

Some Financing Tips

Buying mixed-use properties can sometimes require a larger percentage of the purchase price for the down payment on the mortgage than on loans for home mortgages. But in a competitive financial marketplace, there are many lending programs to choose from. A good mortgage broker can be invaluable when starting out in this field. Traditional lending institutions (banks) hold only a small portion of equity capital for commercial real estate. Pension funds, life insurance companies, and real estate investment trusts (REITs) hold a much larger share.

Joint Ventures

Some investors get 100 percent financing for the purchase of their mixed-use property, plus the cash for refurbishing, remodeling, or conversion by giving up a portion of ownership share to a lender. This form of equity participation is commonly known as a joint venture.

In a joint venture, the investor/developer and the lender become business partners. The lender contributes the money, the investor provides the expertise and the working time. Sometimes the ownership share is 50-50, but other splits are also common. Both conventional lenders and private individuals or groups participate in this type of financing arrangement.

Business Loans

If you are interested in buying a mixed-use property to house your business, remember that you will be adding financial support for the mortgage qualification from the residential rents. Before you begin a hunt for property, however, contact the Small Business Administration, which makes and guarantees small-business loans in the United States (see Digging Deeper below).

DIGGING DEEPER

In addition to start-up loans, the **Small Business Administration (SBA)** offers an immense amount of free information on every aspect of business. The material is organized into four categories:

1. **Starting your business**
2. **Financing your business**
3. **Managing your business**
4. **Business opportunities**

To get answers to your questions, visit the SBA's Web site at http://www.sba.gov or call its "Answer Desk" at 800-827-5722.

The Friends-Only Limited Partnership

Limited partnerships are regulated by the U.S. Securities and Exchange Commission and by laws in each state, called blue-sky laws, intended to protect investors against fraudulent sales practices and activities. While these laws vary from state to state, most states typically require companies making offerings to register their offerings before they can be sold in that particular state. The laws also license brokerage firms, their brokers, and investment advisors.

When a group of family, friends, and associates wishes to raise money to purchase a larger and more expensive investment property, however, there is sometimes an opportunity to create a small limited partnership without undergoing state regulation and fees. *It is essential that you consult a local attorney before pursuing this financial opportunity.* Some state laws are very particular, others are not.

The idea is to form your own limited partnership with yourself as the general partner and friends only as the limited partners. When a business venture is limited to friends only, neither the federal Securities and Exchange Commission (SEC) nor state regulatory agencies will usually create undue restrictions on or expenses for such a business arrangement. Here are some suggestions that will help to keep your limited partnership from being regulated under the laws for larger private or public limited partnerships:

- **Limit your offering to a small group of relatives, friends, and associates.**
- **Do business in the same state as the property you intend to buy.**
- **Make your offering of limited-partnership shares only to residents of the state where you do business and in which the property is located.**
- **Do not advertise your offer publicly.**
- **Comply with all the laws of the state concerning fraud and equity.**

Keep your group of investors under 35 persons and be sure that you can prove you knew everybody before you invited them into the investment project. Be honest and open about disclosing every pertinent fact to every member of your group. And again, use an attorney who knows the state regulations.

This friends-only limited partnership may sound a bit intimidating, but it is a legal way to raise

LEARNING THE LANGUAGE

A **limited partnership** consists of one or more **general partners** who are responsible for complete control and management of all aspects of the business and one or more **limited partners** who invest capital but have no vote in decision making and no responsibility for work. The general partner is liable for losses incurred by the venture. The limited partners are liable only to the extent that they risk the capital they contributed to the project. (For more details, see Chapter 17.)

money for an investment project. If your venture is successful, you, as the general partner, will make a lot of money and your limited partners will also get a handsome return on their investments.

How About a Small Apartment Building?

Buying and owning an all-residential apartment building is very similar to buying and owning a larger mixed-use building, except somewhat simpler because you don't have the concerns of accommodating a commercial tenant. With that exception, the criteria for a good investment are essentially the same. Success will depend on location, the soundness of the structure, operating costs, and the current and future economic health of the community.

Apartment buildings are often good long-term investments showing both positive cash flow and tax benefits. They are such good investments, in fact, that most are being bought up by real estate investment trusts and limited partnerships. These two ownership groups are powerful forces in the marketplace and sometimes make competition for the larger and better buildings overwhelming. Generally, as an independent investor starting out, it's better to stay with the smaller buildings. Once you get your feet wet, however, you may choose to move on to larger properties. Check out the books in Digging Deeper on this page.

DIGGING DEEPER

Before you decide to play in the major leagues of the real estate marketplace, read what some experts have to say:

- *The Complete Guide to Buying and Selling Apartment Buildings* by Steve Berges (John Wiley & Sons, Inc.)
- *How to Buy and Sell Apartment Buildings* by Eugene E. Vollucci and Stephen Vollucci (John Wiley & Sons, Inc.)
- *Make More Money Investing in Multiunits* by Gregory D. Warr (Dearborn Trade Publishing)

KEEP IN MIND

- **A mixed-use building is a high-risk, high-reward purchase.**
- **The three most common reasons for investing in mixed-use buildings** are: income, conversion to create value, and housing for the owner's business.
- **Commercial rents** are higher than residential rents for the same space.
- **Conversion from all-residential to mixed-use** increases the value of a property but demands greater time and work commitments from the investor.
- **The five factors** to be considered when investing in mixed-use real estate are: location (both lot site and surrounding area), physical characteristics, legal constraints, the local market analysis, and the investment analysis.
- **Creative financing** is sometimes available on mixed-use property, including joint ventures and friends-only syndication.
- **Residential apartment buildings** are usually higher-priced but less-complex purchases than mixed-use buildings.

The Challenges of Land

"Think of what you can do with what there is."
Ernest Hemingway (1899–1961), American author

By the time you've read this far, you are certainly aware that real estate investing is not exactly a science. Indeed, there are laws and procedures, theories and probabilities, but then there's the human factor. If you were to gather ten experienced real estate investors in a room and ask them ten easy questions, you'd get an array of opinions on every issue and lots of stories that begin, "That reminds me of the time when . . ."

But there's one judgment that just about everyone agrees on: Undeveloped land is the highest risk among all the real estate investment vehicles. Financial advisors advise against land purchases for almost all independent investors. At best, it is a place to invest only money that you are quite sure you won't be needing.

What makes it so risky? Consider these factors:

- **Most land generates no income** during the period of ownership, leaving property taxes to create negative cash flow.
- **Because land is considered indestructible,** there is no depreciation allowed for federal income-tax purposes.
- **The municipality in which the land** is located governs how the land can be used.
- **Development of land** is subject to environmental testing and regulations.
- **Land is the most nonliquid** investment in real estate, which, as a whole, is considered a nonliquid invest-

> **"Every man holds his property subject to the general right of the community to regulate its use to whatever degree the public welfare may require it."**
>
> Theodore Roosevelt (1858–1919), American statesman

ment. Its sale can take years and some land truly cannot be sold at any price.

Why Buy Land?

With all those negative and high-risk factors, you can't help but wonder: *What could possibly be the appeal of land as an investment?* The answer is money.

From colonial times on, great American fortunes have been made in land. This is an investment vehicle that can often be bought dirt cheap (pardon the pun). With no work effort, it can bring a return that is many, many times its original cost. That's the lure of land. But—and this is a big but—chance and luck play as important a role in successful land investment as foresight and knowledge do.

This investment vehicle brings the best return when the land lies in the path of prosperity. But prosperity is fickle, and its path often changes direction. Increases in land value are almost always dependent on future use, economic growth, and demographics. All of which boils down to supply and demand.

Just as an example, think of the oceanfront land between Miami Beach and Fort Lauderdale, Florida. In the 1950s, there was nothing on that strip but sand, weeds, scrub bushes, and an occasional palm tree or two. The land was cheap by any standard. Some parcels were bought for trailer parks, others for small motels. By the early 1980s, that land had become some of the most valuable in the nation. Many of the trailer park and motel owners sold out to resort hotel and condo developers. Those sellers never had to work another day.

But that investment took almost 25 years to come to fruition. Too long, you say? Okay, in the same state, think about land in the vicinity of Orlando. Everything from residential building lots to large tracts went up in value the day after Disney announced plans for Disney World. And the spiral still goes on as the value of land in an ever-widening circle continues to appreciate. If you had insider information or a hunch about Disney (or were just plain lucky in your choice of investment land), an inexpensive land purchase could have returned a fortune.

To repeat the essential nugget here: Land investment is a combination of foresight and luck. Understanding this investment vehicle can increase your odds for success, however. So let's take a look at it. There are three types of land investment:

1. **Long-term holdings**
2. **Speculation**
3. **Subdivision/development**

Long-Term Holdings

This is a no-work, no-worry form of real estate investment. You buy a tract of land that's considered way out, far from everything. Then you wait for growth and development to move toward your holdings. Or you hope for some major corporation to locate its headquarters or a new branch nearby. As your land becomes less far from everything, its value increases. Then you sell.

The challenge lies in the fact that there is no way to be sure growth will move in your direction, or how long that movement will take. And owning land costs you money. You must pay property taxes during the period of your ownership. Long-term land investment is a good place to put money that you can forget you have.

Speculation

Land speculation looks for a faster return on risk and investment. The speculator usually sees or imagines something coming. The thought goes: Soon there will be both a need and a general desire for a change in the use of this parcel of land. With the change in use, there will be a greater demand for the land and therefore an increase in its value.

Few speculators actually buy and pay for their land investment. We'll talk about how they decrease their cash investment by using options and land contracts in just a bit.

STOP AND THINK!

Unless you're the kind of risk taker who thinks skydiving is a pleasant way to spend a Sunday afternoon, invest in land only money for which you will have no need in the foreseeable future.

Subdivision and Development

Because of the time, expertise, and money involved in the subdivision and development of large tracts of raw land, few individual investors choose this investment vehicle. If you're willing to think smaller, however, there are opportunities to start out in parcels of land that can be subdivided into two or three lots. This entry strategy works especially well when there is a house already on the property. See "Checkpoints for a Good Investment" later in this chapter.

Your Profile for Success

Your profile for success in land investment depends on your intended strategy. Because long-term land holding is a passive investment, it has a low demand in all character-trait categories. So let's consider speculation and subdivision/development. Each character trait will be rated high demand, moderate demand, or low demand.

■ **Assertiveness** (high demand). You will need to be assertive in arranging financing and working with planning and zoning boards. Assertiveness may also be a factor in your ability to find potentially profitable land *and* persuade the owner to sell it.

■ **Attention to detail** (high demand for subdivision/development, moderate demand for speculation). If you choose to be a subdivider or developer, the work is by nature a compilation of details. If speculation is your game, the detail-oriented work is usually in the financing arrangements.

■ **Awareness (high demand).** What you know about the town, its economic and demographic profiles, and local politics can mean the difference between suc-

A PROFILE FOR SUCCESS

Assertiveness:	XXXXXXXXX
Attention to detail:	XXXXXXXXX (subdivision/development)
Attention to detail:	XXXXXX (speculation)
Awareness:	XXXXXXXXX
Creativity:	XXXXXX
Initiative:	XXXXXX
Perseverance:	XXXXXXXXX
Rational judgment:	XXXXXXXXX
Self-confidence:	XXXXXXXXX
Strategic planning:	XXXXXXXXX
Tact:	XXXXXX

cess and failure. Your decision to purchase should also be influenced by research and knowledge regarding nearby suburban areas, the closest metropolitan area, the transportation and pattern of commuting, and plans for future road construction and/or industrial development.

■ **Creativity** (moderate demand). Most of the actual planning work for land development will be done by civil engineers and architects. Your creativity will come into play in visualizing the possibilities for use of the land.

■ **Initiative** (moderate demand). Initiative is needed in behind-the-scenes work. You'll have to spend some time digging through records in the tax assessor's office to see who owns the land around the parcel being considered. At the zoning board office, you'll look at the town's Master Plan to see *where* future development is allowed and *what* exactly is being encouraged.

■ **Perseverance** (high demand). You must learn to believe that "no" can often mean "maybe" when you deal with town officials and environmental engineers. Also sometimes with prospective lenders.

■ **Rational judgment** (high demand). Don't get caught up in the idea of owning a mountaintop or the farm that you vaguely remember from your childhood. Not all land is valuable and value is not necessarily deter-mined by the size of the tract or by its beauty. You must weigh demand and feasibility for development without emotional input.

- **Self-confidence** (high demand). To act upon a vision (or a hunch), you must believe in yourself. Friends and relatives may laugh and say, "That's impossi-ble." Will you have the self-confidence to proceed?
- **Strategic planning** (high demand). In speculation or development, you must know your goal and have a plan for getting to it before you start out. Other-wise, you may find yourself working through the in-vestment process like a blind person in a forest.
- **Tact** (moderate demand). People at zoning-board meetings have been known to get more than a little hot under the collar, as have people negotiating

---

DIGGING DEEPER

If you would like to get a glimpse of the work involved in land development, you might start with a look at these books, which are technical but highly informative:

- *Land Development Calculations: Interactive Tools and Techniques for Site Planning, Analysis and Design* by Walter Martin Hosack (McGraw-Hill)
- *Land Development Handbook* by The Dewberry Companies, Philip C. Champagne, Sidney Dewberry, and Philip Champagne Davis (McGraw-Hill)
- *Practical Manual of Land Development* by Barbara C. Colley (McGraw-Hill)
- *Real Estate Development* by Mike E. Miles, Gayle Berens, and Marc A. Weiss (Urban Land Institute)

If you are considering a rural land purchase that will serve as the site for a vacation home with plans to subdivide and sell some lots at some date in the future, you might profit by reading:

- *Finding and Buying Your Place in the Country* by Les and Carol Scher (Dearborn Trade Publishing)

---

over price on the sale of property. You will need tact to stay cool and courteous while at the same time working toward your personal goal.

Time, Work, and Money

Long-term land investment makes few time demands on the investor. Holding time (usually years) doesn't require your attention, and working time is the time it takes each quarter to write a check for property taxes. Money is usually a cash investment, either paid in a lump sum or over time to the seller. That's the easy side of the street.

Speculation and development require less holding time but usually consume many hours of working time with prospective lenders, civil engineers, surveyors, attorneys, local zoning boards, and environmental groups. Long before any ground is broken for development, there is a significant cash drain for planning and testing work. If you are a developer, cash is also needed for the down payment on seller financing or the outright purchase of the property. If you are a speculator, cash risk and demand can be lowered by using an option.

An option locks in a deal for a future date. The speculator is betting that the property will increase in value before the option expires. Let's look at an example of how this might work.

> **LEARNING THE LANGUAGE**
>
> In the real estate marketplace, **to assign** means to transfer one's interest or rights in a property to another party. Assignment can be used with purchase contracts, leases, deeds of trust, mortgages, options, and even title. If you want the right to assign your interest in a property, state that in writing in the agreement. Some purchase contracts specifically forbid the right to assign. You can make the right a negotiating point.

Farmer Brown has 25 acres of pastureland for sale for $100,000. Tom Speculator has some insider information that General Motors is considering a tract of land in the next town for a new research and office park. If GM locates in the next town and if Farmer Brown's land can be subdivided into building lots for houses, the parcel will be worth much *more than the price Farmer Brown is asking. (Approved building lots of ½ acre are selling for $30,000 to $50,000 in the area.)*

Rather than buy the land and then be stuck with it if General Motors chooses another site and/or the development is not approved by the zoning board, Tom Speculator offers Farmer Brown $2,000 for an option to buy the property at full price 12 months from that date of option agreement.

During the 12-month option period, Farmer Brown cannot sell the land to anyone else. Meanwhile Tom waits and watches the GM deal to see if it goes through. At the same time, if he chooses to do so, Tom can apply for subdivision approval on Farmer Brown's tract.

If all goes as he's betting and he gets the subdivision approved, Tom can exercise his option to buy the land at any time during the 12 months and then begin selling building lots. Or he can sell the whole parcel to a developer. Or he can bypass the buying process entirely by assigning his option to a developer. (He might charge the developer $10,000 for the option, thus pocketing a quick $8,000 and letting the developer do the work of getting zoning board approval.)

If approval for the subdivision is denied or if GM changes its mind, Tom can decide not to exercise his option. Then he will have lost the $2,000 he paid for the option, but will have no responsibility to purchase the parcel.

Checkpoints for a Good Investment

What makes land more or less valuable? Putting economic demand aside, it's how the land can be used. Look at the pyramid in the box on the following page. The uses named at the top of the pyramid bring the highest prices per acre; those at the bottom, the lowest. Significant returns on invested capital are often made when land use can be

THE LAND USE/VALUE PYRAMID

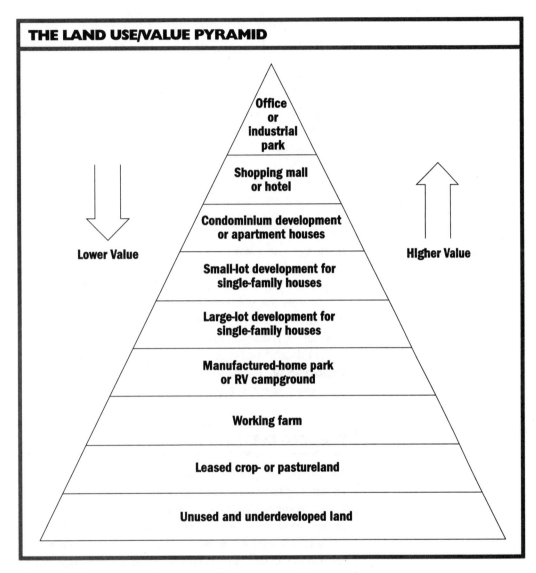

Office or industrial park

Shopping mall or hotel

Condominium development or apartment houses

Small-lot development for single-family houses

Large-lot development for single-family houses

Manufactured-home park or RV campground

Working farm

Leased crop- or pastureland

Unused and underdeveloped land

Lower Value

Higher Value

changed from a category near the bottom of the pyramid to one nearer the top.

Factors in the Use of Land

But like most things in life, determining the best use for land is not quite as simple as a pyramid of value. Because of location, physical characteristics, demographics, and economics, not all land is appropriate for all uses. You'll hear both investors and zoning-board members talk about the "highest and best use" for a parcel. That potential use is affected by many of the following factors:

- **Road access and traffic patterns.** Will existing roadways be adequate after proposed development is completed? Will traffic lights become necessary? Is there access through the property to another outlet and another road or is there only one access to the property?
- **Availability of drinking water.** Can the developer connect into municipal water supply? If private wells are necessary, is the underground water source adequate? Is the water drinkable?
- **Drainage and waste disposal.** Can the developer connect into municipal sewer systems? If private waste disposal systems are required, what type will work best given the soil conditions and topography? Does the land meet percolation standards for adequate drainage? If a significant area of the property is paved for roads and parking, where will the runoff water go?
- **Topography.** Is the topography appropriate for the proposed use change?

DIGGING DEEPER

An understanding of the topography is essential before committing to an investment in land. Fortunately, that's easy to come by. The U.S. Geological Survey is responsible for providing accurate maps that show the topography of the land throughout the nation. The USGS Earth Science Information Centers (ESICs) answer questions, sell maps, and distribute consumer-oriented materials.

- **For the address of the ESIC** nearest you or for answers to other questions, contact the USGS at 888-275-8747.
- **The USGS Web site** features a section on "Finding and Ordering USGS Topographic Maps" at http://mcmcweb.er .usgs.gov/ordering_maps.html.
- **To access topographic maps online,** visit http://www .topozone.com.

■ **Environmental factors.** How will your proposed development affect the surrounding areas? Are wetlands protected from development? Is there a possibility that hazardous materials have been dumped and buried under the topsoil?

Remember that highest and best use may change over time as the demographics and economics of an area also change. Zoning, which regulates the usage of land, is determined by educated opinion and committee consensus. Often, it is subject to challenge and debate.

The Land in Every Season

The parcel of land you are considering may look and feel quite different at another time of the year. You should walk every square foot of a parcel before buying, with topographical maps in hand if possible. Look for dry streambeds that may become roaring rivers in spring. Avoid soggy swampland that will turn away developers who do not want to spend megabucks dealing with drainage problems. Inquire if the area is subject to flooding, severe windstorms, erosion, mud slides, sinkholes, or whatever other local weather or geologic problems might be prevalent.

Take note of any rock outcroppings. Visible rock may be an indication that expensive blasting will be required for development. Pay particular attention to the soil reports that are done with percolation tests. Is there any evidence of contamination from nearby industrial sites or dumping grounds?

Getting Started in Subdivision

If you find the idea of land subdivision and development appealing, but you're intimidated by the big bucks and red tape, you can sample this investment vehicle with a manageable and relatively low-risk investment: an older house on an extra large lot. At mid-20th century when the idea of planned neighborhood development (the early Levittowns) was just catching on, some homebuyers persuaded the builders to include extra land for a small increase to their

DIGGING DEEPER

For information about local independent home-builders and factory-built house manufacturers, you can contact:

The National Association of Home Builders
1201 15th Street, N.W.
Washington, DC 20005
800-368-5242 or 202-266-8200
http://www.nahb.org

The Manufactured Housing Institute
2101 Wilson Boulevard, Suite 610
Arlington, VA 22201
703-558-0400
http://www.mfghome.org

purchase price. In some cases, the extra land was just short of another legal building lot, in others it actually was an additional lot. If you can find one of these properties, it can get you started.

Often you'll see them advertised with leads such as "double lot" or "subdividable property." The more aggressive and assertive investor may even find eligible properties by hunting in the tax records office. On the tax maps, look for vacant lots with the same owner's name on a contiguous lot. Or look for outsize lots in areas where everyone else lives on the standard rectangle. Then make inquiry by mail, phone, or in person to see if the owners will consider selling their house. Many of these homeowners are not aware that the extra land can spell profit.

When you consider buying such a property, you'll be combining the demands and rewards of the single-family fixer-upper with the challenges of land investment. You should be able to make money on both deals. To subdivide the land, you will have to go through all the steps that any large developer would take in subdividing a large tract. You will have to petition the zoning board, draw the new plat, and present your appeal for subdivision.

If you are approved, you can sell the fixer-upper and the new lot separately. Or you can put up a house on the new lot, sell it, and keep the old house as a rental property until you are ready to sell. (You can work with an independent builder for the new house or you can have a factory-built house delivered and assembled on a foundation by a manufactured-housing company.)

If your petition for subdivision is not approved, you can still profit from resale of the fixer-upper.

That's the safety net. In either case, you will have "learned the ropes" of subdivision and development with relatively low risk and small investment. (It also helps that you can get mortgage financing on the fixer-upper, which will help you buy the property in the first place.)

All of this can be even more profitable if you choose to live in the fixer-upper as your home for at least two years. Then you can supervise construction on the newly created lot and you can claim the home-owner tax exemption on your newly fixed-up house when you finally sell at a tremendous profit, a profit influenced by the beautiful new house next door.

Safeguards in the Contract

Contracts to buy land are very much like all other real estate purchase contracts. You want to be assured in writing that you can get clear title and that the contract specifies exactly what you are buying and how much you are paying. Title insurance is available for land just as it is for houses. Be sure to get it. Also insist that the seller provide you with a survey (at the seller's expense) and that the property is marked by monuments.

Make the land-purchase contract contingent on percolation and soil-testing results that are acceptable for the land use you anticipate. If the land does not have access to a public water supply, the contract should specify water rights or be contingent on the availability of well water.

As mentioned, many speculators and developers use an option to secure enough time to get subdivision approval before committing to purchase. If a seller is not amenable to an option, however, a purchase contract can be written contingent on subdivision approval. Getting approval from the local zoning

> ### LEARNING THE LANGUAGE
>
> In the real estate marketplace, a **monument** is a visible, permanent object marked or installed by a surveyor to identify the boundaries of a parcel of land. It may be artificial, such as a wooden or concrete post, or natural, such as a tree or large rock. Most surveyors mark the monuments with "flags," usually brightly colored plastic strips.

or planning board can take several months, so allow at least six months before the contract expires, and include a provision for extension if delay is due to no fault of the buyer.

When you are buying land contingent on approval for a change of use, it's advisable to have the contract drawn by a local attorney who is active in the real estate marketplace. Local politics almost always plays a part in subdivision and development. You will need legal help not only with the filing procedures but also with the planning and presentation of your proposal to the appropriate committees or boards.

Some Financing Tips

Financing land can be a creative venture. In fact, sometimes it's a joint venture with a lending institution or a "silent partner." It's almost always easier if there is a building on the property.

The Farm Fantasy

Many land dreamers think that they can buy a farm from a farmer in financial distress and turn it into an instant cash crop by subdividing for single-family houses. If this were really so bright an opportunity, don't you think the farmer might have thought of it? Or perhaps a professional developer?

The fact of the matter is that most farms are not situated in locations appropriate for current housing-

---

DIGGING DEEPER

If you are interested in buying a farm, Uncle Sam might just help. For information on current programs, contact:

Farm Service Agency (FSA)
U. S. Department of Agriculture
http://www.fsa.usda.gov

In farming areas, you'll find addresses and telephone listings in the phone book in the federal government section.

---

tract development. If you're willing to hold the farm as a long-term investment, however, you may indeed harvest a sizable profit. And unlike raw-land investments, there is financing available for farms, including help from Uncle Sam.

The federal Farm Service Agency (FSA), once known as the Farmers Home Administration (FmHA), makes or insures mortgage loans to farmers and ranchers who can't get credit from other lenders. Often these are low-down-payment loans. FSA mortgage money is also available for the purchase and improvement of farms and the building or rehabilitation of farmhouses and outbuildings.

Unlike other land investment, farms do carry some tax benefits. If the farm is rented, the buildings can be depreciated. Other benefits include tax credits, reduced property-tax rates, and reduced assessments both for farming and for preservation of agricultural land (not developing it).

For some investors, these benefits add to the appeal of a farm as a long-term vacation-home/investment property. The working farm is leased to a farmer while the family builds and enjoys a country house.

Seller Financing

Seller financing is more prevalent with land sales than with any other real estate investment vehicle. Most of these mortgage loans are short-term notes (five years or less) on which the buyer pays interest only, with the entire principal due on sale or maturity. While the seller holds the mortgage, the buyer usually secures subdivision approval or a zoning change. When the buyer/subdivider sells the parcel to a developer, he or she pays off the mortgage held by the seller. When a subdivider or developer wants to sell off individual lots within the parcel, however, a seller-held mort-

> **"Farming looks mighty easy when your plow is a pencil and you're a thousand miles from a cornfield."**
>
> Dwight D. Eisenhower (1890–1969), U.S. Army general and American statesman

---

LEARNING THE LANGUAGE

A **release clause** is a provision in a mortgage-loan agreement that allows for the freeing of a piece of the property when proportionate payment has been made.

Equitable title or **equitable ownership** is legal possession by a person who does not have legal title, such as the buyer under a land contract, or (technically) the trustor under a deed of trust (legal title being in the trustee).

gage can become a problem unless it includes a release clause.

Sometimes seller financing is done with a land contract, also called an "agreement for deed." In this situation, the seller continues to hold legal title to the property while installment payments are being made by the buyer. The buyer, however, assumes equitable title, which allows him to use the land as his own. The advantage to the seller (and risk to the buyer) is that the seller can reclaim rights to the land if the buyer defaults on payments. There is no foreclosure procedure required, and the buyer may lose all the money that has been paid to date.

If you choose to use a land contract, protect yourself from some loss if you default on the payments by having your attorney write in an agreement specifying how much will be forfeited. Not every seller will agree, of course. And even if there is a written agreement, you may not get any money back until the land is sold again, which may be some time.

KEEP IN MIND

- **Land is not only a high-risk investment** but also a nonliquid investment.
- **There are three ways to invest in land:** long-term holdings, speculation, and subdivision/development.
- **Options** are an important tool for the speculator.
- **Profitable land investment** often depends upon a change in the use of the land.
- **Always walk the land before purchase,** giving careful consideration to topography, drainage, and the effects of seasonal weather changes.
- **Have your land-purchase contract drawn by a local attorney** who is active in the real estate marketplace.
- **Be aware of environmental restrictions** in the area.
- **Farms are rarely a source for instant-profit subdivision** but they may be excellent long-term investments.
- **Seller financing** is common in land investment.

Paper Real Estate

"There is a danger of being persuaded before one understands."
Woodrow Wilson (1856–1924), American statesman

Does this chapter belong in this book? Paper may be the product of trees, but it's certainly not a piece of the earth. And buildings are not made of paper—not yet anyway. Is "paper real estate" an oxymoron?

Not any more than "jumbo shrimp." There are ways of owning an interest in real estate without actually taking title to anything. These paper real estate holdings release you from property hunting, estimating value, negotiating, financing, planning, managing, landlording, and marketing for sale. In other words, you can make money in real estate without all the demands and most of the headaches of real estate ownership.

So why bother with the work? Is the concept of fee simple ownership for the independent investor becoming as outmoded as the rotary dial telephone? Perhaps we should choose our real estate investments in the same way that we choose among mutual funds.

Many people are doing just that. Investment in paper real estate has increased dramatically in the past 20 years and is still increasing. In the hope of a good return without the expenditure of time or effort, investors are committing their money; some of them don't realize that money can be lost in this marketplace more easily than it can be lost in fee-simple investment.

Besides time and effort, the one big difference that distinguishes paper real estate investing from traditional real estate ownership is *control*. When you put your money into paper real estate, you are no longer captain of the ship. Decisions regarding the money you invest in this real estate marketplace will be made by someone else.

Think back to the beginning of this book. Chapter 2 discussed control as one of the reasons for choosing to invest in real estate. Lack of investor control over his or her investment makes paper real estate as different from fee-simple ownership as European "football" (soccer) is from American football.

Paper real estate investment is a huge and diverse field. Whole books have been written about its many vehicles and you'll see space allotted to most of those vehicles in major financial publications such as the *Wall Street Journal* or *Business Week*. This chapter will introduce you to some of the most common possibilities for investment, suggest what you should know or learn, and warn you regarding what to watch out for. But this chapter is *preschool,* not even kindergarten, in terms of what there is to know about this field.

Having acknowledged these limitations, let's look into tax sales and tax-sale certificates, public limited partnerships, real estate mutual funds, and real estate investment trusts.

Tax Sales and Tax-Sale Certificates

You've probably heard of property being sold for back taxes. Maybe you've watched some late-night infomercials that promised riches just by using their sponsors' "guaranteed" methods for buying property "on the courthouse steps." Or maybe you've been browsing among the more than 4,000 sites on the Internet if you key "tax+lien+certificate" into a search engine. Most of them want you to subscribe to their advice publications. As you might expect, it's not quite as easy—or risk-free—as they make it seem.

Tax Sales

Tax liens take precedence over all other liens, and governments (federal, state, and local) can *and do* seize and sell property for unpaid taxes. But there are rules—many, many rules—and they are different in each state. Some states issue deeds; others issue certificates when a property is seized and sold for unpaid taxes. The box on page 311 indicates which state does which.

> ### STOP AND THINK!
>
> Tax sale or certificate **redemption periods** are set by each state. They range from 180 days to four years or more. In many states the delinquent owner is allowed to remain on the property. Needless to say, maintenance by the tax-delinquent owner is rarely good and many properties lose value. Carefully study your state's laws on tax liens before you enter this investment vehicle. For information, call your state attorney general's office.

TAX DEEDS. In states that deed the property to the tax-lien buyer, the deeds are issued (although sometimes held unrecorded) at the tax sale. They either wholly or conditionally transfer title to the property from its tax-delinquent owner to the successful bidder.

In cases where a portion of property taxes is not paid with the monthly mortgage payment, the successful bidder is most often the first-mortgage holder. Federal statutes provide that if there is a government-insured loan (FHA, for example) on a property that is sold at a tax-forfeited sale, the government agency has one full year to redeem. So don't count on moving in the day after you purchase a property on the courthouse steps.

In some deed states, after the paper deed is issued, the successful bidder must then deal with the state's statute of redemption (a law that allows the delinquent owner to reclaim the property by paying the back taxes, expenses, and interest during a specified period of time). In all but two states, all lien holders of record must be served notice and they also have an opportunity redeem the property prior to the expiration of the redemption period. Once the deed to the new owner is actually issued, all prior liens are extinguished. In two states, Delaware and New Mexico, liens that are attached to the property prior to the attachment of the tax lien are not extinguished.

TAX SALE CERTIFICATES. In certificate states, forfeiture for tax delinquency does not convey ownership to the property in question. Instead a *tax-lien certificate* creates a first priority lien on the property with a right to foreclosure that is subject to the state's statutory right of redemption.

The buyer of the certificate pays the outstanding tax and expense bill. Then he or she must wait through the period of redemption. During that period in order to redeem the property, the delinquent owner must pay the certificate holder the full amount that he or she paid for the tax certificate, plus interest, and sometimes expenses and penalty fees. (The interest rate on tax lien certificates is set by each municipality and is quite high, commonly 15 percent to 20 percent, and it can be even more.)

If the tax certificate is not redeemed by the tax-delinquent owner or another party with a possible legal interest in the property, such as an heir, an ex-spouse, or even a contractor with a mechanic's lien, the investor must then initiate foreclosure proceedings. The purpose of foreclosure proceedings is to convey title to the holder of the tax lien certificate.

Even when foreclosure proceedings are complete, there may be claims against the property or other problems in getting clear and marketable title. If this occurs, you will find yourself in court for a "quiet title" action. If the court's decision goes in your favor, you will own the real estate. If it goes against you, you will lose the real estate and the money you have invested.

LEARNING THE LANGUAGE

Action to quiet title is a court action to establish ownership of real property when there is a dispute. In every state, all parties with a potential interest in the property are notified that a lawsuit has been filed to determine the validity of the title. The court then hears the case and rules on the matter. The decision establishes **marketable title.**

DEED AND CERTIFICATE TAX SALE STATES

Here is a list showing states that use **tax sales for deed** and **tax lien certificates.** Be aware that this information can be changed at any time by legislation. And, at the end of the day, tax deeds are, in fact, sold in almost every state when the local government acquires property because the tax lien certificates offered for sale remain unsold.

Alabama—tax lien certificates
Alaska—tax sales for deed
Arizona—tax lien certificates
Arkansas—tax sales for deed
California—tax sales for deed (the state legislature has authorized tax lien certificate sales, each county must implement)
Colorado—tax lien certificates
Connecticut—tax sales for deed
Delaware—tax sales for deed
District of Columbia—tax lien certificates
Florida—tax lien certificates
Georgia—tax sales for deed
Hawaii—tax sales for deed
Idaho—tax sales for deed
Illinois—tax lien certificates
Indiana—tax sales for deed and tax lien certificates
Iowa—tax lien certificates
Kansas—tax sales for deed
Kentucky—tax lien certificates
Louisiana—tax lien certificates
Maine—tax sales for deed
Maryland—tax sales for deed and tax lien certificates

Massachusetts—tax sales for deed
Michigan—tax sales for deed and tax lien certificates
Minnesota—tax lien certificates
Mississippi—tax sales for deed and tax lien certificates
Missouri—tax lien certificates
Montana—tax lien certificates
Nebraska—tax lien certificates
Nevada—tax sales for deed
New Hampshire—tax lien certificates
New Jersey—tax lien certificates
New Mexico—tax sales for deed
New York—tax sales for deed and tax lien certificates
North Carolina—tax lien certificates
North Dakota—tax lien certificates
Ohio—tax sales for deed
Oklahoma—tax lien certificates
Oregon—tax sales for deed
Pennsylvania—tax sales for deed
Rhode Island—tax sales for deed
South Carolina—tax sales for deed and tax lien certificates
South Dakota—tax lien certificates
Tennessee—tax sales for deed
Texas—tax sales for deed
Utah—tax sales for deed and tax lien certificates
Vermont—tax lien certificates
Virginia—tax sales for deed
Washington—tax lien certificates
West Virginia—tax lien certificates
Wisconsin—tax lien certificates
Wyoming—tax lien certificates

DIGGING DEEPER

Before you get lost among the thousands of Web sites trying to sell you advice on tax liens, you might curl up on a winter's night with:

- ***Profit by Investing in Real Estate Tax Liens: Earn Safe, Secured, and Fixed Returns Every Time*** by Larry B. Loftis (Dearborn Trade Publishing)
- ***You Can Do It Guide to Success in Tax Lien and Tax Deed Investing*** (2 Vol.) by Lillian Villanova (AuthorHouse)

A Demanding and Sometimes Risky Investment

Dealing in tax deeds and tax sale certificates is not an easy road to riches. It makes intense demands on the investor for assertiveness, perseverance, patience, and knowledge of the law. Although there is little demand for working time during the redemption period, work demands may become overwhelming if the delinquent owner does not redeem the property and the investor must take possession.

Many investors in tax certificates never expect to take over ownership of the property in question. They buy the certificates for their high interest rates, fully expecting the delinquent owner to redeem them. (Some studies show that up to 97 percent of these properties are redeemed.) Tax certificate holders take on a risk, however, for the time and money that will be required for refurbishing and resale if the owner doesn't redeem. Some investors don't see this as much of a risk because of the very high potential profit in a property bought for unpaid taxes.

If you are considering taking on this paper vehicle, do so only if you have investment cash that you can afford to do without indefinitely. Legal proceedings can tie up a property for years, and costs mount up quickly. Also, if worry about what might or could happen to the delinquent owner who can't redeem the certificate will keep you up at night, stay out of this marketplace.

Public Limited Partnerships

In Chapter 15, we discussed forming a small limited partnership or a friends-only syndicate as a means of raising capital to buy a mixed-use property or small apartment building. As the general partner in that small group, you would be actively involved in the management of your investment. In fact, you would be in complete control. That's not the case in the paper real estate investment of private or publicly traded limited partnerships.

If you were to buy shares (often called units) in a publicly traded limited partnership (LP), you would be one of many limited partners, all of whom have no responsibility or authority in the management of holdings. Your financial liability would be limited to the amount of money you invested. The projected life span of the limited partnership would also be spelled out in the prospectus (usually seven to ten years).

Limited partnerships are not limited to real estate. They are a form of investment organization in many industries from agricultural products to mineral mining, from Broadway to Hollywood. Real estate, however, is among the less-risky ventures in this high-risk vehicle because the investment is anchored in tangible ownership (real estate) that has at least some inherent market value.

LEARNING THE LANGUAGE

A **specified limited partnership** tells you in advance exactly what properties it intends to buy. A **blind pool limited partnership** collects your money first and then decides what properties it will buy. In both forms, the general partner has total power. Needless to say, there have been many cases of abuse of funds in this investment vehicle.

Master limited partnerships (MLPs) are limited partnerships that are traded on the New York and American stock exchanges. This trading virtually eliminates their nonliquidity.

"His horse went dead, and his mule went lame, And he lost six cows in a poker game; Then a hurricane came on a summer day, And blew the house where he lived away; An earthquake came when that was gone, And swallowed the land the house stood on. And then the tax collector came around, And charged him up with the hole in the ground."

Anonymous American tale

Some limited partnerships are sold by brokerage firms. Some higher-priced LPs make private offerings only to financially qualified individuals. You must submit a summary of your financial status before the offering will be made to you.

Real estate limited partnerships are able to buy large (and expensive) pieces of property (shopping malls, vacation resorts, apartment complexes) by pooling investor money, just as mutual funds pool money to buy a large and diversified stock portfolio. Buying into a limited partnership, however, is much more expensive than buying into a mutual fund. Brokerage firms that sell limited partnerships charge up-front sales

---

DIGGING DEEPER

For information about the limited partnership industry, visit the Web sites of :

Investment Program Association
1101 17th Street, N.W., Suite 703
Washington, DC 20036
202-775-9750
http://www.ipa-dc.org

National Association of Securities Dealers (NASD)
For the addresses of district offices around the
country, call 301-590-6500.
http://www.nasd.com

Among the many publications and advisory services in this industry is:

The Stanger Report
Robert A. Stanger & Co.
1129 Broad Street
Shrewsbury, NJ 07702
http://www.rastanger.com

Subscriptions to this quarterly cost $475.97. If that seems a bit steep, consider getting a group together to share copies or ask if your library can get copies on interlibrary loan.

---

fees that often total between 8 percent and 10 percent of the investment. Annual management fees can run as much as 3 percent to 4 percent of the investor's assets. Some limited partnerships also charge an incentive fee that can amount to 15 percent of the net proceeds from the asset's sale.

Publicly offered limited partnerships must answer to the rules and supervision of the Securities and Exchange Commission (SEC), which regulates even the form of the offering prospectus. An LP prospectus may run to 100 pages or more and be full of details you'd rather not read. Before you pile it with last week's newspapers, however, think about how much money you are investing, and then think about the fact that you will have no control over its management.

In addition to being expensive and risky, limited partnerships are often a nonliquid investment. You may not be able to sell your units if you should have a need for the money you've invested. Or, more correctly, you may not be able to sell at a profit, or even a break-even figure. There are some brokerage houses and independent firms who will buy limited partnership shares, but at a huge discount. Sometimes the price is less than half of the face value.

Before the Tax Reform Act of 1986, limited partnerships were an attractive investment to many wealthy and high-salaried investors because they allowed depreciation losses to be passed through and deducted against the investor's ordinary income. That is no longer the case. In fact, virtually all of the tax benefits of investing in limited partnerships have been eliminated and some tax-filing headaches have been created. The primary advantage of an LP—the opportunity to participate in the ownership of larger, more-expensive, and potentially very profitable real estate properties—can be overwhelmed by these disadvantages:

- **The high cost of purchasing units**
- **High annual management fees**
- **Nonliquidity**
- **The ever-present chance of mismanagement by the all-powerful general partner**

If you are presented with a limited-partnership opportunity "too good to turn down," make yourself read every word of the prospectus—twice—as a cooling-down exercise. If, after this careful study, you are still convinced that the LP will bring in a good annual return and very profitable liquidation of assets in ten years or so, proceed with caution. If possible, talk with a financial advisor who has no personal interest in the partnership. If you are still determined to buy in, then invest only money that you are quite certain you won't need.

Most financial advisors don't recommend real estate limited partnerships as an investment vehicle, but the industry is still alive and kicking despite the tax reforms that have eliminated most of its advantages. New limited partnerships are being formed by young and hungry entrepreneurs with business degrees in real estate, and people are joining up. In fact, there are those investors who swear that a good LP, invested in when your child is ten, will pay his or her way through college. Maybe. And maybe it'll wipe out enough funds to guarantee financial aid.

DIGGING DEEPER

Brokerage firms will provide you with a wealth of free material describing their offerings. Several mutual fund families offer real estate–oriented funds. Some of them are listed below:

■ **American Century Real Estate Fund**
  800-345-2021
  http://www.americancentury.com

■ **Fidelity Real Estate Investment Portfolio**
  800-343-3548
  http://www.fidelity.com

■ **Franklin Real Estate Securities Fund**
  800-342-5236
  http://www.franklin-templeton.com

■ **U.S. Global Investors Real Estate**
  800-873-8637
  http://www.us-global.com

■ **Van Kampen Real Estate Securities Fund**
  800-341-2911
  http://www.vankampen.com

Real Estate Mutual Funds

There are several mutual funds that focus on real estate. Some buy REITs (discussed next), some buy real estate stocks, some buy the stocks of homebuilders and suppliers to the homebuilding industry, and some buy mortgage-backed securities. The advantages of such investments are similar to those of all other mutual funds:

- **The ability to provide holdings in a widely diversified portfolio**
- **Professional management of investment monies**
- **Relatively low management fees (1 percent of your invested assets is common)**

The process of investing in a mutual fund oriented toward real estate is no different from investing in any other mutual fund. Their market activity, however, is closely related to the response of real estate to current economic conditions. For example, funds heavily invested in equity REITs do better when interest rates are low and occupancy rates and rents are high. Funds heavily invested in homebuilding and homebuilding suppliers do poorly when new housing starts dip for economic reasons.

Many real estate mutual funds confine their investments to U.S. real estate companies. Some funds, however, have charters that permit them to invest globally. As with all market investments, risk and return are usually related in real estate mutual funds. Investors who confine their investments to American soil have a more stable economy and a more secure government behind their investment but smaller potential for sudden and rapid growth. Investors who venture into foreign markets are often seeking out so-called emerging markets where growth potential is tremendous if everything goes well in the economy and government.

Real estate mutual funds are really an investment in the stock market, albeit an investment in a highly specialized selection of stocks. What you know or don't know about real estate will have little effect on your success in this marketplace. What you know or don't know about the stock market in general and mutual funds in particular can make a significant difference.

Real Estate Investment Trusts

In his 1998 book *World Boom Ahead*, Knight Kiplinger wrote:

> *"The biggest structural change ever to hit the commercial real estate industry has occurred in just the past few years, and it will accelerate in the decades to come. It's the shift in ownership of commercial property from wealthy individual developers and small private-investment partnerships to enormous, publicly traded mutual funds called REITs—real estate investment trusts."*

It was an accurate statement and a good prediction. REITs (pronounced reets, rhymes with beets) were created as an investment vehicle by Congress in 1960, but they didn't really catch on until the 1990s. Now they are changing large-scale residential and commercial real estate investment into a financially liquid marketplace that is competing with corporate stocks and bonds for investor attention.

STOP AND THINK!
Dividends paid by REITs to shareholders are taxed as ordinary income, except when a portion of a dividend is considered a return of capital and is therefore not taxed. Check with your accountant before you file.

Most REITs are publicly traded companies. In addition to their focus on real estate, they are distinguished from other companies by their legally established right to avoid taxation at the corporate level as long as they pass 95 percent of their earnings to shareholders each year, paid as dividends.

There are three types of REITs:

1. **Equity REITs** own real estate—their revenues come principally from rents.
2. **Mortgage REITs** hold mortgages or mortgage-backed securities—their revenues come principally from interest.

3. Hybrid REITs combine the investment strategies of equity and mortgage REITs by both owning real estate and holding mortgages.

In 2004, 79 percent of the publicly traded REITs in the United States were of the equity type. These companies own large apartment complexes, malls and shopping centers, hotels and vacation resorts, office buildings, hospitals and health care facilities, industrial parks, storage facilities—even some prisons. Seventeen percent of REITs deal exclusively with mortgages, either originating new loans or buying mortgage-backed securities. Only 3 percent of REITs both own property and originate or buy mortgages.

There were 193 publicly traded REITs in the United States at the end of 2004, with a market capitalization of over $300 billion. In addition there were 20 more REITs registered with the SEC but not publicly traded and approximately 800 REITs that were not registered with the SEC and not traded on any stock exchange.

Ownership in these REITs gives the individual investor a chance to participate in commercial real estate growth, just as ownership of stock allows for participation in corporate growth—or loss. REIT prices go both

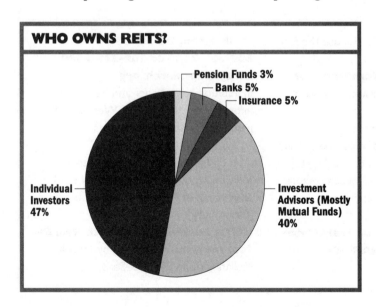

WHO OWNS REITS?

Pension Funds 3%
Banks 5%
Insurance 5%
Individual Investors 47%
Investment Advisors (Mostly Mutual Funds) 40%

up and down. Like stocks, they respond to the state of the national and world economies and to rumors about virtually every major element of those economies. In addition, REITs are sensitive to interest-rate changes and to overbuilding in selected markets.

Of all the paper real estate investments available to the individual investor, REITs are usually the most appealing because:

- **The ability to diversify spreads the risk of property investment.**
- **Professional management allows for knowledgeable investment in geographical areas beyond those familiar to the individual investor and in types of real estate unfamiliar to the individual or beyond his purchasing power.**
- **The investment is liquid; average daily trading volume in REITs is in the millions of dollars.**

Choosing a Good One

So how do you go about choosing a good REIT? Just like everything else in the real estate investment marketplace, it takes some work. Start by becoming famil-

---

DIGGING DEEPER

For more information on REITs, use the following resources:

- **InRealty: Internet Information for Institutional and Commercial Real Estate Investments**
  http://www.inrealty.com
  This Web site provides a multitude of links to sources of information on REITs, real estate mutual funds, sources of demographic and market data, books, and more.

- **National Association of Real Estate Investment Trusts (NAREIT)**
  1875 Eye Street, N.W.

Washington, DC 20006
800-362-7348 or 202-739-9400
http://www.nareit.org
In addition to statistics and background information, the NAREIT Web site offers pamphlets, books, and reports.

For an understanding of the growth and development of the REITs industry read:

- ***Investing in REITs*** by Ralph L. Block (Bloomberg)
- ***REITs: Building Profits with Real Estate Investment Trusts*** by John A. Mullaney (John Wiley & Sons, Inc.)

iar with the industry. You can follow information about it and find statistics that show performance of both the industry and individual REITs in newspapers and publications such as the *Wall Street Journal, Barrons, Kiplinger's Personal Finance Magazine,* and *Business Week.* Financial-reporting services such as Bloomberg, Dow Jones, and Morgan Stanley also publish performance statistics and REIT indexes. The two Web sites in the box on the facing page also provide daily and monthly information.

Once you have learned the terminology and are beginning to get a feel for the industry, start to evaluate individual companies. You can get leads for narrowing down your choices from financial magazines and newspapers. Most experts recommend that you look for the following factors.

> ## LEARNING THE LANGUAGE
>
> **FFO (funds from operation)** is a statistic published by REITs that indicates income without the effect of depreciation. It is a more accurate indication of REIT financial health than net income, which includes tax-allowable depreciation on buildings that may, in fact, be appreciating, and is therefore lower than FFO.

- **Focus.** Top-performing REITs seem to concentrate on buying a certain type of property or on buying within a certain geographic area.
- **Dividends.** Follow statistics on FFO (funds from operation) and the resulting payments in dividends. Note that depreciation allowances will result in payment of more than 100 percent of net income. The best REITs can sustain dividend levels over several years.
- **Comparative performance.** Note how price changes in particular REITs compare with the performance of the industry as a whole. You're looking for better-than-average performance for at least the past five years.
- **Holdings.** Is the type of property held by the REIT in current demand (vacation resorts or long-term care facilities, for example), or an uninteresting but reliable staple (the suburban strip shopping mall, for example), or a combination of both types? Over-building of "hot markets" is a perennial threat in real estate investment.

The Power (and Safety) of Diversification

Specialization has many rewards in real estate investment, just as in life. You become something of an "expert" in your investment vehicle of choice. You know what makes money and what does not. You know where and how to get things done. In other words, you learn the shortcuts to success.

Specialization also has its risks, however. Investing in only one type of property in only one geographical area can make you susceptible to financial loss if that market turns sour, even temporarily. REITs offer investors with a particular interest in real estate the opportunity to diversify their holdings. In return for the diversification, you give up control. But you get liquidity.

KEEP IN MIND

- **You will give up control** of your investment if you choose to put your money into paper real estate.
- **Tax sales for deed** and **tax lien certificates** are more complicated and risky than their advocates would like you to believe.
- **Public limited partnerships** no longer have tax advantages.
- **Buying into a limited partnership** is expensive and annual management fees are usually high.
- **Real estate mutual funds** are traded just like any other mutual funds. Some limit holdings to U.S. companies; other funds invest globally.
- **REITs** have earned a secure place in the American investment marketplace. They allow individual investors to hold a share in commercial real estate that would otherwise be far beyond their means or abilities.
- **One of the major advantages of REITs is their liquidity.**

But Can You Make a Living at It?

"All experience is an arch, to build upon."
Henry Adams (1838–1918), American historian

Do you remember those "career exploration" papers most of us had to write in high school? Hardly anyone ever wrote about careers in real estate. In fact, if you put down "real estate" as your topic, your teacher assumed you meant *selling* real estate, and then looked at you with only a tad more respect than if you had said "used-car salesman."

Even though some of the nation's greatest fortunes have been made in real estate ownership and development, it's usually not the career one plans to enter during the young and starry-eyed stage of life. Many of us, more or less accidentally, stumble into real estate. A few of us are escorted in at the back gate. Many of us choose the field at a time in life when being wet behind the ears is only a distant memory. And some of us make a great deal of money in the real estate marketplace and never call the business anything but a sideline.

"What's wrong with making a little money on the side?" you say.

Absolutely nothing. This entire book has been written with that in mind. But what if you lose your job (or hate your job) partway through your traditional "working life" and you are looking around for a full-time substitute? Can you make a living in one or more of real estate's many investment vehicles? Let's talk about it.

Some Career-Start Tactics

How you get started in a career in the real estate marketplace can make a difference in what you do there and how successful it all turns out to be. Some of the determinants of the *how* and *why* are circumstantial. And some are embedded in your unique character and personality.

Accidentally Stumble In

I see myself in the "accidentally stumbled in" group, but not everyone would agree with that. An astrologer friend who also happened to know my extended family and the fact that I'm a Virgo smugly said, "Not a chance! You were destined!" Well, maybe.

My father's father came from Poland without a penny. When he died at 50, he was one of the largest property owners in the Polish section of town. He was also a good teacher to his seven sons and two daughters, and my father (the middle son) caught the real estate bug. Among my earliest childhood memories are living in an apartment over my parents' grocery store/meat market and sometimes being allowed to go out with my father to collect rents in his buildings. In the next generation, it was my actions that got us (my husband and me) started making money in real estate.

We had just had our second child and were living in a tiny three-bedroom tract house when I noticed an ad in the newspaper for a lakefront acre in the next town. It was a flag lot with a long gravel right-of-way across two other lots. And the acre itself was a steep slope to boot. Oh, but it was so beautiful! Wild mountain laurel blooming everywhere. Swallows sweeping the sky. Yes, our emotions ruled. We dreamed of our dream home and we bought it, with a straight (interest only, due annually) mortgage to be held by the seller.

LEARNING THE LANGUAGE

Flag lot is real estate jargon for a lot that has no road frontage. (The term probably reflects the similarity of the plat map to a flag on a pole— long skinny driveway to a rectangle of land.) The access to a flag lot is either by an easement over the land of a neighbor or neighbors who do have road frontage or by ownership of a strip of land wide enough for a car to pass.

How fast a year flew by. Suddenly, we faced the date the first year's interest was due. And we didn't have the money.

At the time I was taking a graduate course. A friend in that class leaned over and passed me a note that read: "Do you know anyone who wants to sell real estate? Allied Brokers is opening a new office in Branford." Branford was the town just south of us. I applied, read *Principles of Real Estate* over the weekend, took the state licensing exam on Monday, listed a house on Friday, and sold it on Sunday. We had the money for our interest payment and I was hooked.

Five years later, the birth of our third child was keeping me homebound from my work as a Realtor. "Hmm . . . most Realtors can't write," I thought, "and most writers can't 'realt.'" So I wrote *The House Hunt Game* and stumbled into yet another real estate–related field.

A more common stumble-into-the-marketplace situation is buying needed housing for one's own family. Many people get into investment real estate because buying a multifamily or fixer-upper is the only way they can afford to get into the market. When they're successful at their first endeavor, they often try another. And another. Sometimes they hold on to the original properties and work at building a pyramid of value.

Some people are forced into landlording and then find, to their surprise, that it's not such a bad idea. What seems like bad luck when they can't sell their condo or vacation property and must rent it turns out to be the start of a rental property ownership and management career.

And sometimes the need for some extra cash prompts one to look at possibilities in owned real estate. Our older son's experience in real estate development began by subdividing an "almost" double lot and putting up a manufactured house that arrived in four parts.

By the Back Gate

Some people neither stumble into the real estate marketplace nor pay the price of admission. They are wel-

> **"People don't choose their careers; they are engulfed by them."**
>
> John Dos Passos (1896–1970), American writer

comed in through a back gate reserved for "VIPs," who have immediate access because of their "family ties."

My friend Sandra was working as a visiting nurse when her mother die. Sandy inherited seven rental properties. After she moved into her mother's house, she realized that she no longer needed to work at nursing for a living. She efficiently managed the properties, sold two, and bought three others. Many people inherit real estate. Most sell and take the cash. But a few look at the income and the possibilities.

My brother learned the ropes of buying, selling, and managing both residential and commercial property from our father. He went on to establish one of the largest real estate ownership, construction, and management companies in Connecticut. They not only build and manage single-family housing developments and residential apartment buildings but also shopping malls and movie theaters. His son now operates the business. Now *that* is entering by the back gate.

A Matter of Choice

In Connecticut, Butch Bailey built a house for my husband and me during the 1990s. Working with him as our general contractor had none of the earmarks of the usual custom-building nightmare. Everything was completed on time; every detail was attended to, including the several changes that I made, sometimes a bit too late.

Butch began his career as a builder with one house that he built for himself and his family. When they moved into that house, he began building another. The family moved into the new one and sold the old at a large profit. This house exchange had already happened several times when we met Butch. In fact, the house we bought from him had just been framed when we saw it (and modified it). It also had been intended for his own.

Today Butch is a developer, working tracts of several houses at the same time. He began with a high-school education and a knowledge of fine carpentry. He learned the rest, including how to get financing and how to deal with all the red-tape permits and inspections that restrict and determine homebuilding. He is an excellent example of a person who chose real estate as his career.

Bryan Eastman also chose real estate as his career but his story is a very different one. He had college behind him and was working at a "good" job at IBM. But he was not satisfied. He objected to the anonymity of the corporate hierarchy. "You're just a Social Security number there," he said. He objected to the unreliable (often nonexistent) rewards for exceptional work. And he objected to his lack of control over important decisions.

Bryan was young, single, and willing to take risks when he began to explore the real estate marketplace. He started by buying a couple of fixer-uppers. He still owns both as rental properties. Then with a partner, he began a company called Innovative Equity. What do they do? Bryan says, "We wholesale real estate."

"That's a new one!" you say. "Exactly *what* is a real estate wholesale company?"

I had to ask the same question.

Through networking, Innovative Equity has developed a list of over 1,000 people who are interested in buying real estate. That list is the backbone of the business. The day-to-day activity of the business is finding property that owners want to sell.

Bryan and his partner search the marketplace. They watch the for-sale-by-owner ads in the newspaper; they watch the obituaries (people often sell inherited property); they listen to the talk at every social gathering they attend; they read foreclosure notices; they distribute flyers describing their search for property both by mail and by handing them out on the street; and they let it be known that they are willing to pay a finder's fee of $1,000 to anyone who gives them a lead on a property that they actually buy. When they find an interested seller, they inspect the property. If it's appropriate, they make an offer and sign a purchase contract. *Then* they *assign* that right to purchase that property to one of their interested buyers, *for a fee.*

> **"All work is as seed sown; it grows and spreads, and sows itself anew."**
>
> Thomas Carlyle (1795–1881), Scottish historian and writer

Bryan quit his job at IBM and went into real estate full-time in September 2004. The business is thriving. There are no real estate entrepreneurs in Bryan's family. He has chosen (one could almost say "created") this career and developed it on his own.

Building Blocks

So you think real estate might be for you, not just as a sideline to secure your financial future but as your source of the proverbial bread and butter, day-to-day. However, you don't want to stumble in, you have no family ties in the marketplace, and the choices made by Butch and Bryan are just a bit too risky to feel comfortable. There are two other gates to a career in real estate: education and experience.

Books and Classes

It wasn't too long ago that colleges offering a major in real estate were a rarity. About the most you could easily find were a few courses in the business curriculum or perhaps a community college that offered the necessary study to take the state's licensing exams. Today, a college and university search at Peterson's Web site will bring up over 270 colleges in the United States that offer studies in real estate. There are both four-year degree programs and continuing-education courses offered to the community.

The Urban Land Institute (ULI) Web site offers the names of 47 colleges and universities in the United States that offer real estate development and related education programs. The names include University of California at Berkeley, Harvard, and MIT. (Not a bad group at all!) And if you're wondering if anyone else in the world cares about real estate education, you'll also find colleges in Scotland, Spain, Cambridge (UK), London, Dublin, Germany, Hong Kong, Belgium, Singapore, Sydney, Melbourne, Fiji, Northern Ireland, and Canada.

If you wish to go beyond the bachelor's degree, 97 colleges on Peterson's Web site offer graduate degrees in real estate. Some of these are in real estate law and finance, others in building construction and city planning.

The ULI runs a number of nondegree programs, among them the Real Estate Development Certificate and the Real Estate Development Finance Certificate. Programs and seminars in other fields are held throughout the year at various locations across the nation.

DIGGING DEEPER

You can search the Web for profiles of colleges that offer real estate majors. Two good places to start are:

**Peterson's Guide to Four-Year Colleges
http://www.petersons.com**

**The Urban Land Institute
http://www.uli.org**

The ULI has published a number of books on real estate development, finance, and city and regional planning. Explore its Web site for new ideas and an overview of trends in the industry.

The American Resort Development Association (ARDA) also sponsors seminars and study programs throughout the year. Its Web site and address can be found in "Digging Deeper" on page 268 in Chapter 14. It offers a number of books and pamphlets at its bookstore on the Web.

A Start in Sales

Many careers start by selling the product of an employer. In my opinion, there's no better way to learn the ropes and establish a network of support people in the real estate marketplace than by working as a real estate agent for a few years. (Unless, of course, you want to pursue a graduate degree, and that, really, is a different route that usually appeals to a different type of personality.)

By state law, you must begin in the business of selling real estate as a licensed real estate salesperson working under the supervision of a licensed real estate broker. After a number of years (in most states two), you can take the required number of advanced courses, apply for a broker's license, take the test, and (if your test results are satisfactory and your application is approved) open your own office. The period as a salesperson is very much like an apprenticeship, except that your efforts can be rewarded with substantial income.

As a licensed sales agent you will learn real estate law, contracts and procedures for listing and selling property, compliance with zoning and building codes, and real estate finance. Perhaps even more important, however, you will meet virtually all of the people in the real estate marketplace that were discussed in Chapter 5. While earning an income as a sales agent, you can establish the contacts that you will need later as a developer, renovator, or property manager.

Real estate licensing laws are established and enforced state by state so you will need to contact your state regulatory commission for the information that will be pertinent to obtaining a license. Fortunately, this has been facilitated by a trade organization called The Association of Real Estate License Law Officials (ARELLO). In describing itself, it says: *ARELLO is a global, nonprofit association made up of entities involved in regulating the practice of real estate.* Its Web site is a gold mine of information about every facet of the business, with links to many other organizations.

The National Association of Realtors (NAR) also sponsors study programs in many specialized fields of real estate. If you are interested in development, finance, commercial property, or a residential specialty, you can take courses that will illuminate many aspects of these fields. You are eligible to take these courses while working as a licensed salesperson under a Realtor broker. For contact information, see "Digging Deeper" on page 329.

DIGGING DEEPER

On this Web site you can get names, addresses, phone numbers, and e-mail addresses for real estate licensing officials in every state and Canada. You can also read the actual real estate licensing laws for each state. Links are available to other real estate–related organizations.

The Association of Real Estate License Law Officials (ARELLO)
P.O. Box 230159
Montgomery, AL 36123-0159
334-260-2902
http://www.arello.org

Read! Read! Read!

Reading is a way to go beyond training sessions, beyond school-of-hard-knocks experience, and beyond the classroom. Even when you think you know a field, reading a book about that field will often give you a new perspective and strengthen your ability to make your own decisions based upon concepts rather than "procedures and policies." The Digging Deeper box below offers just a few suggestions of the type of books that might be helpful. Find the specialties that interest you, pick some books, grab a cup of coffee or tea at a large bookstore or a comfortable seat at the library, and browse. You can also find listings of books on real estate development and investment at http://www.amazon.com and http://www.barnesandnoble.com. If you see something there that interests you and the price tag is too steep or you'd like to look through it before buying, you can ask your librarian to get it for you through an interlibrary loan.

> **"Any investment in knowledge always pays the best interest."**
>
> Benjamin Franklin
> (1706–1790), American statesman

DIGGING DEEPER

Here are a few examples of the kind of extra reading you may choose to do.

- *Construction Funding: The Process of Real Estate Development, Appraisal, and Finance* by Nathan S. Collier, Don A. Halperin, and Courtland A. Collier (John Wiley & Sons, Inc.)
- *Developing Timeshare and Vacation Ownership Properties* by Diane R. Suchman (Urban Land Institute)
- *Fundamentals of Building Construction: Materials and Methods* by Edward Allen and Joseph Iano (John Wiley & Sons, Inc.)
- *Multifamily Housing Development Handbook* by Adrienne Schmitz, Karen Danielsen, and Kenneth Beck (Urban Land Institute)
- *Professional Real Estate Development: The ULI Guide to the Business* by Richard B. Peiser and Anne B. Frej (Urban Land Institute)
- *Secrets of a Millionaire Real Estate Developer* by Mark B. Weiss (Dearborn Trade Publishing)

Winning

People outside the real estate marketplace often look with a shade of envy at the investor or the professional who holds a dozen income-producing properties and calculates his or her net worth in the millions. "Boy! She's lucky!" they say. Or "Man! Everything he touches turns to gold." And sometimes there *is* a stroke of good luck or a hint of the Midas touch in a person's real estate investment story. But it's never the whole story.

Success in any field is usually the result of talent and experience, not to mention hard work. The enabling power behind talent and experience, however, is the mastery of certain concepts, skills, and strategies essential to working in that particular endeavor. The goal of this book has been to make you aware of the concepts and strategies needed to succeed in real estate. Only you can hone the skills and do the hard work.

I'd like to leave you with a summary of ten important areas of focus in the real estate marketplace. Or, as your grandmother might say: *a few things to remember.* You can always turn back to them whenever you embark on a new venture or are caught in a disquieting dilemma.

Negotiate

Professionals in all areas of real estate routinely talk about a real estate purchase/sale contract as a "meeting of the minds." Because real estate transactions contain so many elements, they are one of the last remaining investment arenas where minds can indeed meet after considerable give-and-take. In other words, in the real estate marketplace, there are many bargaining chips besides money. Investors routinely put together successful deals by negotiating over:

- **Land.** Depending on the particular deal, you might be able to negotiate for a change of boundary line, change in the contour, drainage control, additional landscaping, or a change in parking areas.

- **Buildings.** Investors have negotiated for every kind of change, from putting on an addition or a new roof to tearing the structure down and clearing the property.
- **Legal restrictions.** Many deals have been put together using a zoning change or subdivision approval as a negotiating element.
- **Time constraints.** One of the most common negotiating tools is the closing date.
- **Promises and contingencies.** "Here's what I'll do for you" is an often-heard negotiating phrase in the real estate marketplace. On the other side of the fence is "This must be done before the transaction is closed." Or sometimes before the contract is even binding.
- **Leases.** Getting tenants in or out can be as important as the price.
- **Financing.** Many sellers have made their deals by playing a part in the financing, either by holding a mortgage or paying points and fees.

Virtually every aspect of a real estate deal is negotiable to some degree. It is essential that you become a little wary whenever you hear the word "standard" in the real estate marketplace. For example, there may be a "usual and customary" real estate commission in a given area, but there is no standard that must be adhered to. There is no standard price for a given square footage. There is no standard rule for who will pay the closing costs. When a deal seems to be falling apart, you can often negotiate with elements of the transaction that may have been overlooked.

Know the Marketplace

Most experts agree that the best investments are usually local investments. "Local" here means properties in or near an area where you live or have lived for a period of time. This advice holds true because real estate is affected by what's happening around it on two levels: environmentally and economically. To be successful in investment real estate, you must maintain awareness on both levels. Awareness to new trends or

> ## "Never take anything for granted."
>
> Benjamin Disraeli (1804–1881), British statesman and author

to other gradual changes in neighborhoods or supply and demand usually requires your physical presence at least part of each year.

Environmental awareness includes all the physical elements that surround your property: land, weather, pests and critters, other buildings, neighborhood, and the character of the municipality. Economic awareness includes not only statistics such as the local unemployment rate and the local per capita income but also the pace of the real estate marketplace. You must know whether you are working in a seller's or a buyer's market. You must be aware of local property values, buyer demands, and preferences.

Set Guidelines and Goals

Guidelines and goals are the road signs and destination points for your real estate investment vehicle. Without them, you can lose direction on many levels: negotiating price, holding time, cash flow and tax advantages, improvements, and selling, for example. By taking the time to think through a situation before it becomes an issue and then setting out a goal and some working guidelines, you can keep yourself from going beyond the point of optimum profit.

Let's look at the role of setting goals and guidelines in the five examples just mentioned:

- **Negotiating price.** You've read about establishing your steal-it price and your top-dollar price and doing a fair market value estimate. By doing this work before you begin negotiating, you can keep from getting caught up in tough dealing or in a bidding war and paying too much.
- **Holding time.** One of the goals of almost every real estate investor is to sell at the optimum price and the optimum time. It's easy to continue owning a piece of real estate, especially if the cash flow is positive. You can keep your awareness of holding time keen by setting out an ownership goal when you purchase a property and then reevaluating it each year. Weigh how much positive cash flow you are getting and how much the property is appreciating against the possi-

bility of using your equity to get into other investment opportunities.

- **Cash flow and tax advantages.** Some investors fall
  into a just-keep-marching-along mode when they
  have hired someone else to manage the building,
  collect the rents, and do federal tax returns. Try to
  calibrate the importance of cash flow and tax advantages in your investment plan when you are considering a purchase. Then at the end of each year of
  ownership (or at tax time), reconsider those goals
  and evaluate the property's performance. It may be
  time for a tax-deferred exchange.

- **Improvements.** There are two dangers that come
  with making physical changes to real estate: doing
  too many improvements and choosing the wrong
  improvements. Before you buy a property that needs
  some renovation or refurbishing, before you choose
  to do improvements to support a rent increase, or
  before you spruce up in the hopes of bringing in a
  better selling price, set goals for the return on your
  investment of time and money. Then crunch the
  numbers to see if your goals can be realistically met.

- **Selling.** Setting a realistic goal for the time and price
  at which to sell is often the key to collecting and
  pocketing the money you have "made" on paper as
  your property is appreciating. To do so, use the
  tools for estimating fair market value. Most Realtors
  will do a comparative market analysis (CMA) for prospective sellers without charge.

The tricky thing about setting goals and guidelines is that they change over time and according to
circumstances. Keep this factor in mind and make
frequent reevaluations.

Keep Your Brain in Control

There is no place in the investment real estate marketplace for emotion. Each investment property is a
business deal and you are the entrepreneur. Base your
decisions on facts and rational evaluations, not on feelings. Emotions such as anger, fear, aggression, preju-

dice, greed, and pride almost always sour the investment pie.

Respect the Importance of Location

It's the oldest joke in real estate: What are the three most important factors in a deal? Location! Location! Location!

This cliché has bounced around through generation after generation of real estate investors because it reflects reality. Nothing affects value as much as location.

There are three elements that comprise location: town, neighborhood, and lot. Before you make a purchase, evaluate the property by considering each of these elements. Will the economics and character of the town support the type of investment real estate you are considering? Is the neighborhood desirable? Does your property fit in? Is the land on which the buildings stand conducive to its current use or to the use you intend for it in the future?

A periodic location reevaluation is just as important as the prepurchase evaluation. Because changes generally take place gradually and over relatively long periods of time in real estate, some investors continue to hold property, unaware of the incremental creep that is changing the character of the local marketplace. Don't be lulled into a false security regarding property value and potential appreciation. Once a year, redo the location evaluation.

Take Good Care

Condition can affect profit almost as much as location can affect value. Repair costs that are incurred after you take title are out-of-pocket expenditures. They can wipe out the benefits of leveraging.

Never purchase a building without securing a careful inspection (preferably by professional inspectors) and getting accurate estimates for the necessary repairs (also from professionals). Then factor the cost of repairs into your negotiating. Whenever feasible, cover the cost of repairs in the mortgage financing. This can be done by having the seller do the repairs (to your approval) and agreeing to pay a slightly higher price, by creative financing that factors future improvements into the mortgage ratio (the 203(k) program at HUD, for example), or by hunting down the best possible mortgage deal (high loan-to-value ratio and low interest rate).

Condition also counts during holding time and at selling time. Generally, good maintenance is a factor in the amount of rent you can charge. It also affects turnover and vacancy rates. If you want top dollar when it's time to sell, all the mantras for homeselling are applicable to selling an investment property:

- **Cleanliness is next to Godliness**
- **Neutral colors**
- **No clutter**
- **A coat of paint can return ten times its cost**
- **Curb appeal**
- **Plenty of lighting**
- **No creaky stairs, broken windows, doorknobs that come off in your hand, cracks at the doorjambs**
- **Keep appliances and operating systems in good working order**
- **Keep evidence, on paper, of repair work that has been done and its warranties.**

Get It in Writing

Paper can be the real estate investor's best friend. Purchase and sale contracts, promises, contingencies, agreements, test results, approvals by municipal officials, work orders, price estimates, leases, rules of occupancy, warranties, expenditures, rent receipts, and tax returns are but a few of the instances where good written records are essential.

Beyond documenting your investment from purchase to sale, however, there's another use for print on paper in your investment program. It's important to document your periodic reevaluations. There's no benefit to *doing* periodic reevaluations of the local marketplace, your investment goals and guidelines, or the location and condition of the property, if you do them and then forget them. Write down your findings and opinions so that you can compare each evaluation with those of previous years. Chronological files will help you to see trends developing in the local marketplace or changes in your needs, goals, preferences, abilities, and interests.

Shop for Financing

The cost of borrowing money is a factor in almost every real estate investment. Financing is now available on a nationwide basis. Don't rely on one source for mortgage information. Use local and national newspapers, reporting services, the Internet, and a good mortgage broker to seek out the best possible deal.

In addition, go beyond the traditional mortgage hunt. Be creative. Financing is another arena where homebuying and investment real estate can be different. In most cases, buying a home means taking out one mortgage loan. Buying investment property can mean creating a pastiche of lending agreements.

Explore the possibilities of short-term financing from the seller for a part of the purchase price. When considering the cost of fix-up or rehab, look into private deals for second or third mortgages. (These can come from friends, associates, or relatives, not necessarily traditional lenders.) Consider balloon or interest-only instruments. And if you are investing in inner-city properties, don't leave a stone unturned in your research of private-sector, community-assistance groups, state-government programs, federal programs, and community-revitalization programs sponsored by traditional lending institutions. Even the secondary mortgage market (Fannie Mae) is getting into this act.

But as creative as you might get in seeking out the money to finance your investment property, always keep in mind your goals and the essential numbers in the deal. Rational evaluation must act as an overriding control mechanism.

Because money is readily available in today's marketplace, there is the danger of borrowing too much. Always remember that every loan must be repaid along with an additional fee (interest) for every day that you hold and use the borrowed money. Too much financing can create a negative cash flow that can sometimes be painful enough to force a sale before the investment has reached its maximum potential return, or even a good return.

Know Yourself

One factor that makes this book different from other investment real estate guides is its central premise: *You are an important element in the success of every deal.* Most books on real estate ignore the human element. That oversight undermines effectiveness because it is a person (or group of persons) who chooses an investment property, negotiates a contract, manages a building, and decides to sell.

Look at yourself just as carefully as you look at the property you are considering. Use the information in this book to compare the demands of different investment vehicles with the skills, interests, goals, and personality traits that you bring to the marketplace. And just as you periodically reevaluate the local marketplace and the condition and location of your property, reevaluate yourself as a real estate investor. Ask yourself, "Am I still suited to the investments that I am holding?"

Let yourself grow in the marketplace. Be willing to explore new opportunities. Be open to change. If you choose investments that are right for you, you will have the satisfaction of making money based on your own unique blend of interests and abilities.

Take Time

My father ended most telephone conversations with the words "Have fun!" And I'll leave those words with you as my last bit of advice in the real estate marketplace.

Whether as an investment vehicle or as a profession, real estate can be a demanding mistress. It is almost never an eight-to-five job. Success usually stimulates a desire for more of the same. Risk taking often brings high rewards and the desire for yet higher challenges. Failures can bring out fanatic drives to do better, to be successful. The real estate marketplace is full of metaphorical demons that sit on investors' shoulders and whisper, *"Just a little more time, just a little more work, just a little more money."*

Take time, *make* time for enjoyment. Schedule days off. Don't feel guilty when you're not working. Have fun.

Index

Index

Share the message!

Bulk discounts
Discounts start at only 10 copies and range from 30% to 55% off retail price based on quantity.

Custom publishing
Private label a cover with your organization's name and logo. Or, tailor information to your needs with a custom pamphlet that highlights specific chapters.

Ancillaries
Workshop outlines, videos, and other products are available on select titles.

Dynamic speakers
Engaging authors are available to share their expertise and insight at your event.

**Call Dearborn Trade Special Sales at
1-800-621-9621, ext. 4444,
or e-mail trade@dearborn.com**

Dearborn™
Trade Publishing
A **Kaplan Professional** Company